THE COMING OF THE FRONTIER PRESS

Medill School of Journalism
VISIONS *of the* AMERICAN PRESS

GENERAL EDITOR
David Abrahamson

Selected titles in this series

MAURINE H. BEASLEY
First Ladies and the Press: The Unfinished Partnership of the Media Age

PATRICIA BRADLEY
Women and the Press: The Struggle for Equality

DAVID A. COPELAND
The Idea of a Free Press: The Enlightenment and Its Unruly Legacy

MICHAEL SWEENEY
The Military and the Press: An Uneasy Truce

PATRICK S. WASHBURN
The African American Newspaper: Voice of Freedom

DAVID R. SPENCER
The Yellow Journalism: The Press and America's Emergence as World Power

KARLA GOWER
Public Relations and the Press: The Troubled Embrace

TOM GOLDSTEIN
Journalism and Truth: Strange Bedfellows

NORMAN SIMS
True Stories: A Century of Literary Journalism

THE COMING OF THE FRONTIER PRESS

HOW THE WEST WAS REALLY WON

Barbara Cloud

Foreword by Alan K. Simpson

MEDILL SCHOOL OF JOURNALISM

Northwestern University Press
Evanston, Illinois

Northwestern University Press
www.nupress.northwestern.edu

Printed in the United States of America

10 9 8 7 6 5 4 3 2 1

Library of Congress Cataloging-in-Publication Data

Cloud, Barbara Lee.
    The coming of the frontier press : how the West was really won / Barbara
Cloud ; foreword by Alan K. Simpson.
       p. cm.—(Medill School of Journalism Visions of the American press)
    Includes bibliographical references and index.
    ISBN 978-0-8101-2508-7 (pbk. : alk. paper)
    1. American newspapers—West (U.S.)—History. 2. Press—West (U.S.)—
History. 3. Journalism—West (U.S.)—History. 4. Frontier and pioneer life—
West (U.S.) I. Simpson, Alan K. II. Title. III. Series: Visions of the American
press.
    PN4894.C56 2008
    071.809—dc22

                                             2008013795

To William Ames for helping me on the path to historical research and to my husband, Stan, for helping me travel it

CONTENTS

TABLES

FOREWORD

Alan K. Simpson

I've been known to get tangled up in a pretty good argument now and then, and surely there is an argument still to be made that the West is "truly different." There are so many contrasting regions in this remarkable United States, but the American West—both the land itself and its claim on our national imagination—is a very special and unique place. How it came to be so is certainly a tale worth telling. And an important part of that story, so ably told in this volume by Barbara Cloud, is the role the frontier press has played in the settling, growth, and development of the West. My hometown, Cody, Wyoming, was founded by William F. "Buffalo Bill" Cody himself, and the first thing he did to make it a real community was to bring in an old friend from the East, Colonel John Peake, to start up the Cody *Enterprise*. The newspaper celebrated its 108th anniversary in 2008. Perhaps Old Bison Willie knew what was most important in making a "civilized" town.

I think part of the reason the West has always been so magical to people—both in fact and in our collective memory—is that compared to the rest of the country, the West is still a place of great open spaces. Take the drive from Shoshoni to Casper, Wyoming, and you'll know why. The green (sometimes) of the range grass, the grey of the sage, the brown of the distant hills, the blue of the distant mountains, and the white of the snow upon them—marvelous! But this land is also known as "the big sky" country and the "high plains." The great mountain ranges have plenty of "elbow room" and a lot of "room to grow." It is also a place where you can state clearly, and without contradiction, "I want to be left alone!"

What this means is that there is a great deal of natural beauty but relatively few people. My dear dad, who was governor of Wyoming and a U.S. senator, once said it was "the land of high altitude and low multitude!" So those good folks who traditionally made their home in the West came to relate to each other—as well as to their communities, their economic circumstances, and their own political traditions—in ways that set them apart. Which just may be why the press in the West has such a special role for the citizens here. It has well fulfilled a vital purpose in helping to define the region's significant social and political choices, in raising the tough issues such as conservation, land use, and development (many of which are also of great concern and interest to the nation as a whole), and in serving as a means simply to bring people together. It has been community journalism at its best.

I suspect that being raised in a small town such as Cody may add special meaning to that last comment, and it is my guess that many of my fellow citizens in the West feel the same way. The newspapers and magazines that have long served the western cities and towns have had a historic role in keeping us connected to each other. More than that, the press plays a great part in helping us find common ground on a range of critically important topics—many of which have been more than just a wee bit controversial. If you want a little more information on that, try talking about grizzlies, wolves, land-use planning, and public lands out here in this neck of the woods.

Professor Cloud's wonderful history of the frontier press brings to mind another thought that might be worth sharing.

The legacy of the western press has much in common with the legacy of the American West itself. The frontier may well be gone, but my hunch is that its view of life—its values and its methods of communication—still resonates with the American people from coast to coast. For example, when a public figure, with plain-spoken language and a clear-eyed point of view, levels honestly with his or her audience, we call it "straight talking." It is a somewhat rare form of human behavior these days, a bit unusual in this Age of Spin. But I think it is universally regarded as refreshing when a person has something to say and says it with thoughtfulness, ease, frankness, and maybe just a tad of humor. It's an old custom, a way of looking at the world, handed down from our once-frontier society. My great-grandfather Finn Burnett came to Wyoming in the 1860s, and now the sixth generation of our family is still here helping to make it a place where people love to come. That is the way we westerners try to talk, and I can make another argument that we would all be a little better off if more folks everywhere did the same.

I earlier mentioned the place of the American West in the country's imagination. Since the opening of the West in the nineteenth century, both the local and national media have played a central role in fostering this. So I have to confess that I have always been proudly impressed by the genuine affection and regard that the rest of the nation seems to feel for my part of the country. I live here in the heart of Absaroka Mountain country; Yellowstone Park is fifty-two miles away, and the Grand Tetons are "over the Divide." It's the nation's playground. So much of the rest of America has often looked to the West for inspiration, for opportunity, for natural resources, for recreation, and for a unique perspective on life. The American national character is so complex that I realize almost any generality about it is quite foolish. But no matter where you live, there is a pretty good chance that somewhere in your imagination—back there in the eye of your mind—rest ideas you associate with the frontier West. Some may even be a bit contradictory. Honesty, integrity, as well as a playful sense of humor. Steadfast strength, maybe even stubbornness, as well as risk taking. And perhaps most importantly of all, self-reliance, as well as having a genuine concern for your fellow man and woman. After all, the Wyoming Territory's government was the first in the Western world to give women the right to vote in 1869.

So if you, like so many of our fellow citizens, do associate those values with the American West, I would say to you that we are in complete agreement. Or, to put it another way, even though I do love 'em, we have no argument.

Why would people pack all their earthly goods into a wagon with their children and possibly other relatives or friends and head out to an unknown land fraught with both natural and human dangers? What possesses people to give up whatever comforts they have for what they hope will be—but cannot predict with any certainty—a better life? Western pioneers had to be able to purchase a wagon and a team of oxen, as well as supplies for a journey of several months; they weren't destitute; the West was not, for most of them, a last resort.

The movement in the nineteenth century of thousands of people from settled homes in the eastern half of the United States to the then-wilderness of the western half has long held my interest. It was the topic I first wanted to pursue when I decided to enroll in a doctoral program in journalism history at the University of Washington. Conventional wisdom says that newspapers played an important role in attracting migrants; certainly townspeople thought so, and they went to great pains to ensure that their towns had newspapers. As I learned more about the effort to fulfill what some people called the nation's "manifest destiny" to populate the land from "sea to shining sea," I realized that the railroads, too, were significant in encouraging and facilitating that movement. So I thought this might be a good dissertation topic. But it presented the probable need for many years of reading newspaper microfilm from around the nation, and because I was by then already a "mature" student, I keenly felt the need to finish my degree and get on with my life. As a result, I turned to a narrower, more accessible topic closer to home and examined the history of the press of the Territory of Washington.

By the time I arrived in Seattle, I myself had gone to live in a distant land, one with many unknowns for me—because I could learn little about it in advance—but one without the dangers the western pioneers encountered along the trail. Yet eight years in Australia in the 1960s and 1970s were, for an American, something of a pioneer exercise. While offering a perfectly agreeable lifestyle, the land Down Under did not yet find essential some of the things we considered necessities in the States, or at least they were not common for people in our financial bracket: automatic washing machines, clothes dryers, and dishwashers, for example. We also had to relearn how to deal with a bottle of milk with cream on top. Hardly a primitive experience, yet not the same as "home." Although we avoided ghettoizing ourselves with other Americans, we still grasped at news from home to maintain that important link, much as the thousands who moved to the American West did.

Still, I expect that even in my limited away-from-home experiences, I shared with those nineteenth-century pioneers on the California and Oregon trails some sense of the answer to the questions I posed at the start of this preface. Whatever the difficulties and privations, or in my case the lack thereof, there was an adventure to be enjoyed. Just as some people cannot bear to move outside the bosom of their family and stay in one place all their lives, others among us cannot bear to stay there forever. We want to know what the rest of the world holds for us.

At the time of our adventure—we went to Australia so my husband could take up a postdoctoral fellowship at the Australian

National University in Canberra—Australia attracted attention from the American media only when something sensational happened. About all I could find about the country in this pre-Google period were stories about the drowning of the prime minister. Harold E. Holt went swimming in the sea off the coast of the state of Victoria on December 17, 1967, and never returned. It was all very mysterious. Thirty-five years later things have not changed much when it comes to coverage of Australia by the American press. Sensation rules, but in a way that's only fair, because while I was living in Australia, most of the news I got about the United States was sensational.

The story of the coverage of the American West by nineteenth-century newspapers in the American East still has not been written—and this is not it. This is the story of newspapers in the American West, as written mostly by those western newspapers. I hope it helps place both the West and its newspapers in the context of American history where they belong: not just in footnotes or old Hollywood Westerns, but as central to the growth and development of the nation as a whole. Western newspapers were part of the story of town building, of railroad expansion, and of political discourse, among other things.

In putting this book together, I was both pleased and dismayed at the amount of research being done on western journalism. Pleased, because there is some fine new work in recent years, but dismayed by the gaps that remain. For example, although several books have been written about the *Los Angeles Times,* the best work is a biography of one of its more recent owner-publishers, not an in-depth look at the newspaper in historical context. Documentation for the conventional wisdom noted earlier—that many migrants were influenced by stories in their local newspapers—is still wanting, and I hope that this volume will prompt a new look by more historians interested in western journalism. The West is, after all, roughly half of the continental United States, and it remains today, as it was 150 years ago, a focus for both those seeking adventure and those hoping for a better life. Today they come on freeways and in airplanes, or sometimes crammed into unheated or uncooled trucks, experiences rather different from steep mountains and balky oxen teams, yet with their own perils. Those migrants who come of their own volition still identify with the early settlers. Cancer researcher Nam Dang, chief of hematological malignancies at the Nevada Cancer Institute in Las Vegas, told the *Las Vegas Review-Journal*'s Annette Wells that "you have to have that cowboy spirit" to face the prospect of practicing medicine in Nevada, and he likened it to "heading west during the gold rush."[1] Some parts of the West still claim to be the "last frontier," but even Nevada, certainly one of the longest holdouts for individual rights, recently passed a law banning smoking in public places, moving it a little farther from the time and place where one could say that "anything goes."

I have said what this book is not about. It *is* about a chapter in American history that is still being written. This volume will give attention to phenomena such as the mining camp and booster press; the press's important role in bringing "civilization" to the wilderness; its symbiosis with the railroads; its contribution to the development of western politics; and ultimately its contributions to journalism more generally. The emphasis is on the early years, up to about 1890, but we will take a quick look at some key issues and developments in the twentieth and even the twenty-first centuries. While the West's major newspapers have their roots in the nineteenth century, for most their real story finds fulfillment in the twentieth century and beyond.

Those who say history never repeats itself have only to look at the western press to see the echoes of previous generations of journalism in the United States. Politically, western journalism strongly resembles what some have called the "Dark Ages of American journalism," that period in the early nineteenth century when editors chose sides and used their newspapers to promote their particular democratic ideals. The same thing happened on the frontier, where the first settlers in an area had to build the political structure by which it would be governed. Much of this civic discourse took place in the pages of the newspapers because distance made citizen get-togethers difficult. A newspaper of one political persuasion soon begat another of an opposing view. Eventually, in the West as nationally, economic forces turned most communities into one-newspaper towns.

Like their forebears on the Atlantic seaboard, westerners increasingly used the press for their special interests—women's issues, medicine, entertainment, business, religion, temperance, and so on—but in the boom-and-bust atmosphere of the West, newspaper subject matter diversified faster than it did in the East.

If the western press is just a reflection of the journalism that came before, what makes it worthy of separate consideration? The western press is as integral a part of the making of the nation as is the region in which it thrived, and the West as both place and process has attracted a wide array of scholars. Whether one accepts Frederick Jackson Turner's argument that the free land in the West created the impetus for its development, as well as shaped the attitudes of its settlers, or the more modern view of Patricia Limerick and others that the history of western America is one of conquest, journalists were on the front lines. Although the western press has inevitably been dominated by mainstream journalism, in its history can be found the great diversity that Limerick and other "new western historians" have decried as missing from too many accounts of western history.

One other thought about what this book is about—like all history, it is about people. I have tried to bring to life for the reader some of the people associated with the growth of the frontier press, and I've especially tried to tap into what motivated them to do as they did. Thousands of newspapers were started over the course of the decades examined here, so it has been necessary to be highly selective in citing examples. If I have omitted someone's favorite story about a favorite newspaper, it is to keep this volume manageable.

In developing this story of the West and its newspapers, I am grateful to the many who have written before me, from nineteenth-century newspapermen like Clarence Bagley, Edward Kemble, and Alfred Doten, who were concerned enough about their legacy to record in considerable detail not only their own lives but also journalism and the world around them, to the many students of western journalism history like Wendell Ashton and Ralph Dyar, who have written about particular newspapers or newspapermen or who, like William Lyon and Porter Stratton, have brought together information about the press in a particular area.

I consider myself a westerner, through and through—born in California, schooled in Montana and Idaho, and with a higher education in California, Oregon, and Washington. My adult life has been spent in the West (including Western Australia). I know the West to be not only a geographic location but also a state of mind. I recall attending a get-together with a number of historians from across the country where one of them said he pitied me, living out here on the fringes of mainstream American culture. It was so much better to be, as he was, near the Library of Congress and the other great libraries of the nation.

I've never pitied myself at all for living outside that culture. The West is rich in its own resources. True, I would have been grateful had more editors left diaries, as Alfred Doten did, rather than simply let their newspapers speak for them, but every historian has that kind of complaint. Editors generally have had a sense of the place they would play in history. A twentieth-century journalist gets the credit for applying the phrase "first rough draft of history" to journalism, but nineteenth-century frontier editors knew they were participating in something important, and those who did leave records understood that the West needed its repository of history just as much as the East did. The West has been good to me as well as to thousands of other individuals, and I hope to return the favor by telling its story in the greater context of American history.

My thanks to David Abrahamson for allowing me to be part of this important series about the impact of journalism in the nation's history; to my husband, Stan, for his patience and willingness to climb over the stacks of books that accumulated in my study; to many friends for encouragement and counsel; and to my editor, Jess Paumier, for helping me avoid at least some of my bloopers.

THE COMING OF THE FRONTIER PRESS

ONE

INTRODUCTION

What would the West be today had there been no frontier newspapers?

Many would claim that it would be no different. Indeed, historians of the West, including those who study growth and urbanization, use newspapers as primary sources, but often they do not give the press much credit for contributing to western development.[1]

However, journalism historian Oliver Knight notes, "Although there is a question whether the mass media generally are dynamic elements or simply transmission belts for ideas, it appears likely that the frontier newspaper was an active agent in Western urbanization." Knight goes on to call the frontier newspaper a "catalyst in social change in the Trans-Mississippi West."[2]

Knight uses a small mining camp newspaper, the *Owyhee* (or *Idaho*) *Avalanche* in Silver City, in southwestern Idaho, as the foundation for his argument. He calls the *Avalanche* a "steadying force in the face of threatening economic conditions" and argues that the editors' adherence to their salutatory—"a paper faithfully devoted to local affairs is of incalculable value to the community in which it is published"—helped "create a sense of community in place of centrifugal individualism."[3] (A salutatory was a statement new publishers printed to introduce themselves to their readers and lay out their goals.)

Can you imagine a town or city without a newspaper? The hundreds of thousands of people who came west for gold, for land, and for other kinds of new beginnings could not. To them a newspaper legitimized their towns, provided a link to the life they had left behind, gave them a forum for political discussion, offered a printing shop where they could get posters, tickets, and stationery printed, and provided a channel to advertise goods and services; in sum, it brought them a life much like the civilized life they had left behind when they climbed into their wagons, cracked the whip over the bullocks' heads, and shouted their version of "Let's roll!"

In 1863 a Nevada woman expressed the feelings of many settlers when she wrote to the newly established *Gold Hill News,* "I am so glad that you've brought here your civilizer—your printing press . . . however civilized a place may be, the addition of an enlightened public journal to its institutions will serve as the best of all civilizing processes in use."[4]

Residents saw clear benefits from having a newspaper in town. When Dayton, in eastern Washington, was named a county seat, one contemporary observer commented on the rivalry between Dayton and nearby Marengo for the honor: "Dayton had a newspaper, while Marengo had nothing but a store, a mill in prospect and an abundance of hope."[5]

From the first small paragraph published in the *Californian* on March 15, 1848, testifying to the discovery of gold at Sutter's Mill, it is clear that the frontier press did far more than provide an artifact for modern historians. Without it, it is unlikely that the West would have developed as quickly as it did—and in some cases, in the direction it took. And without growth, the press would have gone nowhere. Evidence for this symbiotic relationship is pervasive throughout the West, whether in the mining camps, the railroad towns, or the booster-built cities.

THE PRESS'S "PREHISTORY"

Given that the definition of a newspaper requires that it be reproduced mechanically—by a printing press—the frontier press can even claim a *prehistory* of sorts, a period when the newspaper was so important to the community that individuals were willing to take the time not only to collect information or write essays to share with their fellow citizens, but also to write out multiple copies by hand: not a lot of copies, to be sure, but enough to guarantee writer's cramp on the part of the editor-scribe.[6]

There was, for example, Charles Edward Pickett, better known to his fellow Oregonians as the Curltail Coon, the editor's name he put at the top of his handwritten newspaper. Pickett cared so deeply about discussion of the political future of the growing area in which he lived that he wrote out multiple copies of the *Flumgudgeon Gazette and Bumble Bee Budget* while delegates were meeting in 1843 at Champoeg in Oregon's Willamette Valley to discuss the formation of a provisional government under the aegis of the United States. Preparing roughly eight pages of script, he is thought to have distributed about a dozen copies expressing his view of the desirability of splitting from Great Britain, with which the United States then shared governance of the region.[7]

Others, such as the Mormons in Utah, were equally committed to the concept of newspapers as a means of communicating with one another, and church youth groups throughout the territory handwrote their community's news in newspaper format, supplementing it with literary material as well as religious doctrine. For example, in Hyrum, Utah, which in 1890 had a population of 1,423, the Young Men's and Young Ladies' Mutual Improvement Associations created manuscript publications called the *Knowledge Seeker, Young Ladies' Thoughts,* and the *Evening Star.* These weekly publications started in the mid-1880s and consisted of six to ten legal-size sheets. They continued into the early 1890s.[8]

In American Fork, Utah, R. G. Eccles handwrote the *Weekly Gazette* in 1868. He produced at least twelve issues of varied content. A year earlier in Utah, F. C. Robinson had started the *Manti Herald,* which consisted of one legal-size page, with three columns of advertisements, local news, and some telegraphic news taken from Salt Lake City newspapers—all handwritten. The author of this newspaper was eventually identified as Robinson, the county clerk, and in one edition he apologized to subscribers for missing an issue: "By way of explanation, [we] may say that the 'type' we had previously used proved defective, and we concluded to wait until we could get a fresh supply!" Utah journalism historian Cecil Alter comments, "Some humor, since the editor drew each letter with his quill."[9]

Robinson took pride in his calligraphy, carefully forming each letter of his text. Meanwhile, David Candland, in nearby Mount Pleasant, used what Robinson described as "common orthography" when the *Manti* editor acknowledged the first issue of Candland's the *Sanpitcher* (March 1867) in his own *Manti Herald.* The *Salt Lake Telegraph* called the *Sanpitcher* a "pithy little manuscript effusion" at the start, and when it took note of the

"Editor's Valedictory" in issue number 13 three months later, the *Telegraph* commented, "But in a private communication, we are assured of its resumption at the solicitation of its many friends. . . . It is a medium of circulating news, and it is not without its influence."[10]

MORE MANUSCRIPT PAPERS

Nevada's first news publication also came in manuscript form. However, when the first edition of the *Gold-Cañon Switch* came out around 1854, its home, Johntown, was in Utah Territory. Writer Joseph Webb, a partner of "Old Virginy" Fenimore, for whom Virginia City, Nevada, was later named, probably issued it monthly and—consistent with most manuscript publications—distributed only a few copies.[11] Another Nevada manuscript newspaper, the *Scorpion,* was started three years later in Genoa, then also known as Mormon Station, a trading post to serve Salt Lake City Mormons heading for the California mines. The founder was an even earlier settler of the Carson Valley, Stephen A. Kinsey. The *Scorpion's* motto was "Fear no man, and do justice to all." A monthly, it is thought to have expired before the year was out, and it was succeeded by perhaps the frontier's most famous newspaper, Nevada's *Territorial Enterprise.*[12]

It is impossible to prove the impact of the early western press, because we cannot go back and do a controlled experiment with and without its presence. But there is plenty of circumstantial evidence that shows the importance communities placed on having a newspaper. The effort just described to produce hand-written papers is one example, and the comments of the Gold Hill, Nevada, resident cited earlier is another. The newspaper played a vital role in the urbanization of the West to that woman and to the people of nearby Como, who held a ball to raise funds and welcome the *Como Sentinel*—"the Paper that is going to start here soon."[13] The paper also played a vital role to all the town builders, such as the Portland boosters, who recruited Thomas Jefferson Dryer to establish the *Oregonian,* and to Edmund Sylvester, who owned most of the Olympia, Washington, town site and who, in turn, recruited Dryer to send an editor to start the *Columbian.* Sylvester was sure a newspaper would help Washington gain territorial status and thus attract settlers to whom he could sell lots.[14]

HIGH LITERACY IN THE WEST

Many newspapers in the West owed much—but not all—of their success to the high level of literacy of the forty-niners and their fellow immigrants, who thought the western territories held the key to their fortunes. Although the mining camp image is one of rough-and-ready men whom one would not expect to be versed in Shakespeare or Browning, many of those who answered the siren call of gold knew also of the Sirens who unsuccessfully tempted Odysseus.

The twentieth-century scholar William Lyon, one of the earliest researchers to address the growth of the western press, listed the desire of a literate population for reading matter as one of four key reasons for the rapid spread of newspapers across the frontier.[15]

Much earlier, nineteenth-century newspaperman Frederic Hudson of the *New York Herald* offered evidence for this desire when he recorded that it took four to six weeks for the *Herald*'s special California editions to reach the Pacific, and copies were read until the ink was worn off.[16] In addition, when copies of the New York periodical reached the Pacific coast, baskets of newspapers were set out on the honor system, and reading-hungry miners tossed in the expected silver dollars.[17]

In 1857, while discussing its purpose in life and its circulation, the *New York Tribune* commented that it sent 6,000 of its total 230,800 copies (including the daily, weekly, and semiweekly editions) to California and Europe.[18]

Historian Allan Nevins has written that "never in the history of the world has there been such an articulate body of pioneers."[19] Alfred McClung Lee suggests that westerners were so desperate for something to read that they would read anything. "One must remember that the men who blazed the trail through the Western wilds were not discriminating readers," Lee writes. "Their respect was commanded only by the editor who could fight with his guns as well as his pen," thus fostering the myth of the editor with a Colt revolver in one hand and a composing stick in the other.[20] The cache of diaries kept by gold field inhabitants is further evidence of their literacy, and the census data support these conclusions.[21]

U.S. census data for 1880, the earliest census for which a full report on literacy is available, showed that what would become the far western region of the United States had a remarkably low rate of illiteracy (the census reported "illiteracy" rather than "literacy," but if illiteracy is low, one might deduce that literacy is high). Several western locations did better, for example, than Massachusetts, the cradle of American journalism. (See table 1.1.)

TABLE 1.1 Selected Illiteracy Rates, 1880

State/ Territory	Total Population	% Illiterate Whites Under 21 Years	% Illiterate Whites over 21 Years
Arizona	40,440	23	15
California	894,694	2	5
Colorado	194,327	8	6
Idaho	14,999	3	3
Montana	39,159	2	2
Nevada	62,266	2	5
New Mexico	119,565	62	62
Oregon	174,768	2	4
Utah	143,963	5	9
Washington	75,116	1	3
Wyoming	20,789	2	2
United States	50,189,209	7	9
Massachusetts	1,783,085	3	8
New York	5,082,871	2	6

Source: Tenth U.S. Census, "Miscellaneous Statistics," 922–23.

Mining camps generally had bookstores, often in the newspaper office, some run by stationers (who sometimes were also part of the newspaper office). For example, in 1867 the *Owyhee Avalanche* in Silver City, Idaho, carried advertisements for three booksellers in the tiny, remote mining camp.[22]

In examining table 1.1, the reader will note that territories such as Arizona and New Mexico stand out with high illiteracy rates because of their large Native American and Spanish populations. Far western Indian tribes did not have written languages at the time, and the U.S. government apparently did not care if the Spanish-speaking inhabitants could read and write in their own language. A caveat: census taking in the nineteenth century had little precision. Census errors of the current age are minuscule compared with those of a century or more ago, except, of course, that the numbers involved are so much greater now.

GOD BEFORE GOLD

Although the California gold rush gets the most credit for impelling people in the eastern half of the United States to move to the western half, more than a decade earlier another group of citizens packed their wagons and moved into the largely uncharted lands of the West. In 1834 Methodist missionary Jason Lee, assigned originally to work with the Native Americans of the Pacific Northwest mountains, in particular the Nez Perce and Flatheads in Idaho, decided the Indians in the Willamette Valley farther west would be more sympathetic to his message and settled there instead.[23] Four years later, Marcus Whitman determined to fulfill Lee's original goal of serving the inland Indian nations and established a Methodist mission to the Cayuse near Waiilatpu, now Walla Walla, Washington.[24]

Just as religion motivated so many of the earliest immigrants to the western territories—the Whitmans, Lee, the French Catholic missionaries in the Northwest and their followers, and the Spanish Catholic friars in California, Arizona, and New Mexico—so, too, did the first printing presses arrive in the West at the instigation of the religious pioneers. The Presbyterians transferred a printing press they had used at their mission in Hawaii to the Lap Wai Mission that served the Nez Perce on the Clearwater River in Idaho. The Whitmans at Waiilatpu also expected to use the press and planned to cart it the 110 miles between the two missions every six months or so. "On the first trip back to Walla Walla, however, the packhorse fell over a cliff and came to grief at the bottom of a canyon, along with the press, which was abandoned as a total loss."[25] The first printing presses in California came with the Catholic priests who were part of the Spanish colonization of Mexico and the West Coast.[26] A trader used New Mexico's first press briefly for a newspaper, but later the Catholic missionaries printed religious materials on it.[27]

Most of these presses printed religious tracts for missionary work, but the press at the mission at Monterey also served the Spanish authorities for printing official documents until it was appropriated by Walter Colton and Robert Semple for sectarian use in 1846: to print California's first newspaper, the *Californian*.[28] The Spanish authorities had recognized the potential value of a newspaper some years previously when the Spanish governor Manuel Micheltorana talked about having a newspaper in Monterey "in which citizens might read and criticize the acts of the government in their behalf," and asked the residents in Monterey to look into it. The administrator of customs, Manual Castañares, and the director of establishment of education, Don Enrique Camburton, responded by saying they would issue such a paper to contribute to the governor's "enlightened views." This pleased Micheltorana, but the two bureaucrats never got beyond printing a proclamation.[29]

With the stability and security represented by the missions, settlers followed. Those settlers wrote home about the wonders of their new homes, a boosterism to be replicated in the newspapers that soon were established. And, of course, some of those settlers found gold and other mineral resources on which they would build their fortunes and attract even more attention—and settlers—to the West.

ANTICIPATING GROWTH

Daniel Boorstin and others have suggested that poor itinerant printers wandered the West looking for a good place to set up shop and build a town around them.[30] The itinerant printer was, indeed, a fact of western newspapering; the ability to set type proved a good way to see the world. But the men who started newspapers generally had or could get enough money to hire someone with a wagon to haul equipment over difficult, rutted roads. They needed the help. The image of the printer wandering the country with his press on his back and a shirttail full of type defies logic. The Ramage and Washington hand presses used in so many frontier print shops weighed about 1,500 pounds, even when built partly of wood, and carts or wagons were required to transport them. Enough type to fill a four-page newspaper would quickly have ripped through that shirttail. The printer was a sturdy fellow but not a superman.

Many newspaper publishers took their chances that the veins of precious metals would last long enough for them to build a community, but most wanted something more solid—the arrival of a railroad, for example. Western frontier towns competed to have major railroad facilities that would ensure jobs, as well as access to transportation, and many newspapers started in time to herald the arrival of the first iron horse.

Another attraction to a would-be publisher was the promise of a frontier town becoming a government center—a county seat or, better yet, the territorial or state capital. If a publisher was a member of the governing party, this meant contracts for printing laws and ordinances as well as the numerous forms and stationery required to run a government. In addition, land-use laws generally called for the publication of legal notices when a would-be owner sought to acquire government land, such as for mining or a homestead. In any case, a seat of government offered more opportunities to publishers and printers. Even a territorial prison or university was considered a plus because of the jobs and economic activity it could bring. For some publishers, the lively political discourse that came with publishing in a political center was its own reward. Others were happy to exercise influence over one or more politicians.

A study of the beginnings of Washington Territory newspapers cited railroads and government activity as two major signals to a printer that a location was a good prospect for a newspaper. A third was a mineral find, and fourth were other economic events such as a major mill expansion or a major addition to the town. Emphasis shifted as the region matured and had fewer major mineral discoveries. In all, 81 percent of the Washington Territory towns had a significant and identifiable event that could be expected to bring growth about the time of the establishment of their first newspapers.[31] Printers may have been naive about some aspects of the business, but they understood the importance of having an increasing population.

THE TRANS-MISSISSIPPI WEST

A word is necessary about the time and space discussed in this volume. Every part of the United States has had its "West" at some time in its history, making the "frontier" a moving target.

The original charter for some New England colonies stretched westward with no limit except the Pacific Ocean. Kentucky and Tennessee were home to famous frontiersmen like Davy Crockett. Abe Lincoln is often referred to as a "frontier" lawyer. This study examines the trans-Mississippi West, starting on the west side of the Mississippi River where Joseph Charless, in St. Louis in 1808, with encouragement and fiscal support from Meriwether Lewis, then governor of the Missouri Territory, started the *Missouri Gazette,* the first newspaper in the western half of the United States.

Most Americans have a sense of what they consider "the West." Shaped largely by movies, Zane Grey, Louis L'Amour, and Larry McMurtry, this idea matches to a great degree the U.S. Census Bureau's definition of the frontier, which is based on a limited number of people per square mile. That concept of the West still exists today, and the easterner who plans a "western" vacation is probably heading for California, Nevada, Montana, or adjacent states, not those states immediately west of the Mississippi, such as Charless's Missouri, which has been settled long enough that it no longer fits the popular image.

Much of what is written here can be applied to all trans-Mississippi frontiers because they shared similar challenges in the beginning, but the specific examples discussed in this book will come from farther west, typically west of the 100th meridian, which runs north-south just east of Denver and through San Angelo, Texas, and Dodge City, Kansas. These three cities have popular images that fit comfortably into the region commonly considered "the West." Texas, however, is a region unto itself, and little attention is paid to that state here. Nor do we look at the Great Plains or the northern reaches of the Mississippi River. We start essentially with Denver, nestled on the eastern flanks of the Rocky Mountains, and move westward to include the Great Basin and the Pacific Coast from Mexico to Canada—more than a million square miles of forests and deserts, mountains and valleys that make up one-third of the continental United States.[32]

DEFINING PLACE AND TIME

I have chosen not to get involved in the arguments about whether *frontier* is a legitimate word to use regarding western development. To this day, individuals and organizations try to agree on a definition. To the extent that *frontier* implies self-sufficiency, it does not apply to newspapers. However resourceful a western publisher might be—sometimes building his press, carving his own type, and printing on wallpaper or cigar wrappers when supplies of newsprint failed to arrive—he was, nevertheless, heavily reliant on the outside world. Except in Utah, where the Mormons established paper mills to serve the *Deseret News,* publishers needed connections with the outside world for paper, usually for ink (although some tried making their own ink), and most certainly for at least some of their news. As will be seen, western editors served their readers a rich menu of local news, but they also recognized the importance of including national and international information in their publication if they truly wanted it to qualify as a "newspaper."

To the extent that the word *frontier* implied exploitation, as suggested by "new" western historians such as Patricia Limerick, Clyde A. Milner II, Charles E. Rankin, and others in *Trails: Toward a New Western History* and other works, the fit is better.[33] Western newspaper publishers eagerly took advantage of land booms, ore discoveries, and other opportunities the West offered to the entrepreneurial and adventurous. Some became quite wealthy, usually not because of their newspapers, but because by being early on the scene, they had access to those opportunities. Find a frontier editor and you will probably find a land speculator.

In any case, although *pioneer* may be a better term than *frontier* for describing the initial set of newspapers established in the West, because of its common use, *frontier* will be used interchangeably with *western*.

As for time, choosing dates within which to present a historical thesis is always arbitrary. If we were to include the colonies whose charters often had a West that extended across the continent, we would have to begin in the eighteenth century. Charless established the first newspaper west of the Mississippi River in 1808. But the first newspapers in the area of emphasis in this study appeared more than thirty years later, in the 1840s, and the West of the American imagination is a mid-nineteenth-century phenomenon. The Frontier Period is often considered to have ended in 1890, the year the U.S. Census Bureau, which defined *frontier* as an area with a population of fewer than two people per square mile on average, declared that the population of the nation had exceeded that number and therefore there was no more "frontier."

Historian Frederick Jackson Turner's scholarly paper crediting free land as the impetus for the westward movement was built on the notion that the end of the frontier came in 1890, when the population had increased enough presumably to restrict the amount of free land available. But when 1890 began, six states had yet to be admitted to the Union: Idaho (1890), Wyoming (1890), Utah (1896), Oklahoma (1907), Arizona (1912), and New Mexico (1912).[34] Of these latecomers, only Utah and Oklahoma—the latter outside the geographic scope of this study—had populations that met the Census Bureau's post-frontier definition. Of those already admitted to the Union, Nevada and Montana were still "frontier" states in terms of population density.[35] Even so, early in the twenty-first century, Nevada and Montana, along with Alaska, still bragged about being the "last frontiers" because of their wide-open spaces and independent mind-sets.

This discussion of the frontier/pioneer press, then, will focus primarily on the middle and late nineteenth century, starting in the 1840s and emphasizing English-language publications, but also exploring the diversity of the press that developed during this time frame. It will also move into the twentieth and even the twenty-first centuries as appropriate to highlight the development of some of today's western newspapers. This is the traditional West—of cowboys and Indians, cattlemen, sheepherders, sod busters, dance-hall girls, and the "miners forty-niners."[36]

MINER-PRINTERS, PRINTER-MINERS

The thousands of people moving west—whether on the Oregon Trail to settle in the Pacific Northwest, on the Gila Trail to the drier climate of the Southwest, or, most likely, on the California Trail heading for the gold fields—included men who had in their former lives been associated with newspapers. Like the other young men who heard the news of the discovery of gold in California, these newspapermen thought first to make their fortunes in the mines.

Often mild-mannered and unused to long days of hard manual labor outdoors, some of these men turned away from the violence in the mining camps and the physical effort required to discover and mine gold. Sickness in the camps also deterred some, such as Thornton L. McElroy, the son of a Middleton, Pennsylvania, minister. At age eighteen McElroy left home for Pittsfield, Illinois, to learn the printer's trade.

In 1849 McElroy took the sea route to California, lured by the prospect of picking his nest egg off the ground. Not wanting to risk the illnesses current in the mines that would undo his dreams of taking riches home to Sally, his bride-to-be, he returned to his previous calling in printing, first working in San Francisco newspapers and later moving to Portland, Oregon, where he worked for Thomas Jefferson Dryer, publisher of the new *Oregonian*.[37] McElroy impressed Dryer sufficiently that the latter selected him to start a newspaper for the prospective territory of Washington, and in 1852 Dryer sent McElroy to Olympia with a partner, James W. Wiley, and the necessary equipment.[38]

McElroy was typical of frontier editor-publishers in many ways: he moved from his original role of setting type in the back shop of the newspaper plant and working the printing press to the front-office functions of editing and managing the newspaper. On September 18, 1852, the *Oregonian* acknowledged the first issue of the *Columbian,* with McElroy as coeditor with Wiley. A month later, the *Oregonian* printed an extract from the *Columbian* about the marvels of Olympia, the typical booster effort that the Olympia sponsors hoped for, paid for, and expected from their newspaper.

This kind of boosterism was typical of the impetus for starting newspapers on the frontier, but it was not the only stimulant for the establishment of a press in a town. Frontier newspaper entrepreneurs knew that just as ore veins were fickle, so were advertisers, so they looked for more than mere promises that a locality would grow and flourish. Printers' criteria for setting up shop included the requirement that some signal justify the expectation that the location would continue to attract settlers, including businessmen who would buy advertising in the newspaper, as well as residents who would subscribe to read it.

The kind of signal shifted as the region matured and had fewer major mineral discoveries.

WANDERING THE WEST

The journeyman printer who moved about the country was generally either hired by someone who had already started a newspaper or by a politician who wanted to start one but did not know how to set type or pull a page from the press. Sometimes the printer decided to borrow some money and start a newspaper on his own, but he was quickly beholden to the politician, banker, or local businessman who funded him.

Editors, printers, publishers, journalists, owners—these were technically very specific jobs, but for our purposes they were usually one and the same individual because, like the early American colonists, most frontiersmen wore several hats, so we'll just call them newspapermen unless a specific distinction is necessary. These newspapermen moved from place to place, often with their printing presses, hauling them not on their backs but in wagons at risk of getting stuck in the mud of the miserable western trails. Like McElroy, these men may have started out heading for the mines, but they detoured to San Francisco or one of the other cities that sprang up early in western development, where they could earn an income by pursuing their craft. Then they heard of an opportunity, perhaps another discovery of silver or gold, or an offer of sponsorship by town developers convinced that a newspaper would help them sell land; and then, perhaps, they heard of another opportunity, and then another, and they kept searching for the pot of gold at the end of their particular ink-stained rainbow. One newspaperman has been tracked through at least eight different towns and mining camps.[39]

Newspapermen rarely stayed in one place more than a couple of years. The boom-and-bust economy of the frontier made the newspaper business as unstable as the many other frontier enterprises established to serve communities dependent on the latest mineral discovery. Even in an area like Washington Territory, which was less reliant on the richness of ore veins than Idaho and Nevada, two years in a town was a long stay for a newspaperman.[40] On the other hand, a few newspapermen found the right place right away and stayed to build their newspaper and their town. William Byers published the *Rocky Mountain News* in Denver for twenty years; John Miller Murphy published the *Washington Standard* in Olympia for fifty years; and in a later era C. P. Squires edited the *Las Vegas Age* for nearly forty years.

Journeyman printers ran most newspaper offices. They had learned their craft at the type case; setting type by hand, one letter at a time, gave a man a good education both in general and about newspaper production. Unfortunately, typesetting did not necessarily enhance their knowledge of the financial end of the operation. Reporters were rare in frontier newspaper offices in the mid-nineteenth century, except in the cities or at particularly prosperous endeavors such as the *Territorial Enterprise* in Virginia City, Nevada, which had Mark Twain and Dan DeQuille writing "locals," the small paragraphs about what was going on in town.

Sometimes the journeyman printer arrived in town at a fortuitous moment. Perhaps an election was in the offing and those in opposition to the existing newspaper wanted their own organ to press their politics. Most first newspapers in a town, recognizing the economic dangers of offending perhaps half of their potential clientele, were politically neutral—until the first election came along. Then a lawyer or doctor or merchant with a political agenda he wanted to spread throughout the area would hire a printer to achieve his goals. This, in turn, led the editor of the existing newspaper to feel the need to respond to whatever political position was being put forward. His partisan leanings bubbled up and the partisan battle was engaged.[41]

Frontier editors faced challenges their eastern counterparts lacked. Although encounters with outlaws were not daily events, as one might assume from some Western movies, frontier towns' isolation and long supply lines made it difficult to publish a newspaper. The mail provided an especially critical service because that was how the frontier newspaper got much of its news, whether national or regional. McElroy wrote his wife, Sally, on January 11, 1853, that he had received no mail for six weeks because of the winter weather. In that letter he also retracted anything he had previously written about a "delightful climate." Western Washington had three feet of snow that year. It stayed on the ground for three weeks, cattle starved, and then three weeks of rain caused flooding.[42]

A SENSE OF WORTH

Welcomed from the beginning, as we have seen, newspapers were valued members of the frontier community—and they were not shy about saying so. For example, in its salutatory (inaugural editorial), the *Esmeralda Star* in Aurora, California, referred to the "exalting influence of the Press." The press is, the editors wrote, "deemed an indispensable appendage to society." [43]

Some communities, such as Salt Lake City, celebrated their newspapers with special annual banquets. The first such banquet in the Salt Lake Valley was attended by the Mormon leader Brigham Young himself in 1852, two years after the founding of the church-sponsored *Deseret News*. Toasts at the dinner included:

> The Press—The greatest preacher of righteousness in the world; makes it thousands of proselytes where man can make but one; may the time speedily come, when every nation, kindred, tongue and people, will have such a minister, conducted by the saints of God, within their midst.

> The Deseret News: The Trumpet of the Vallies [*sic*] which sounds the true notes that every saint understands, and is a silent preacher in every habitation; may it continue under the same conductor, guided by the same Spirit, the type set by the same hands, and perused by all in the world, in time, and in eternity.

> The Spirit, the Pen, and the Press—The Spirit to dictate, the Pen to indite [*sic*], and the Press, with the truth, to the world shall give light. [44]

In 1873 the *Idaho Avalanche,* which had moved from Ruby City to Silver City, Idaho, published an article on how people were increasingly appreciating newspapers. "Few families are content with a single newspaper," the article said. "The village news-paper is eagerly sought after and its contents eagerly [devoured]. Then comes the demand for county news, State news, national and foreign news." The article concluded, "The newspaper is just as necessary to fitting a man for his true position in life as food or raiment."[45] John A. Lewis and John McElroy, founders of the *Los Angeles Star,* commented, "The Press is a main auxiliary to all the means of prosperity" and is the "offspring of enlight-enment of our age."[46]

LOOKING AHEAD

Journalism has always had its foundations in the economics of its time. It costs money to publish, and, as is often remarked, "he who pays the piper calls the tune," or "freedom of the press belongs to the man who owns one." But publishers' desire for profit and well-being was tempered in the early years of the republic by the religious underpinnings of society and the polit-ical urgency of revolution. As a whole, however, in spite of the religious origins of many presses, frontier attitudes were less often influenced by religious notions. Rather, they were leav-ened by the wealth promised by gold and other minerals, as well as by the availability of land and other natural resources waiting to be exploited. Only a few people moved westward for freedom's sake or with an eye to heaven; most went expecting to improve their lot in life on earth. Some of the exceptions— the Mormons and several utopian colonies—are discussed in chapter 7.

In spite of their seemingly laid-back ways, westerners have been people in a hurry to transplant themselves and their culture into the wide-open spaces and snowcapped peaks common to the West. And to get rich quick. Nevadans have exploited that desire with casino gambling since the 1930s; in addition, the joint operating agreements that help make newspapers more profitable originated in the West.[47]

Australian historian Geoffrey Blainey titled a history of his country *The Tyranny of Distance*.[48] Australia was at the end of the road—or sea-lane—on a global scale, but its challenge was to develop despite the long umbilical cord tying it to the mother country. Westerners, too, including the western editor, had to deal with geography. They waited for supplies and news to cross the deserts and mountains, a lesser challenge, perhaps, than months at sea tossed about by waves and storms, but nevertheless a test that tried the patience and, often, the pocketbook. In this, the editor experienced the same inconveniences his eastern forerunners had to live with, but instead of waiting two weeks for mail from Boston to New York, the frontier publisher more often had to wait months for the news from the East. This long communication time is one reason the press and the railroads had the symbiotic relationship to be discussed in chapter 6. Newspapermen wanted railroads not only for the benefits they would bring to a community but also for the benefits the newspaper itself would receive in terms of faster news and supplies.

Geography, then, with its corollaries of distance and climate, is a key factor setting the western press apart from its fellows east of the Mississippi River.

Another issue for the frontier publisher was the lack of permanence. This created a set of problems different from those an eastern publisher might face. The men who came west did not intend to stay. With varying personalities, some adventurous, some restless, some more stable, the gold seekers planned to pick the gold off the ground and return to the bosom of their families as soon as they were rich. Once on the frontier, they realized that getting rich required more effort than they had expected—and some discovered that effort was best employed in conning other men out of their money—but rather than return home, many chose to stay and engage in other enterprises, such as printing or land speculation. Historian Earl Pomeroy quotes the San Francisco poet Prentice Mulford:

> Five years at most was to be given to rifling California of her treasures . . . and the rich adventurers would spend the remainder of their days in wealth, peace, and prosperity in their Eastern homes. No one talked then of going out "to build up the glorious State of California." No one then ever took pride in the thought that he might be called a "Californian." So they went.[49]

And they still come today. Some western cities, such as Las Vegas, Nevada, are still viewed as places where money, jobs, and a better life can be easily obtained. Like students attending a commuter university, people pass through, staying long enough to win—or lose—their fortunes at the gambling tables or in land speculation but with little interest in being called a "Nevadan." For journalists, the media markets of the West are but stepping-stones to what are perceived as the more "legitimate" markets of the East, and local journalism suffers because the steady turnover results in many journalists who do not stay long enough to get to know the character and history of the area. Yet, as we shall see, this is a broad generalization, because sometimes the frontiersmen stayed, as today some stay to help build their adopted towns.

TWO

THE WEST
AS A REGION

The study of the history of regions in the United States, as opposed to historical themes such as politics and culture, people and limited geographical locales, has not caught on with journalism historians as much as it has for those examining the broader scope of history. Other than the press in the South and West, the literature of journalism history offers little that might define press development in connection with an area of the nation larger than a state.

REGIONAL HISTORY

The question of region is both geographical and mythological because in both senses regions are difficult to define. The West, for example, is laden with image, legend, and myth; it was once likened to the Garden of Eden, supposedly representative of the pure of heart. That, of course, was before people recognized the harshness of the desert that covers much of the Southwest or the earthquakes and rain that bring havoc to the Pacific Coast. Even today, in some circles, the West has an image of somehow being "better" than the crowded cities of the East. The oft-told tale of the country mouse and city mouse—the former an innocent, the latter too wise and experienced for his own good—permeates our literature and our thinking, and although the West has never been particularly rural in the usual sense, it remains something of a country mouse, albeit with a big hat and cowboy boots rather than a pitchfork and a piece of straw in his teeth. The white and black hats of mid-twentieth-century cowboy films and television are embedded in our consciousness, and the cowboys in white hats surely represent goodness every bit as much as the country mouse does. In fact, almost all of those who braved the rigors of the Oregon, California, or Gila trails to be pioneers in the new land are by definition "good," at least in spirit, even when we know that many of them were as ready, able, and willing to take advantage of others in the interest of self-advancement as we could find anywhere else.

At the same time, no one can agree on exactly what the West's physical boundaries are. Generally it has been considered to end at the Pacific Ocean, but the addition of Hawaii and Alaska to the roster of states makes even that simple border obsolete. Indeed, many have suggested the West is more a state of mind than a physical reality. Similar arguments are made about the South.

While we could consider studies of the colonial period to be regional in nature, since the original colonies were all on or near the Atlantic seaboard, research that covers the press of more than one part of the colonies, such as David A. Copeland's work, centers on social or political themes, rather than regionalism per se.[1] In addition, psychologist Max Sugar argues in *Regional Identity and Behavior* that the colonies were actually four separate cultures that were so different from one another they could not

be considered a "region."[2] Historian David Hackett Fischer identified four distinct cultures in New England alone, while also
noting that regions reinvent themselves.[3] For example, he points
to Puritan origins of New England that continue to be evident,
even though the ethnic and religious makeup of the region
changed significantly with the arrival of Roman Catholics from
Ireland, who "learned to play by Yankee rules."[4]

Regional history has had its ups and downs in popularity
among the broader scholarly community, and has its own
themes and conflicts. The principal debate has been led by
geographers, some of whom say that the physical nature of a
region is of primary importance, while others argue for pushing
cultural concerns to the foreground. But, of course, the most
useful studies are those that recognize that culture and physical
geography interact. People take their cultures with them when
they move from one place to another, but they must also adapt
to the environment in which they find themselves. The aridity
of much of the West has challenged cultures built on the ready
availability of water, for example.[5]

Sociologist Louis Wirth said it well: "Nature sets the stage,
but it is man that is the actor."[6] Frederick Jackson Turner relied
heavily on the physical nature of the West when developing
his famous frontier theory that the immense amount of free
land was an important impetus in shaping the West, but the
availability of land would not have mattered had not culture
determined people's belief that land ownership was important
and desirable.[7] It is nature versus nurture on a big scale.

In the chapters of this book, the tendency of the western
press to mimic the newspapers of the more settled regions is
frequently noted. Certainly the West was peopled by immigrants who brought with them not only their pianos to play,

seeds to plant, books to read, and other accoutrements of "civilized" living, but also their likes and dislikes, their attitudes, their political organizations, and their dreams, not so much of replacing the life they left behind but of improving on it. In catering to this audience, the western press had little need to step out of the box and be significantly different in any way.

However, because historians have not looked at the press of other regions of the country in quite the same way they have studied newspapers of the West (or South), we do not really know the extent of any differences that might exist between the press in these various regions. Thus, attempting to compare journalism in the West with that in other parts of the nation—geographical or mythological—is probably foolhardy.

Increased access, online and on microform, to nineteenth-century newspapers around the nation will allow greater opportunities for researchers to examine more and varied newspapers in order to answer some of the questions raised about regional differences.[8] For the time being, however, we will rely on one source that provides data for all parts of the United States and even conveniently designates regional groupings: the United States census. In 1880 the U.S. Census Bureau engaged in a special report on the newspaper and periodical press of the United States. The bureau hired Simon Newton Dexter North to conduct a survey as part of a series on business and industry, and his work provides a detailed look at the economics, in particular, of publishing in that era.[9] As with all census data, the reader should remember its shortcomings. In this case, census-taker error is not so much at issue, but the data are self-reported, and we know that not all newspapers returned the survey instrument; the report is, therefore, incomplete.[10] A similar but less extensive report was prepared in 1890 as well.

Nevertheless, the 1880 report contains data for 3,407 printing establishments; the 1890 report covers 16,566, illustrating the great growth in journalism in that last decade of the nineteenth century.[11] The 1880 census data placed the value of all products from printing and publishing at $90,789,341; by 1890, it had tripled to $275,452,515.[12] The total number of employees and total wages had also tripled. As would be expected, the data for the two decades show that the rapidly growing western population was served by a rapidly growing newspaper population. Much of the growth was in the hinterland and in readership for existing publications. Because the data were reported by states or territories, and sometimes even by cities, a picture can be drawn of the press in various parts of the nation.

By 1880 San Francisco had achieved national status as a newspaper and periodical city; its reputation as a literate city was already established, and it was number three on a list of twenty-two newspaper cities across the nation in terms of the numbers of copies of daily newspapers issued compared to population. With twenty-one daily newspapers, San Francisco's ratio was one copy for every 1.63 people. New York, second with twenty-nine daily newspapers, published one copy for every 1.58 people. Ten years later, on a list of twenty-nine newspaper cities, New York had fifty daily newspapers and led the nation in copies per person, actually printing more copies than it had population— 1:0.89. San Francisco had the same number of daily newspapers as in 1880 but, thanks to a 143 percent increase in aggregate circulation, now provided a copy for every 1.04 people. In spite of that large circulation growth, the city had dropped to fourth place on the national list in copies per person. Pittsburgh had taken over third place at 1:1.03, and Boston was now second at 1:0.96. The only other western city to make the 1890 list,

Denver, was eighteenth with five daily newspapers and one copy for every 2.22 residents.[13] Nationally, in 1890 daily newspapers printed one copy for every 2.55 people; considering all kinds of periodicals, the ratio was 1:0.91.[14]

The 1880 census divided the nation into five areas: North Atlantic,[15] South Atlantic,[16] North Central,[17] South Central,[18] and Western.[19] These divisions had little similarity in terms of population or area—ranging from more than twenty-two million people in the North Central division to three million residents in the West—but since they apparently had some significance for nineteenth-century observers, in this chapter, I will also use the word *regions* to refer to these groupings of states and territories. As with so much numerical data, the census numbers show that something is, but not necessarily why it is that way. Often numerical data confirm what "everybody knows"—or at least suspects—but occasionally there are surprises. All of the following calculations are based on the North report on newspapers in the 1880 census, or on a similar report in 1890.[20]

It is, for example, no surprise that the South Central division, comprised mostly of southern states devastated in the Civil War, was often the poorest of the divisions. Nor is it surprising that the North Atlantic division, which includes Boston, Philadelphia, and New York City, was generally the wealthiest division regardless of the enormous influx of poor European immigrants in that period. But the benefits to newspaper publishing were spread among the regions.

For example, consider wages, one of the many pieces of information in the 1880 census. The data show that the best place for men employed in some aspect of the newspaper business was the North Central division, where annual wages paid to men averaged more than $1,000. The total includes office, editorial, and printing staff, as well as pieceworkers. Women were better off in the West, where their wages averaged $445.95 a year. Western women in each category except editorial earned more on the average than their counterparts in any of the other divisions. Western men topped the list only in the clerk and piecework categories. In terms of women's pay as a percentage of men's, women in the South Central division fared best; their wages amounted to 56 percent of men's wages in that division. Fifty-six percent of men's wages was not much in the south-central United States, where the actual annual amounts earned were only $343.75 and $613.81, respectively. The relatively well-paid western women achieved almost 50 percent of parity with western men, and earned 30 percent more than their sisters in the South.

It is not clear from the available information how publishers reported the amounts paid to family employees, if any. It is possible that they counted unpaid family members as workers, but listed no amount paid to them, skewing the averages. For example, according to the report, the 2,628 women working as operators in the North Atlantic region averaged annual wages of $1.10. This may be a typographical error on the part of the government printer, but it is as likely to represent unpaid females who operated small job-printing presses for the family business. Examination of the average wage paid to men and women in four job categories—clerk, editorial, operators (those actually doing the printing), and pieceworkers (compositors)—shows that male operators in the North Atlantic division had the highest average wage: $3,485.55 a year. Male editorial workers in the North Central area took home the highest average wages in their category. The report also includes data on nearly six thousand children younger than fifteen years who worked for newspapers and periodicals; their average annual wage for all divisions was $107.67.

TABLE 2.1 Newspaper Industry Growth, 1880 and 1890, by Region

Region	Population 1880	Population 1890	% Change	No. of Dailies (% Change)	Avg. Newspaper Circulation per Region (% Change)	Value of Advertising/ Subscriptions (% Change)
North Atlantic	1,611,944	1,934,108	20	37	54	81
South Atlantic	844,133	984,214	17	31	108	47
North Central	1,447,133	1,867,535	29	53	82	85
South Central	1,134,672	1,376,290	21	44	104	54
Western	160,700	282,024	76	42	20	82

Source: Tenth and Eleventh U.S. Censuses.

Table 2.1 shows that the growth of the newspaper industry between 1880 and 1890 far outstripped population growth in most of the nation. The population increase ranged from a low of 17 percent in the South Atlantic region to a high of 76 percent in the West. Newspaper circulation growth ranged from a low of 20 percent in the West to a high of 108 percent in the South Atlantic. Circulation also more than doubled in the South Central division. The impressive circulation growth in many of the southern states likely reflects the return to something approaching normalcy after the Civil War, when newspapers closed so their staffs could join the Confederate Army. The poor showing in the West suggests that the later waves of immigrants there were of a different character than the initial influx of people, and were perhaps not as interested in reading as the pioneers were. It may also reflect the fact that by 1880 the railroads had spanned the continent and mail service was vastly improved. Faster access to letters and literature from "home" may have reduced the need to read the local newspaper. By then, too, many areas of the West had stabilized, and competition for government entities and for newspapers was no longer so great.

The transient nature of residence in the West may also account for some of the low circulation figures. Even in the twenty-first century, newspaper circulation does not necessarily keep pace with growth in the West, which has some of the fastest-growing cities in the nation.[21] In a mobile nation such as the United States, after someone has made the initial move from wherever he or she called "home," it is easier to keep moving until a new "home" feels right. Many of the immigrants of the mid-nineteenth century changed locations several times.

For example, longtime Las Vegas, Nevada, editor Charles Pember Squires moved as a child with his family from his birthplace in Wisconsin to what his father thought would be a more agreeable location in Minnesota. Later his asthmatic sister, Helen, moved to Walla Walla, Washington, but her health was only marginally better there so she was willing to move again when Squires and other family members decided to try southern California. Their first stop was Pasadena, but Helen pronounced its air unsatisfactory—even before the automobile. They tried San Bernardino, but it wasn't until they arrived in the new town of Redlands that Helen stepped out of the stagecoach, took a deep breath, and said, "This is all right, I can live here."[22]

This kind of mobility continues, and it affects newspaper circulation. Cities growing rapidly in the South, as well as the West, tend to have the least impressive newspaper circulations. For example, as of spring 2007, circulation reported to the Audit Bureau of Circulation and the latest metropolitan-area population figures in the *World Almanac 2006* showed that in Las Vegas, which through the 1990s was the fastest-growing city in the nation, its major newspaper printed enough copies for only 15 percent of the city's population. Portland, Oregon, and Orlando, Florida, also had relatively low circulation figures, producing enough copies for only 19 percent of their population. Newspapers in Nashville, Tennessee, and Austin, Texas, had circulations in the teens as well, in contrast to more settled locales such as Raleigh, North Carolina, at 64 percent; Omaha, Nebraska, at 30 percent; and Little Rock, Arkansas, at 41 percent.[23] Mobility is not the only link to circulation, of course; competition from other media, including the Internet, has impacted newspaper readership, but studies have shown that stability of population is integral to newspaper readership. People need to stay in a town long enough to begin to care about what goes on in it. This, of course, applied to the publisher as well as to his audience. The publishers of one Las Vegas, Nevada, pioneer newspaper gave their enterprise barely six months' attention before they were off starting newspapers in what they hoped would be more congenial circumstances.

Even with aggregate circulation up in the late nineteenth century, income from subscriptions lagged for western newspapers. In the early frontier days, publishers often went broke following the "Law of Newspapers."[24] This "law" put the burden of paying for or stopping a subscription on the subscriber. The custom allowed the publisher to continue to deliver or mail the paper on the assumption that the reader would eventually pay. A reader may have moved to a mining camp hundreds of miles away, but the publisher continued to print a newspaper for him. Newspaper owners also continued to publish advertisements even if the business did not pay for them. Publishers felt that a newspaper full of ads indicated a successful newspaper. Plus, the ads were already set in type, so except in those circumstances where the newspaper did not have room for all the advertisers who were begging to have their ads in the paper, the publisher could see no great disadvantage to continuing to print the ads of a nonpaying advertiser. Early on, many frontier papers foundered on this policy. Later, some publishers seemed to think that chasing down subscribers to make them pay was more bother than it was worth. Publishers who printed the list of delinquent subscribers in their newspapers usually regretted the loss of good will. Generally, their time and effort were better spent contacting advertisers.

Table 2.2 compares newspaper income (from both subscriptions and advertising) in the five regions in 1880 and 1890; although circulation had not kept pace with population growth, Western newspaper income was up substantially thanks to advertising. From the earliest days when approximately 50 percent of a newspaper's content was advertising, to the twentieth century when the *Los Angeles Times* boasted more classified advertising linage than any other newspaper, advertising has been key to the success of the western press.[25]

TABLE 2.2 Newspaper Income (Advertising and Subscription Revenue), 1880 and 1890, by Region

	1880			1890		
Region	Total Income	Number of Newspapers	Income per Newspaper	Total Income	Number of Newspapers	Income per Newspaper
North Atlantic	17,269,875	3,501	4,932	32,568,469	5,027	6,478
South Atlantic	2,562,643	984	2,604	3,790,568	1,311	2,891
North Central	12,824,431	4,920	2,606	24,065,563	8,097	2,972
South Central	2,847,485	1,155	2,466	4,435,825	1,770	2,506
Western	3,470,856	684	5,074	6,343,567	1,401	4,549

Note: Income is given in U.S. dollars.
Source: Tenth and Eleventh U.S. Censuses.

This is not to suggest that publishers in other parts of the nation did not care about advertising and making a profit; of course they did, and American newspapers have long been known for their high profit margins.[26] But if you combine this data with the development of the joint operating agreement, it points to a mind-set among western publishers as more financially focused, even though they may not have realized it themselves. Many editors readily admitted their devotion to financial success—see the earlier references to salutatories—yet a few scorned the notion of being in the West to make money. An editorial in the *Sacramento Union* in 1851 took readers to task for being more interested in making money than in building California. A few months later, however, the *Union* showed its own true color to be green. It reported that it did not want to get into a damaging price war and had come to an agreement with the competition, the *Sacramento Times* and the *Transcript,* for common subscription and advertising rates.[27]

CAPITAL INVESTMENT

At least two other items of census data are of interest. The first is the value of each newspaper establishment in terms of capital investment. This information is available from the 1890 census and is shown in table 2.3. The North Atlantic and North Central divisions clearly led the way with total capital reported at nearly $60 million for the former (an average of $11,933 per establishment) and $43 million for the latter ($5,353). The West came third with nearly $9 million in total investment, or an average of $6,335 per establishment (second highest of the five regions).

TABLE 2.3 Newspaper Capitalization, 1880 and 1890, by Region

Region	Total Newspaper Capitalization	Number of Newspapers	Capitalization/ Newspaper
North Atlantic	$59,987,463	5,027	$11,933
South Atlantic	$5,938,534	1,311	$4,530
North Central	$43,342,271	8,097	$5,353
South Central	$8,102,807	1,770	$4,578
Western	$8,875,020	1,401	$6,335

Note: Monetary unit is the U.S. dollar.
Source: Tenth and Eleventh U.S. Censuses.

The second noteworthy item is the comparison of area served. It was suggested in chapter 1 that geography influenced newspapers in the West: it created the long supply lines that frequently experienced interruptions, thereby hindering publication, and it created the need to reach beyond a core community to residents living on ranches, farms, and in mining and lumber camps, sometimes at considerable distances, thanks to the massive size of the West. These distances also contributed to the diversity of the press. Special interests, such as the utopian colonies, relied on newspapers to create a virtual community of members who sometimes lived at considerable distances from one another. The size differences between the regions are shown vividly in table 2.4.

Modern communication has largely eliminated many of the disadvantages created by western geography. At the same time, however, it has created a demand for immediacy. The newspaper subscriber of the frontier period was relatively content if the "news" was only a month old, and the subscriber appreciated the editor's assurances that he had at least tried to

TABLE 2.4 Area of Geographic Regions, 1880–1890

Region	Square Miles
North Atlantic	162,065
South Atlantic	268,620
North Central	605,850
South Central	540,385
Western	1,175,550

Source: Tenth and Eleventh U.S. Censuses.

check its veracity; today's news consumers want their information to be transmitted almost instantaneously, and they do not seem to care whether it has been vetted for accuracy by anyone.[28]

The changes in newspapers that have occurred in the decade leading up to the publication of this volume are not, of course, unique to the western press. All newspapers have been subject to the inroads made on their audiences by television in the mid-twentieth century and by the Internet in the late twentieth and early twenty-first centuries.

Frontier newspapers had no such competition. And yet the West is infamous for the number of newspapers that were started and failed during the nineteenth century. Generally the blame is laid upon the readers—or lack thereof. The assumption is that the newspaper was not good enough to attract readers and therefore it failed. This is not exactly true. There were as many reasons for the failure of newspapers in the hundreds of small western communities that had so looked forward to having their own press as there were for starting newspapers, but rarely was rejection by the community one of them. Sometimes it was true that the publishers did not pay enough attention to the desires of their constituents; sometimes they belonged to the wrong party; or they filled their columns with so much advertising they could not meet the needs of readers desperate for literature of any kind. Sometimes, as in Whatcom on Bellingham Bay in Washington Territory, the audience moved on because of separate political and economic circumstances. But as often as not, despite their confident statements about their commitment to financial success, frontier publishers did not make good business decisions. Like small business owners in many places and many times, they overextended themselves and could not repay those who had lent them money, resulting in bankruptcy and foreclosure.[29]

THREE

THE MINING CAMP PRESS

Although they were not the only attraction the West offered to easterners, gold and other precious metals have stood out in much of the literature about western growth, especially in certain areas such as the western slopes of the Sierra Nevada range in California, where gold was discovered in 1848, launching a major cross-continent migration.

The mining camps that sprang up to house and supply prospectors were a colorful addition to western history, full (mostly) of men who, according to the lore, worked hard during the day to make their fortunes and worked equally hard at night to spend them by getting drunk, gambling, and whoring. Mining camps generally had a sprinkling of women and children: among the former were adventurous wives who wanted to see the West for themselves and were unwilling to wait until their husbands struck pay dirt and sent for them, prostitutes who saw opportunity among miners who were either unmarried or far from the tender mercies of their beloveds, and a few women who were miners in their own right.[1]

But it is the men who stand out in the images we have (created primarily by the movies) of a mining camp: mostly unshaven, wearing wide-brimmed hats and well-worn boots, often waving a bottle of whiskey as they stagger or swagger down the street. Sometimes we see a miner carrying a pick and wide, flat metal pan for swirling gold flakes from the waters of the Sierra slopes or trudging through desolate country, tugging a rope tied to a stubborn mule.

Rarely do we see a miner reading a book or a newspaper, even though the newspaper office is a fixture in the cinematic mining camp. Usually there is just one newspaper office in such depictions, but in reality the more prosperous mining camps— the Virginia Cities in Nevada and Montana, and Tombstone in Arizona, among others—had more than one.[2]

Despite the stereotypical rough image of the miners, culture thrived in the camps. Historian Ray Allen Billington records that schools, literary societies, and theaters for plays and concerts were common and that performers liked to play the mining camps because they might be rewarded with bags of gold.[3]

These mining camps also had bookstores, frequently located in the newspaper office or the stationery store, which often were the same place. We usually do not see these in the film versions of the camps. We do see the frontier editor taking a photograph with his fiery magnesium flash, and although the depiction of the photographic method may be accurate, the implication that the photo would appear in the newspaper the next day or even week was not.

Until the late 1880s and the development of the halftone, newspapers had to use engravings for illustrations, so a photo would be sent away to an engraver who reproduced the image on a metal printing plate.[4] For the isolated mining camp newspapers of the West, far from big-city services, this took days or weeks, and while authorities found the engraving process useful for "wanted" posters that remained timely for an extended period—unless the villain was particularly unlucky and was caught or killed quickly—it could not be used on a day-to-day basis except in the metropolitan centers. Both engraving and the cheaper halftone process were also generally too expensive for mining camp newspapers that typically had only five hundred or so subscribers, most of whom were delinquent in paying for their newspapers, if the newspapers' frequent pleas to readers to meet their obligations are any indication.[5] Even after the invention of the halftone, equipment for the process was too expensive for the typical small weekly newspaper. Few of them printed photographs until the early twentieth century.

HEAVY WORK

Throughout most of the nineteenth century, the production of a frontier newspaper was little different from the methods Gutenberg used in the sixteenth century to print his famous Bibles. After stories were written or selected from other newspapers, the type had to be set one letter at a time, much like playing Scrabble on a massive board with tiny tiles—this was called "sticking type" after the holder or "stick" into which the letters were first placed. The completed story was put in the "chase," a metal frame set on the "stone," a flat surface. The chase held the type tight while leather balls were used to spread ink over the surface. A lightly dampened sheet of paper was carefully placed over the inked type, and a metal plate the size of the page was screwed, or sometimes levered, depending on the particular kind of press, down on top of it for an even impression of the ink. The plate was raised, and the paper was carefully removed, so as not to smudge the ink, and allowed to dry before being printed on the other side. This was repeated for as many sheets as needed—usually only one, which was printed two pages at a time (pages one and four, two and three) and folded in half for a four-page newspaper. It was a slow process and generally took two men.

The press was heavy and hard to work, one reason we do not see a great many women starting newspapers. Women did, however, find employment setting type; their usually smaller fingers were generally considered more nimble at extracting the tiny letters from the type case. Many newspaper printing shops had women typesetters, as old photographs that show them standing in their long skirts at the type cases bear witness.

Often the women were wives or daughters of the editor-publisher.[6] Keeping the business in the family helped keep costs down, but at least one Nevada newspaper took on single women as apprentices.[7]

LOCALS EDITOR TWAIN

In most ways, the mining camp newspaper was typical of other bastions of the press on the western frontier. Physically, editorial and printing activities were in separate rooms, and the men often slept and ate in the building. Only the larger newspapers actually had "reporters"—people who went out looking for news and returned to the office to write columns of "locals," the bits of news they had culled from their wanderings around town. Samuel Clemens was a locals writer for one of those larger papers, the *Territorial Enterprise* in Virginia City, Nevada, a town which at the height of the Comstock fever claimed a population of more than fifteen thousand.[8] If his own accounts are to be believed—and a biographer suggests they are as creative as some of his later fiction written under the name Mark Twain—one of his first stories was manufactured at the behest of his editor, Joe Goodman.

Although Goodman is generally praised as what later generations would consider a responsible journalist, he apparently did nothing to discourage the twenty-seven-year-old Clemens's use of imagination in reporting, thus facilitating his transition to Twain. According to *Enterprise* lore, on Clemens's first day at the newspaper in 1862, Goodman sent him out to find the local news. When he came back empty-handed, Goodman chided him, told him how another *Enterprise* writer, William Wright (Dan DeQuille), could turn a routine town event into a major happening, and sent him back out on the street.[9]

Clemens soon obliged with a story magnifying the arrival of a lowly wagon full of hay into an invasion of hay wagons. "I multiplied it by sixteen, brought it into town from sixteen different directions, made sixteen separate items of it, and got up such another sweat about hay as Virginia City had never seen in the world before," Twain said later, explaining how he filled his two-column quota.[10] On another occasion, he turned the passage of an immigrant wagon train through hostile Indian territory into "an Indian fight with no parallel in history," and in his account wiped out all parties of one of the wagons. In *Roughing It,* Twain's account of his life in the West, he says plainly that he didn't like facts getting in the way of a good story and that only the likelihood that he would get caught kept him from more exaggeration.[11] He also admits, however, that once he discovered he could hold his own against the other journalists in Virginia City, he was less inclined to make things up. His career, however, is marked by stories that stretch credulity.

Twain had come to Nevada from Hannibal, Missouri, where he had more or less mastered his trade on the *Courier* as a print shop apprentice. He had learned to set type, a skill that made highly literate men out of many who engaged in it, thanks to the focus on words.[12]

In 1861, when his brother Orion Clemens was appointed secretary to the Nevada Territorial governor, James Warren Nye, Twain decided to accompany him to the territory's headquarters in Carson City. The Comstock rush was but two years old, and young Sam could not wait to join the hundreds of men probing the Nevada earth for riches. As he notes in *Roughing It,* he had tried—and failed at—many potential occupations by that time. In any case, he headed for the tiny mining camp of Aurora, seat of the newly formed Esmeralda County on the California-Nevada border, and one of the first five towns incorporated by the new Nevada Territorial legislature. In 1860 Aurora had been the site of "the first important mining discovery outside the Comstock," on the eastern side of the Sierra Nevada.[13] It experienced the typical mining camp boom: in 1864 Aurora supported two daily newspapers, and in less than ten years it produced more than twenty-nine million dollars in gold ore; then the town and its ore field rapidly declined, and over the next eighty years it produced only another two million dollars.[14] Aurora lost the county seat to Hawthorne in 1883.[15]

Twain went to Aurora with prospecting in mind, but, never one for hard physical labor, after about a day of shoveling earth, he inquired about becoming a compositor at the *Esmeralda Union.* He admits, however, that typesetting was one of the careers in which he had failed; he was exceedingly slow at sticking type, and when the *Union* had no openings, he does not seem to have been upset. In the meantime he had been writing letters to the *Territorial Enterprise,* the Comstock area's first printed newspaper, which, to his purported surprise, had printed them. He was much relieved to be able to walk away from pick and shovel duty when the *Enterprise* offered him a job writing locals for twenty-five dollars a week. He says at that point he realized that writing might be the career he had been seeking.[16]

As noted, Twain had no qualms about fudging the line between fact and fiction, and since much of what is known of his years in Nevada comes from his own pen, much of it is therefore suspect.[17] However, some of what he says is corroborated by fellow journalists in Virginia City who, with some exceptions, were apparently not above engaging in fiction themselves while appearing to report the news.[18]

While it might seem that the use by Twain and his colleagues of literary license to play fast and loose with facts should deny them the right to the title *journalist,* research by journalism historian Hazel Dicken-Garcia places him firmly in his journalistic times. Dicken-Garcia has documented the prevalence and acceptance of what she calls "news manufacturing" in late-nineteenth-century America.[19] Twain clearly indulged in this practice, and did it with more pizzazz than most of his cohorts.

In Montana, Henry N. Blake, of the *Montana Post* in another Virginia City, said he also made mountains out of molehills, "dressed to the best of my ability in attractive phrases."[20] He added that he had to make as much of the news as possible because there was so little of it.

JOE GOODMAN

Twain's boss, Joe Goodman, who at twenty-three was even younger than the future literary giant, worked hard to make the *Territorial Enterprise* a newspaper of record for the Comstock area, particularly for mining news. He and his brother joined the western immigration in the 1850s, and Goodman set type for the *Golden Era* in San Francisco. His experience on this literary publication clearly influenced his future management of the *Enterprise,* because he not only tolerated Twain's literary forays but stressed good writing from all of the staff he hired, and he brought to the Nevada newspaper a number of journalists with literary connections, including Rollin Daggett, the former editor of the *Golden Era.*[21] While setting type for the *Era,* Goodman had met Denis McCarthy, and the two of them formed a business partnership in 1861 to purchase the *Enterprise.*

In his biographical sketch of Goodman, historian Lawrence I. Berkove calls him "fiercely and fearlessly independent" and describes his many exposés of mining scams, as well as his destruction of the senatorial hopes of William Sharon.[22] Not only was Goodman a competent journalist, but the paper he edited was a financial success. This achievement may have resulted from a good journalistic product, belying Alfred McClung Lee's statement that miners were not discriminating readers, or, more likely, it resulted from being in the right place at the right time, when miners had tapped a rich vein of ore so that they and those who supplied their needs had lots of money. *Enterprise* lore symbolizes Goodman and McCarthy's success by having them carry buckets of silver dollars to the bank. In 1865 Goodman bought out McCarthy, who proceeded to lose his substantial wealth playing the stock exchange in San Francisco; he returned to Virginia City to work as foreman in the *Enterprise* print shop.[23] Goodman edited the newspaper until 1874, when the man he had attacked editorially, William Sharon, revealed that he had quietly acquired enough stock to control the *Enterprise.* Goodman refused to work for the politician and retired to San Francisco, but like most of the frontier newspapermen, he could not stay away from publishing for very long. He worked on a number of San Francisco newspapers, and the *Enterprise* published his letters from a European trip. In 1877 he tried his hand at being a stockbroker, but like his partner before him, he soon lost all his money. Offered an opportunity to repurchase the *Enterprise,* Goodman recognized that the Comstock's glory days had passed and the camps were in decline. In 1884 he started his own literary journal, *San Franciscan,* but soon sold it. Central America and newly discovered Mayan ruins caught his attention, and he took up the study of the Mayan hieroglyphs. He was able to decipher enough to realize that they represented the Mayan calendar and that the calendar had played a central role in Mayan culture. Goodman's work is still recognized as part of the Goodman-Thompson-Martinez hypothesis.[24]

Generally, locals editors like Twain filled one of the four pages of the weekly newspaper with short items, some of which were clearly advertising notices, but who is to say that advertising is not news to its readers? Some editors admitted that the inclusion of some local items was related to the generosity of their subject. A wedding notice might depend on how much cake or liquor the wedding party sent to the newspaper office, or a fish merchant's plug of a fresh supply on how many fish he gave the printers.[25]

For example, the *Marysville Appeal* in California printed the following locals in its inaugural issue on January 23, 1860: first, a plug to attract advertisers to the new newspaper:

> READING MATTER.—It will be observed that we have distributed our reading matter upon the four pages of the APPEAL. By this arrangement the eye of the reader is attracted to all parts of the paper, and advertisements command equal notice wherever placed.

And a thank-you to the local saloon keeper for acknowledging the new paper:

> CHAMPAGNE.—Simultaneously with the adjustment of our press upon its apportioned place on the office floor, came an offering of Champagne from Harry Dougherty of the Union Saloon. It speedily had resting places under printers' jackets. Thank you Harry.

In the *Placer Times* in Sacramento, April 22, 1850, the locals columns included these promotional paragraphs for the local entertainment:

> AMUSEMENTS THIS EVENING—Mr. Massett's Concert at the New Hall, assisted by Mr. Nichols,—a full house, of course.
>
> At the Theatre, "Don Caesar de Bazan," "A Day in Paris," and "The Happy Man," are to be presented. Mr. and Mrs. Hambleton, Mr. Campbell, Mr. Wilson, and other favorites of the San Francisco public, make their first appearance here.

> The spirit of Sir John Falstaff will "visit the glimpse of the moon" tonight, and occupy, during its terrestial [*sic*] sojourn, the mortal body of "Baron" Hackett. Were we a spiritualist, we should point to Hackett as a living proof of our creed. Falstaff will look upon us worthy of the dust, from the stage of the theatre, this evening.

Editors had plenty of material for their mining camp newspapers—they reported new finds of ore veins, business developments, activities at the local opera house, and stock prices. Reporters like Twain were often rewarded with "feet" (stock) in new mines after—or even before—they wrote positive stories about the prospects of an enterprise. Reporters learned how to be ambiguous and vague, writing about how the *indications were good* for the mine, or that it *resembled* the Comstock. Sometimes the stock proved to be valuable for the journalist; often it was worthless. Twain said that when Goodman increased his salary to forty dollars a week, he rarely collected it because he had "plenty of other resources." On one occasion he held on to some "feet" a little too long as he watched the stock soar and then plunge faster than technology stocks fell in 2000–2001.[26]

Comstock editor Wells Drury tells of finding a gold nugget in the craw of a chicken one morning at breakfast. "By camp custom this treasure trove was handed over to the *restaurateur,* Charlie Legate. The precious metal when later assayed totaled $4.85, just about a British pound sterling; and I bought it, carrying the gold around with me in the form of cuff-links, to recall my first 'strike' on the Comstock."[27]

Twain and others covered the Nevada Territorial legislature, another generous subject. The legislature used journalists' reports as the official record of the proceedings and paid them for it because otherwise the lawmakers would have had to hire a stenographer to record the deliberations. In 1861 they paid three dollars a day; the following year the payment was doubled to six dollars.[28]

TRUE TALES OF THE *ENTERPRISE*

The *Territorial Enterprise*'s history is full of colorful stories, not all of them revolving around Twain, and some probably apocryphal.

Enterprise founder William L. Jernegan felt cheated out of his interest in the newspaper, and when nearing death he cursed it and Nevada: "I call on God to curse the *Enterprise* and all, dead or alive, who robbed me, and I also call down the curses of the Great Jehovah on Nevada by quarter sections and subdivisions." By the time Jernegan wrote this in his diary, his partner Jonathan Williams had committed suicide. Future editors of the *Enterprise* sometimes recalled Jernegan's curse as Nevada lost population—and the *Enterprise* lost money—while territories all around were gaining settlers.[29]

One day, *Enterprise* printers dropped the type-filled pages of the newspaper while putting them on the press, dumping thousands of tiny letters on the print shop floor, thoroughly "pi-ing the type," according to print shop jargon. The typesetters sorted through the mess and recovered enough type to print part of the newspaper but left some pages blank. According to the neighboring *Gold Hill News,* "Subscribers to the Territorial Enterprise were greatly astonished this morning on discovering that the inside of the paper was blank." The *News* explained that the composing room was on the third floor of the *Enterprise* office building, and the press was in the basement. The chase— the frame that holds the type tightly for the press—had slipped as it was being carried to the basement, dumping three hundred pounds of fifteen or twenty different kinds of type. One of the "boys" gave a copy of the blank paper to Old Dufferdink, one of the town drunks, and suggested he might want to read about the rape, arson, and other news. The poor fellow looked at the blank pages, started to weep, declared, "I'm struck stone blind," and passed out.[30]

Once clearing one thousand dollars' profit a day, by 1893 the *Enterprise* had no audience left and died quietly, but not unnoticed: the Society of Pacific Coast Pioneers flew its flag at half mast.[31] The newspaper's name has been revived periodically by publishers hoping to profit from the historic name, most recently in 1952. That effort ended in 1969.[32]

NORTHERN LIGHT

The arrival of a newspaper press in a mining camp was often an occasion for festivities. Like the booster-driven town, mining camp residents saw value in having a newspaper. In the first place, many of them hoped the camp would be permanent and grow into a proper community. However high their awareness of the boom-and-bust nature of mining, they always thought their location would be different. The newspaper helped by providing legitimacy, but, of course, if the miners suddenly moved on in the chase for another vein of precious metal, the newspaper might go along, too, or simply close down.

Such was the case of the *Northern Light* of Bellingham Bay, in Washington Territory. In 1858 San Francisco newspaperman William Bausman heard of the discovery of gold on Canada's Fraser River. The Pennsylvanian had come west to seek his fortune in the northern California gold fields but, like so many of his craft, soon tired of pick and shovel duty and turned back to the composing stick and press, editing a mining camp newspaper, the *Hydraulic Press,* in North San Juan in northern California. Subsequently he bought an interest in the *Daily Sun* in San Francisco. When the discovery of gold in the Fraser River district of British Columbia, Canada, stirred interest as far south as San Francisco, Bausman decided there would be more profit in supplying the miners with reading matter than in joining them in the mines, and he boarded a steamer for Bellingham Bay with a printing press, not a gold pan, in his luggage.[33]

On the steamer, Bausman influenced others to join him at Bellingham (then known as Whatcom) rather than go on to Victoria, Canada. "When they heard there was a printing press aboard going to Whatcom, they supposed the owner had inside information and changed their destination," Bausman wrote later.[34]

Bausman was welcomed to Bellingham by its developer, Captain Henry Roeder, who had big plans for the building lots he had purchased around the bay and gave Bausman property on which to locate his newspaper. Bausman was happy to do his part in boosting Whatcom, and promised in his first issue on July 3, 1858, to help Whatcom become "THE American town of the North."[35]

At the time of Bausman's first issue of *Northern Light,* Whatcom had at least a dozen grocers, three hotels, eight cafes, eighty houses, 130 tents, and other businesses, surely the heart of a new community. Because Whatcom was the start of a short route to the Fraser River diggings, and because it was under American control, American prospectors were happy to use Bellingham Bay as a staging point.

The observant British, however, looked across the waters of Puget Sound and saw the wealth starting to flow to Whatcom. They wanted the business for themselves and, since the mines were actually in British North America, were able to call the shots. They issued an edict that all prospectors had to get a license before going to the gold fields and declared that the license could be obtained only in Victoria on Vancouver Island. From there, a return to Whatcom significantly lengthened the trip to the Fraser River, and access to gold being more important to a miner than town building, Whatcom's value as a staging point plummeted. By September Whatcom had reverted to being a quiet sawmill village, and the thirty-eight-year-old Bausman suspended his newspaper, ruefully telling friends, "Whatcom has gone in and the Light has gone out."[36] He returned to California and later served as private secretary to Governor J. Neely Johnson. Bausman died in 1893.[37]

EDITORS' STAMPEDE

About seven months after the Whatcom boom and bust, an area in the Colorado Rockies, a few hundred miles southeast of the Washington coastal town, had its own boom, and although the accompanying competition was not as formidable as that of the British government, it nevertheless led one printer to give up his plans to publish a newspaper; he sold his press and headed for the mines himself.

What historian David Halaas calls a "dramatic stampede of editors and printers to Cherry Creek [the future Denver] in the Spring of Fifty-nine" came on the heels of a gold discovery on Pike's Peak, and just as being the first to discover a rich vein promised riches, so did being first on the streets with a newspaper ensure a publisher's future.[38]

Leading the pack to Cherry Creek were a sometime surveyor and successful town promoter from Omaha, William N. Byers, and a journeyman printer from Leavenworth, Kansas, Jack Merrick. Merrick, hauling an old Mormon press recovered from the Missouri River where an angry anti-Mormon mob had thrown it, arrived in the camps of Cherry Creek and

Auraria in early April 1859, a few days ahead of Byers.[39] Byers, however, anticipating that conditions in the camps would be less than optimal for newspaper publishing, had printed one side of his four-page sheet before leaving Omaha, which gave him a head start on getting a newspaper into the hands of readers. Upon arrival in the Colorado camp, he quickly acquired office space and set about filling the other side of the sheet. As Halaas tells it:

> On April 22 [1859], three days after Byers' arrival, a whiskey-excited crowd "vibrated" between the competing print offices, watching latest developments and placing bets on the outcome of the "Battle of the Newspapers." Finally, at ten o'clock in the evening, Byers hurriedly distributed copies of his *Rocky Mountain News* to the awaiting populace. Jack Merrick's *Cherry Creek Pioneer* appeared but twenty minutes later, prompting a "self-constituted newspaper committee" to declare Byers the victor. The following morning, a disappointed Merrick sold his press and type to his rival and set off for the mountains to pick gold instead of stick type.[40]

Because the Denver area offered easier access for eastern journalists to major mining camps than did Bellingham Bay, Fraser River, or even San Francisco, a steady flow of "scribblers" followed Byers and Merrick to the Rocky Mountains. Many of them, not finding appropriate work in the growing city, went on into the mountains to start camp newspapers of their own.

The farther a mining camp was from a city, the greater the challenge to the publisher to produce a newspaper. The more isolated the camp, the harder it was to get news because the mail carrying the essential newspaper exchanges did not always get through, especially in the winter snow. Neither did freight, on which newspapermen depended for their supplies. In 1859 the Virginia City, Nevada, *Territorial Enterprise* relied on mountain expressmen for rescue when it ran out of paper: John "Snow Shoe" Thompson was famous for making his way across the mountains on his snowshoes, and on at least one occasion another expressman, John A. Trumbo, "toil[ed] over the snow-clad summit of the mountains with the paper on his back—to [the] peril [of] his own life." [41] Regardless of their efforts, sometimes the *Enterprise* skipped an issue because it had no newsprint or paper of any kind; at other times it printed on wallpaper or whatever material the staff could locate in Virginia City.

To a degree, the weather was the great equalizer between the isolated camps and the metropolitan areas. In the primitive building conditions of the time, a blizzard, ice storm, or even just a good rainstorm could cause almost as much distress in town as in a remote settlement. In both locations, printers stretched cobwebs of strings from the print shop ceiling, channeling the water that came through leaky roofs along the lines so that it would not drip onto type and precious paper.

Like frontiersmen in general, printers were resourceful. When they bought an assortment of type that lacked enough of some letters, they carved the missing letters; when they ran out of *w*'s, they put two *v*'s together; lacking *v*'s, they used *u*'s. When a press part was needed, they made it from whatever materials they had. An editor in Oregon City declared that the wooden press he built would "tell the truth quite as well as an iron one." [42]

As already noted, when they ran out of newsprint, they used whatever paper was available: cigar wrappers, notebook paper, wallpaper, wrapping paper, and so on. When composition rollers replaced leather balls for inking type, printers made their own rollers from glue and glycerin or molasses. Dry western climates made rollers brittle; hot western climates sometimes melted them.[43] The Mormons' *Deseret News* once asked readers to donate molasses so it could make more rollers. When a paper mill was established in Utah to supply newsprint for the *News,* the editor frequently begged readers for rags.[44]

Byers's foresight in preprinting half of his newspaper foreshadowed what would, after the Civil War, become a common practice and an aid to the establishment of many a western newspaper. Preprinted pages, known as "patent 'sides," insides for pages two and three of a four-page paper, or outsides for pages one and four, were developed to help a newspaper whose staff had gone off to war, as so many did after 1860. For would-be frontier publishers, who were usually short-staffed anyway, preprints greatly reduced their labor needs, while providing subscribers with news and literary efforts they might not otherwise have received. Companies sprang up in major centers such as Chicago and, later in the West, San Francisco, Portland, and Spokane, to service small newspapers with preprints so they needed fewer typesetters and less time to complete publication.[45]

The preprint companies hired staffs who culled news, fiction, and poetry from the exchanges of eastern newspapers, looking for timeless items. Given the weeks or months it took most news to reach the West Coast, preprint staffers could choose from plenty of stories that would be new to western readers. Editors of the patent 'sides knew that their content would be as fresh as most other news a frontier newspaper could come up with, other than the locals, because their clients also relied on the oft-delayed exchanges. The preprint producers in the cities received newspaper exchanges more speedily than the frontier newspaper offices did, plus they had easy access to the big-city papers. Preprint editors had access to a greater variety of news and literary material than the typical frontier editor had, and they received it faster, working generally from offices in big cities with aggressive newspapers. The frontier editor kept copies of literary classics handy to copy from if he had a slow news week, but that would not have been popular with any of his subscribers who were well read.

Preprints were controversial. Some editors scorned those who relied on patent 'sides, insisting that they did not properly serve their readers if they did not select every story themselves. One Washington Territory publisher refused to use them, even though he knew they would save him money. "To publish a paper entirely of home print, entails more than twice the expense of a patent outside," he said.[46] He said his paper would carry only the "choicest miscellany" and "nothing but the very latest news," carefully selected, typeset, and printed by his office. One anti-preprint editor in New Mexico called the users "emasculated humbugs," and another editor remarked that a neighboring paper that had failed "was a patent-outside, weakly, milk-and-water sort of weekly, and its death creates no aching void in the journalism of Nevada." When a Yakima, Washington, paper failed to publish one week because its preprints did not arrive, a competitor saw that as one more reason to avoid their use.[47]

Certainly preprints would have saved the publisher money. Preprint providers could buy paper in bulk and could use some of the same stories in several versions sold to many different newspapers. They sold advertising for their publications. They would customize their product for a specific client so that it looked more like the local paper. Meanwhile, the frontier editor did not have to hire as many compositors or printers, and his production time was greatly reduced, allowing his staff to work on job printing that might be more remunerative.[48] Byers probably would not have won the printing competition in Cherry Creek, and he, instead of Merrick, might have been the one to sell his press and go prospecting, had he not done his own preprinting before heading for Colorado.

Regardless of whether preprints were involved, the typical camp newspaper published weekly, but the arrival of the mail was often the occasion for an extra. Sometimes only a single page, the extra gave the miners the latest news—which still might be months old.

A few mining camps grew large enough to support daily newspapers, as well as multiple newspapers. Virginia City, Nevada, at the heart of the Comstock gold and silver boom, is perhaps the best known of the larger mining camps. Its preeminent newspaper, the *Territorial Enterprise,* actually began in Genoa, a tiny settlement in 1858 and the county seat of Carson County, Utah Territory. Cofounder William Jernegan was running from his California creditors, and Genoa was sufficiently isolated to suit his purpose.

In less than a year Jernegan moved the operation to Carson City, a few miles to the south, but his creditors soon caught up with him, so his then-partner, Jonathan Williams, moved it again to booming Virginia City at the heart of the Comstock silver excitement. The paper changed hands every few years, eventually closing in 1893. The name has been revived periodically.

GOOD WILL IN THE PRINTING FRATERNITY

Scattered throughout the West, particularly in the mountains, were hundreds of mining camps, most of which worked to establish their legitimacy by supporting, at least for a time, a newspaper. Some of these newspapers are known only because some other newspaper acknowledged their debut, the custom among newspapermen being to salute their new competition and wish the upstart well. This good will carried over into times of crisis. If a brother editor was shut down by fire, earthquake, flood, or other disaster, his cohorts came to his rescue with the loan of type, presses, paper, scissors—whatever he needed to meet his production schedule. What they couldn't provide, however, was a replacement for the advertising that might disappear if the disaster severely damaged the businesses in the affected town. In 1878 the tiny central Nevada town of Austin, nestled in a steep canyon as so many mining camps were, experienced one of Nevada's gully-washers. This flash flood tore through the town and damaged the building of the town's newspaper, the *Reese River Reveille*. The newspaper and its town were barely back in business when they were hit by a second flash flood. The *Reveille*'s editor noted that the townspeople were coping but wrote, "The Reveille, however, wants relief." His "cherished scissors" were washed away in the flood. "We cannot conduct the Reveille successfully as a first class family journal without scissors."[49] A few days later, he acknowledged the receipt of a pair of rusty scissors that enabled him to clip from the exchanges. By using type borrowed from a neighborly printer, he could then fill his columns with the latest news from afar.

Most mining camp newspapers were individually owned, although the owners may have been deep in debt to a wealthy mine owner or a mining company–controlled bank. Exceptions include the first newspaper in Arizona, started by a group of mining companies in Tubac to promote independence for

Arizonans. Other exceptions were the newspapers of Montana. Nearly all the major newspapers in Montana were started by or came under the control of the Anaconda Copper Company. At the University of Montana, Dennis Swibold's research into Montana journalism history shows two thirty-year periods for the "copper dailies," as the company-owned newspapers came to be called. The first three decades essentially started in 1899, during the War of the Copper Kings. "You have all these tycoons in Montana duking it out for political and economic control," he told the author of an article about his work that appeared in the University of Montana magazine *Vision*.[50] One of these contenders was Marcus Daly, the mining engineer who founded the Anaconda company in the 1880s, and who in 1889 "decided like all other tycoons in Montana he needed a newspaper to advance his political and economic agenda."

Daly's newspaper was the *Anaconda Standard,* and Swibold says it "had everything a metropolitan daily would have in Manhattan. . . . You couldn't have found a better newspaper. You wouldn't have found the depth of its national and international reporting" even in big-city newspapers. At the same time, readers would not have found anything negative or controversial about the Anaconda company in the paper. Anaconda built a chain of newspapers throughout Montana, becoming what Swibold calls "this 10,000-pound elephant in the middle of the room." Swibold says that in the first thirty years, the copper dailies "were aggressively championing the company and attacking its enemies. . . . But in the last thirty, not only did they produce really bad journalism, but they had no credibility, so they weren't a good PR vehicle for the company."[51]

Anaconda's primary interest, of course, was mining; it "really didn't understand or care about journalism." In the mid–twentieth century Anaconda decided to get out of the newspaper business and sold its publications to Lee Enterprises, a small midwestern media chain. "Though Lee wasn't the highest bidder for the papers, it won out, Swibold says, 'because Anaconda felt comfortable with Lee's representative, [Don] Anderson. The Montana-born Anderson had been editing Lee's *Wisconsin State Journal* when he got the call to assist in the negotiations with Anaconda. He understood Montana, and the company felt that not only would the papers be in good hands, but the company would probably get pretty favorable treatment from Lee.'"[52]

According to Swibold, however, the newspaper proprietors had no intention of agreeing to go easy on the mining company as part of a deal to buy the Montana papers. "They had agreed to break off talks at the first hint that Anaconda expected favorable treatment as a condition of the sale," Swibold says.[53] Montana readers were shocked, therefore, when the papers covered a strike in Butte and both sides of the story were printed.

Despite general agreement that Montana's papers were in better hands with the Lee purchase, many also expressed concern that almost all of the state's dailies were in this single set of hands.[54] Swibold concludes that thanks to the considerable local autonomy that Lee management grants to individual papers, Montana is not likely to experience the kind of press control it had during the Anaconda reign.

Anaconda's keen rival in the copper wars was the Amalgamated Copper Company headed by Senator William A. Clark, owner of the *Butte Miner.* Anaconda's Daly and Clark were bitter foes, the latter having bought his way into the Senate, a common practice before the approval of the Seventeenth Amendment calling for the popular election of senators. Daly wanted to unseat Clark, who had helped prevent Daly's company town,

Anaconda, from becoming capital of the state.[55] Remarkably, given the decline in the quality of the Anaconda-owned papers later, when Daly initially financed the *Anaconda Standard,* he also hired an outstanding editor, John Hurst Durston, formerly of Syracuse, New York, to turn it into a fine newspaper. Although some would probably not consider an endorsement by William Randolph Hearst a plus, the California publisher said he had studied the *Standard* and considered it "as able and enterprising as any in the nation."[56]

In 1899 the *Standard* celebrated its tenth anniversary by playing host to the Montana Press Association. The copper wars heated up; Daly was temporarily successful in removing Clark from the Senate, but the latter retrieved his seat "thanks in part to a spree of newspaper buying unmatched in the state's short history."[57]

The Montana Press Association did not meet again for six years. "Its convention reports would resume again in 1906 with the account of a boozy 1,700-mile junket from Butte to Los Angeles that traveled extensively over William A. Clark's new railroad, the San Pedro, Los Angeles, and Salt Lake. To the astonishment of the train's porters, the Montana scribblers ran out of whiskey somewhere near present-day Las Vegas."[58] This Montana connection reappears in the story of Las Vegas, in chapter 5.

FOUR

THE BOOSTER PRESS

Western immigrants considered a newspaper a "legitimizer," that is, it gave their communities credibility and made them "real" towns, because a real town in the mid-nineteenth century had at least one newspaper. So it is not surprising that the settlers who were first on the scene, men who laid claim to as much of the land as they could with the intention of plotting a town and selling lots, usually wanted a newspaper to help boost their communities, and thereby their fortunes.

For town boosters—hence the label "booster press"—a newspaper not only granted the legitimacy that settlers were seeking but was also useful in promoting the town. While it might seem that a newspaper was preaching to the converted when it told its readers how wonderful the climate might be, how rich the soil or minerals were in the vicinity, and how many new enterprises had started in recent months, publishers made use of the "exchanges" to make sure that people outside of their community heard about the town's virtues.[1]

One of the common—and misleading—myths of journalism history is that the thousands of small papers that sprang up across the nation as settlements spread through the continent did not include local information—that they did not print local news.

William Lyon, for example, claimed that the pioneer editor was not a chronicler of his local community.[2] John Cameron Sim insisted that to locals, "news" was something from outside their communities. He argued that local news or personal items "began appearing regularly only around the 1890s," adding that "readers didn't really expect to find local news in their papers; some might even have resented it. . . . The newspaper asks us for news, prints it, and then asks us to buy it."[3] In his biography of the frontier journalist Legh Freeman, Thomas Heuterman contended that Freeman and his brother were not typical of frontier editors who, Heuterman said, ignored local news because they lacked reportorial techniques or felt readers already knew of local events.[4]

Oliver Knight, on the other hand, knew that local news was important to small-town editors and their readers. His content analysis of the *Owyhee Avalanche,* a mining camp paper in southwestern Idaho, showed that 58 percent of the four-page weekly was devoted to news of various kinds and about half of that was local news (the other 42 percent was advertising). The *Avalanche* editors, John and Joseph Wasson, positioned their newspaper as "faithfully devoted to local news."

While it is true that in the sense of "covering" local news, western newspapers fell short because as a rule only the big-city newspapers had the staff to "cover" anything, it is certainly incorrect to say they had no local content. Most of these newspapers were four pages, sometimes about the size of a magazine, sometimes broadsheets so big that a full stretch of the arms could not hold them open. Generally one-quarter to one-half of the newspaper—certainly half if you count the advertising—was devoted to items of local interest.

Prosperous mining camp newspapers in Nevada had their "locals" editors who combed the streets of the camps for items to put in the papers. The *Territorial Enterprise* in Virginia City had Mark Twain and Dan DeQuille; the nearby *Gold Hill News* had Alfred Doten, who later served the same function for the *Enterprise* and for the *Reese River Reveille* in Austin after the failure of the *News* sent him looking for another job. In 1866 the *Arizona Miner* in Prescott pledged to emphasize local affairs, a promise many frontier editors made to their readers.[5]

For the most part, covering local affairs included the bad news as well as the good, even in newspapers committed to boosting their towns. Indian raids, violence, and bad weather all made it into the columns of the typical frontier newspaper, as editors took seriously their responsibility to keep readers updated on their environment. The *Leader* in Cheyenne, Wyoming, had a name for those who dared speak ill of their towns, however, and especially of Cheyenne. "Croakers," the *Leader* called anyone who had anything negative to say.[6]

The *Leader* would no doubt have called the *Oregonian* a "croaker" after it published this negative but remarkably candid and realistic appraisal of Portland weather in 1873:

Dirty days hath September,
April, June and November,
From January up to May
The rain it raineth every day.
All the rest have 31
Without a blessed gleam of sun
And if any of them had 2 and 30,
They'd be just as wet and twice as dirty.[7]

In contrast, the editors of the *Mendocino Democrat* in California were soul mates of the Cheyenne journalists and would have avoided the "croaker" epithet. In 1875 the *Carson Valley News* in Nevada Territory reprinted a paragraph from the *Democrat:*

> It's bad taste for a country newspaper to rake up every little disreputable transaction that occurs in its locality, spread it out in the biggest and most degrading dimensions, dish it up in its columns and send it out to the outside public as a specimen of the town characteristics. The duty of a local paper is to build up, defend, and advance the interest, good name and prosperity of the place in which it has support and being, and not to decry it, and bring it into bad repute. And the paper that does this duty in this respect should receive the countenance and support of the community as a true and much-to-be cherished friend, while the one of a contrary character should be met with discountenance and repudiation.

USING THE EXCHANGES

In the days before the telegraph, and even after its service became readily available, frontier newspapers relied on the exchanges for out-of-area news. They benefited greatly from federal postal laws that at various times in the nineteenth century allowed newspapers to mail copies to one another postage-free. Booster editors were particularly heavy users of the exchanges. They not only drew upon the exchanges they received for news to fill their own columns, but they published positive stories about their communities with the intention that these would be copied by editors in the eastern states. Sometimes credit was given, sometimes it was not. Sometimes a story was perceived as coming from a town whose newspaper copied it from a newspaper in another town but neglected to cite the source.

The eastern newspapers did, in fact, pick up stories from the frontier press, but booster newspapers sought additional ways, other than the mailed exchanges, to get their stories into the hands of potential residents. For example, they promoted multiple subscriptions by their primary readers, urging them to send copies of the newspaper to their friends and relatives "back home." Both the *Calico Print* in southern California and the *Belmont Courier* in central Nevada promoted sales to relatives, the *Courier* pointing out that "[it] would not only save frequent correspondence, but it would carry a weekly reflex of all local matters, as well as invaluable information regarding the resources of the country in which you are living."[8] Implicit in this plea was the hope that the relative who received the newspaper would take it to his local editor who might, in turn, select a story or stories from the booster's pages to reprint in his own publication. Personal letters from the frontier were often shared with the recipient's wider community in the same way. Occasionally a frontier editor would introduce a story with a "Wisconsin papers please copy" or similar alert to catch another editor's attention if a story had particular relevance to a region, such as a death.

Although the success of exchanges in attracting settlers to the frontier is taken largely on faith at present because little study has been given to tracing the complex paths that communications took in helping the pioneers decide to pack up and move to some part of the West, we know something of how it worked for at least one group of immigrants—the forty-niners.

At first the residents of San Francisco were in no hurry to broadcast the discovery of gold at Sutter's Creek to the world. It took several months before even the Maine-born Mormon Sam Brannan, San Francisco's brash, principal booster, decided that it was time to spread the word.

According to legend, Brannan shouted the news of the gold discovery at Sutter's Fort in the streets of Yerba Buena (the original name for San Francisco), launching the gold rush.[9] Actually, according to his biographer, the announcement was not quite so dramatic. Instead, in May—about four months after the discovery—Brannan held forth to a small group of citizens outside his newspaper office just before he printed a story about the gold discovery in the *California Star,* California's second newspaper, and then sent a special edition of about two thousand copies overland to the eastern states.[10]

Hindsight lets us see the enormous impact the discovery of gold had not only on the West but also on the rest of the nation. Given that knowledge, we can speculate as to why the San Francisco newspapers—Brannan had a competitor, the *Californian,* which, as we have already seen, was originally started on an old Spanish-mission press in Monterey and later moved to the growing village on San Francisco Bay—neglected the story for two months. Were they poor journalists who did not recognize a good story? Did they think the story was too good to be true? Did they anticipate the way employees in the city's businesses, including their own, would desert their posts and empty the city to head for the diggings? Did they want to keep the news to themselves so they alone could benefit? No doubt the answer to all of these questions is a qualified "yes," but clearly at some point Brannan must have realized that the lots he had acquired in the city would be more valuable with an influx of residents wanting land, and so he, as we would say today, "broke the story."[11]

Eventually, Brannan's special edition, as well as word of mouth, reached the eastern seaboard. It still took until August before the *New York Herald* printed a small story and the find was acknowledged by the politicians in Washington, D.C., who were, no doubt, exceedingly glad they had moved to take over the Spanish territories of the southwestern part of the continent.

THE CRADLE OF WESTERN JOURNALISM

San Francisco was to western development and its press as Boston was to the colonies and colonial journalism. The City by the Bay served as the entry port for many would-be settlers and prospectors, as well as for most of the news and supplies from the East that were shipped around Cape Horn or by the sea/land route via Panama. It became the financial center for the West, the place where fortunes were made and lost speculating on the mines. Although the first newspaper in California, the *Californian,* was established about 180 miles down the coast at the Monterey mission and later moved to San Francisco, the second, the *California Star,* emerged in the city itself, and the two eventually combined into the long-running and influential *Alta California.* Within ten years 89 newspapers were being sold on the streets of San Francisco, and by 1880 there were 140, including 24 foreign-language newspapers.[12] Many, if not most, of the editors and publishers of the thousands of little upstart newspapers around the West worked on a San Francisco newspaper before moving inland. The first literary publications in the West were produced beside the San Francisco Bay, as were numerous religious periodicals.

If San Francisco was the West Coast's Boston, Sam Brannan was its Benjamin Harris and John Campbell rolled into one. Like the rabble-rouser Harris, who founded the nation's first newspaper, *Publick Occurrences,* which was promptly shut down by Massachusetts Bay Colony authorities because Harris neglected to ask permission to publish, and Campbell, the thoughtful postmaster who dutifully obtained official permission before going into the newspaper business with the longer-lasting *Boston Newsletter,* Brannan was both boisterous and strategic.

The youngest of five children of Irish immigrants who settled near Portland, Maine, Brannan left home in his teens to get away from his abusive, drunken father. He went to live with his sister in Ohio, where he apprenticed himself to a printer, starting that career as well as one in land speculation. At the conclusion of his four-year apprenticeship Brannan was penniless, thanks to his real estate activities, but he was ready to see the world, which, for him in 1837, started in New Orleans where a brother had settled. Sam and his brother lived among poets, artists, and musicians and started a small bohemian newspaper.[13]

When a fever epidemic took his brother's life, Brannan could not get far enough away from the gulf city. Working his way north, he paused in Indianapolis, eventually sent for the printing press he had left in New Orleans, and again published a small newspaper, the *Gazette.*

Brannan returned to his sister's home in Ohio, not far from Kirtland where the prophet Joseph Smith was preaching his new religion, Mormonism. Brannan's sister and brother-in-law were Mormon converts. Although Brannan liked listening to Smith, he demurred on immediate conversion whenever his relatives or Smith approached him about it. But love conquers all, and when Brannan fell in love with another of Smith's converts, Harriet

Hatch, he submitted to church doctrine and he and Hatch were "sealed" by Smith. It was a case of opposites attracting: the good-looking, passionate Brannan and the docile Harriet, described by Brannan's biographer as "handsome in a rather bovine fashion."[14]

Soon pregnant, Harriet neglected her wifely duties, both in bed and out, and Brannan looked elsewhere for satisfaction. Harriet threatened to divorce him and he walked out, again heading for a big city, this time New York. Lonely among the strangers in the big city, Brannan sought out William Smith, Joseph Smith's brother, who was proselytizing for the new church. Brannan accompanied Smith on a tour of New England after the missionary promised to raise money for a press so Brannan could start a newspaper. Believing he could be more effective with the Smiths if he were actually a member of the church, Brannan allowed William Smith to baptize him.

After successful fund-raising in New England, Brannan, with Joseph Smith's authorization, started the *Prophet,* a Mormon newspaper. On the side Brannan did job-shop printing for extra income. Also on the side, he found Lisa Ann Corwin, a graceful young woman who reminded him somewhat of his mother.

Meanwhile, the Mormon Church was undergoing growing pains with the emergence of a second leader, the pragmatic Brigham Young, a much better executive than the dreamer Smith. Some of Young's supporters tried to convince Brannan that Young had the executive skills needed to help the church prosper, but Brannan criticized Young and stayed loyal to Smith. Soon the question became moot: Joseph Smith was killed by a mob in Nauvoo, Illinois, and Young took over.

In the turmoil of leadership change, Brannan and Mormon leaders changed the *Prophet* to the *Messenger,* with Brannan arguing that non-Mormons would be less likely to attack the newspaper under its less overtly challenging name. Brannan also decided he would marry Lisa Ann, a non-Mormon. Because he wanted to keep peace with the Young faction in the church, Brannan persuaded his new wife to have both the Episcopal ceremony her faith required and the Mormon "sealing" rite. Before the weddings, Brannan returned to Ohio to find his existing wife, Harriet, to give her money to get a divorce. He couldn't find her.

Not long after the marriage, Brannan's earlier intemperate comments about Young resulted in his excommunication by the new Mormon leader, but the glib Brannan successfully defended himself and was reinstated. Brannan was thus well positioned when Young decided his followers should move to the West. In 1846, while Young was leading the main party of Mormons overland to the valley of the Great Salt Lake, Brannan was escorting another group of the faithful to the West Coast by ship. The original intention was for the two groups to come together, and in spring 1847 Brannan's group traveled from San Francisco to Utah to meet up with Young and his followers. Unsuccessful at persuading Young to bring his flock all the way to San Francisco Bay, Brannan returned to San Francisco where he generally proceeded to ignore his Mormon connections, except when it was convenient for him, and subsequently made a fortune in real estate.

The Brannan-led Mormon expedition had originally expected to establish a self-sufficient colony on the coast, perhaps in Baja, California. Thus, all requisite trades were represented among the immigrants, and Brannan made sure to include a printing press. On January 1, 1847, a newspaper extra preceded the first issue of the *California Star*. The extra, "known only through a reprint in the English *Millennial Star*," told of the Mormon colony, provided information on travel, and announced plans for a newspaper "by the sanction of Colonel Freemont" [i.e., John C. Frémont], to begin the following week.[15] Eight days later, January 9, the *California Star* debuted under the leadership of Sam Brannan.[16]

Meanwhile, Brannan himself was also busy opening stores to supply the miners. With a partner, he soon had a store at New Helvetia, later known as Sacramento, and another at Coloma, closer to the diggings, as well as one in San Francisco itself. He successfully ran for the San Francisco City Council, but he had a poor attendance record at meetings because he gave his business interests higher priority than his civic duties. However, when he decided the city needed some action, particularly something that would benefit Sam Brannan, he gave it his full attention and it usually got done.

For example, when San Francisco needed a place to house its criminals, Brannan suggested the purchase of a brigantine that lay in the harbor. Its crew had deserted to the gold fields, so the ship could be had for a small sum and converted to a prison ship. The city council loved the idea, as did the police chief, who quickly filled the available cells and shocked the council with a bill for food and maintenance. It was Brannan who then persuaded the council that the prisoners should be made to work, and chain gangs were formed to repair streets and roads.[17]

By this time Brannan was putting little energy into the newspaper, and in 1848 he sold it to Edward C. Kemble, a young editor who had worked with him in New York and traveled west with the Mormon contingent, although Kemble himself was not a Mormon.[18] Kemble also acquired the *Californian,* and it was he who combined the two newspapers into the *Alta California.*[19]

EDWARD C. KEMBLE

Brannan's successor, Kemble, clearly had printer's ink in his blood. Although he responded to Captain John C. Frémont's call for volunteers for his California Battalion of Mounted Riflemen instead of staying to help Brannan establish the *California Star,* Kemble left the army as soon as he could and was back at work in Brannan's printing shop about a week after the Battle of Santa Barbara.[20]

An article in the September 7, 1866, San Jose *Pioneer* described Kemble:

> We see him now, through our mental vision, precisely as he then appeared [in 1848]. He was attired in a neatly fitting light-blue roundabout or jacket; his nether garment was of fine black cloth; his vest of similar texture and color. His cheeks were like a ripe peach, rosy and smooth as velvet; his eye sparkled and scintillated with tender emotion—it was as black as coal; and his beautiful glossy hair, of similar hue, fell gracefully on either side of his tranquil brow . . . he was a gentleman of strict integrity and moral worth—of the most tender susceptibilities—unassuming, generous, and magnanimous; and . . . his writings were always couched in elegant phraseology and of high moral tone.[21]

Kemble persuaded another printer, Edward Gilbert, to join him in the newspaper business, and their company expanded in 1849 by establishing a newspaper, the *Placer Times,* in Sacramento. Later that year Kemble joined Gilbert—by then one of California's first congressmen—on a trip to Washington, and a toast at the farewell staged at Delmonico's by other San

Francisco journalists and printers called the twenty-two-year-old Kemble "the father of the California Press," technically an exaggeration but testifying to the high regard in which his colleagues held him.[22]

Kemble and Gilbert returned to San Francisco two years later and got caught up in the city's Vigilance Committee excitement. Tempers ran high, and the following summer Gilbert was killed in a duel with James W. Denver—the namesake of the future Colorado city. Devastated by the loss of his friend, Kemble managed to make it through the following year, then went to Europe, ostensibly to cover the Crimean War, but illness prevented him from seeing any fighting. On his return in November 1854 the *Alta California* was bankrupt, so he sold it.[23]

In 1857, after another trip to the East Coast, marriage, newspaper editing, and participation in a California immigration project, Kemble decided to record the history of the California press. He sent a questionnaire to newspapers in the state, as well as to present or former journalists, asking for specific names, dates, and interesting sidelights.[24]

In his report of the survey results, Kemble noted that more than a thousand people had been in San Francisco journalism at one time or another and contended, "No country under the sun can show so large a proportion of what are termed 'newspaper men,' from their past or present connection with journals, to the number of newspaper readers as California."[25]

The *Sacramento Union,* which he then edited, published the results in a special Christmas issue in 1858. Comment in the *Alta California* noted that five of that issue's eight pages were devoted to the "longest article we have ever seen in any paper, and a valuable contribution to the literature and history of the

State."[26] The history appeared without Kemble's byline, but his project was well known around the state, and he was soon widely credited with authorship.[27] In the introduction to his article he writes:

> Before undertaking a task so novel, and, to the majority of readers, of such questionable utility and interest as the compiling of a history of newspapers, it is very proper that we should offer a word of explanation. It is undoubtedly true that there is very little in the bare newspaper chronology of any State, the perusal of which can either amuse or edify those who are not now, or who have not been, in the profession. It is moreover true that the newspaper history of California, extensive and remarkable as it is in comparison, is neither old enough to delight the antiquarian nor sufficiently eventful to give it prominence in the general interest over similar histories of other States. And, lastly, it *is* a fact that newspapers in California have monopolized a larger share of public attention in the recital of incidents laudatory of their growth and development than their years, wisdom or influence entitle them to.[28]

THE PACIFIC NORTHWEST

Newspaper exchanges provided an important channel to inform prospective settlers about an area, but certainly not the only one. By the time of the major westward movement in the 1840s, would-be settlers had a substantial information bank on which to draw, one that would only increase as the years progressed and more people contributed to it.

Acquisition of the Louisiana Territory and Lewis and Clark's subsequent exploratory journey created early interest in the West, particularly its northern regions. Representative John Floyd of Virginia, an early booster of the Pacific Northwest in particular, repeatedly introduced bills calling for the United States to take over the region from the British and open it to American settlement by acquiring lands from the native inhabitants.[29] These bills kept the Oregon issue alive in Congress from 1820 to 1829, when Floyd turned his attention to governing Virginia. Senator Thomas Hart Benton and Representative Francis Baylies of Massachusetts supported Floyd's efforts, but none of the measures made it through the legislative process, dying in committee, on the table, or because no money was appropriated. After Floyd's final effort failed, the *National Intelligencer* commented that "this decision is rather contrary to our expectations. Much talent and zeal have been enlisted in its support."[30] But "manifest destiny" was not to be rushed.[31]

Debates on the topic in Congress in the 1820s, 1830s, and 1840s were printed in the newspapers and thus widely disseminated. Some were issued in pamphlet form. Newspapers also printed letters and reports from fur traders, travelers, and government agents who had been to the Oregon country or California. Not everything published in the newspapers was factual; the information bank included plenty of *mis*information. For example, in its October 17, 1818, issue, *Niles' Register* reported: "Wonderful fact. A Philadelphia writer says, there is at present a practicable inland navigation from Philadelphia to the Columbia River which empties into the Pacific Ocean, with the exception of 75 miles portage!" Crossing the Continental Divide in the Rocky Mountains required a somewhat longer portage than this optimist estimated.

The American Board of Commissioners for Foreign Missions began collecting and spreading information about Oregon as early as 1828, and home visits of the missionaries had considerable influence.[32] Members of the Peoria Party, said to be the first organized group to make the westward trek, said a lecture by missionary Jason Lee sparked their "impulse" to go to Oregon.[33]

After new arrivals got established in the western states, their letters home influenced others, especially family members. Often printed in hometown newspapers, these letters became another important source of information for future pioneers. In addition, visitors to the West published books; the writings of explorers such as John C. Frémont further added to the data bank.

A few private individuals took it upon themselves to stump for the West. For example, Hall J. Kelley became widely known for his espousal of emigration to Oregon. In the 1820s, John Cleves Symmes in Kentucky wrote and talked much about Oregon and volunteered to lead a group of settlers west.[34] Midwestern newspapers reported lectures about the Pacific Northwest by an emigrant named Peter Burnett in the 1840s.[35]

And there were emigration societies—Kelley formed one—which held meetings, published pamphlets and magazines, hosted lecturers, and placed articles and letters in newspapers.

Finally, there were the railroads. Awarded large amounts of land which they were to sell to finance their own westward building, the railroads had a vested interest in attracting settlers to the West. The Union Pacific/Central Pacific, which met at Promontory Point in Utah in 1869, as well as the Great Northern and Northern Pacific railroads of the Pacific Northwest, had extensive programs to promote immigration. For the railroads, immigration meant buyers for the lands they had been given by the government in order to finance the building of the tracks; it also meant ticket sales to westward-bound passengers (and when they returned to their hometowns for visits), and, of course, it meant freight to be shipped to and from the West. The railroads had special departments to promote migration, but they also saw the value of the newspaper press.

FIVE

THE PRESS
AND THE IRON HORSE

During the Civil War, while conflict threatened a permanent split between North and South, the U.S. Congress chartered railroads in order to strengthen the connections between East and West. The move was a natural consequence of such developments as the discovery of gold in California, the growing industrial capacity of the Northeast, which required new markets, and the passage of the Homestead Act in 1862.

The Homestead Act had fulfilled the 1860 Republican platform promise of free land to settlers in the West, and the building of the railroads was the next step in making it possible for people to claim their portions of this land.[1]

The first transcontinental line was completed in 1869 when the Union Pacific, heading west from Omaha, and the Central Pacific, east from California, met at Promontory Point, Utah, a few miles northwest of Salt Lake City. Immediately the pace of westward migration to California and other parts of the frontier accelerated. Movement to the Pacific Northwest—Oregon and Washington—stepped up as well, despite the fact that for fourteen more years that region of the West had no direct rail link to the East or even to California. It was not until 1883 that the transcontinental Northern Pacific Railroad was completed, linking the Pacific Northwest by rail to the rest of the nation.

In the meantime, migrants to the future states of Washington, Oregon, and Idaho had to travel overland by wagon along the Oregon Trail or make a sea or land journey north from San Francisco, either way a matter of some discomfort, danger, and inconvenience. That so many did so—historian James B. Hedges estimates that at least eighteen thousand migrants arrived in Portland, Oregon, in 1877 alone—is testimony to the railroads' efforts to promote the region as a desirable destination, as well as that of the booster press, and the efforts of the missionaries to attract civilized folks to set a good example for the Indians.[2] The railroads worked side by side with the newspapers in boosting western locations for settlement, and in some cases they appear to have been working hand in glove with the press.

Why would the railroads promote migration long before they were operating in an area, and what role did newspapers play in this promotion?

One answer to the first question is that railroad builders recognized that without people there would be no need for railroads, and it was preferable to create the market first than to have expensive rolling stock moving about empty. Another key factor was land. Although the railroads—the Northern Pacific was to be the initial important line into the Pacific Northwest, but the Union Pacific had spurs into the region—had no rails or locomotives in the Pacific Northwest, they already had land that they could sell or give away. Congress had made substantial grants of territory in addition to the necessary railroad right-of-way. The plan had been for the railroads to sell the land to help finance the laying of the tracks; to do so, they had to persuade immigrants to move to the region. As Hedges has written about a major railroad promoter with journalistic links, Henry Villard, builder of the Northern Pacific:

> It has been characteristic of the builders of railroads that they did not leave to chance the important work of settling the lands through which tracks were already laid or into which they were to be built. So with Villard! He inaugurated a vigorous campaign for promoting immigration to the Northwest, and a complete history of the colonization of that region cannot be written without giving ample space to the part played by the various transportation companies in that section of the country.[3]

Posters, press releases, excursions for editors and prospective settlers, advertising, testimonials, letter-writing campaigns, lectures, pamphlets, and magazines—and probably their own newspapers—were among the tools used by railroads in those campaigns. Men who had presumably never heard of market research nevertheless carefully considered their markets and planned their campaigns with the care that any modern marketing or public relations manager might use.[4]

They watched for areas of discontent in the eastern states and the Midwest. They assured victims of crop failure and bad weather that the Pacific Northwest offered a prosperous and healthful climate. Moreover, during this period of great migration to the United States from Europe, the railroads established foreign offices to spread the message of the benefits of settling the western lands they held.

Historians have observed that the competition for settlers was so keen that the railroads expended considerable foresight, ingenuity, and money on the problem. The Illinois Central spent twenty-nine thousand dollars for advertising and printing in one year, a large budget for that time. Hedges says there were 632,590 copies of Northern Pacific publications issued, again suggesting the magnitude of the operation.

HENRY VILLARD

At the heart of much of this activity for several decades was a journalist-turned-railroad financier, Henry Villard. Born in Bavaria as Ferdinand Heinrich Gustav Hilgard in 1835, the son of a jurist who became a Bavarian supreme court judge, Villard attended the universities of Munich and Würzburg. In 1853, after a fight with his father, he immigrated to America where, to make it difficult for his father to track him down, he changed his name to Villard. He moved westward and in 1855–56 settled in Belleville, Illinois, where he read law, sold books and real estate, and edited a small-town newspaper.

Initially working primarily for German-American news-papers, such as the *Staats-Zeitung* of New York, for which he reported the Lincoln-Douglas debates, Villard rapidly mastered the English language and subsequently worked for the *Cincinnati Commercial,* the *Missouri Democrat* of St. Louis, the *New York Herald,* and the *New York Tribune,* among others. One of his biographers notes that he "corresponded freely with Western newspapers" ("Western" at that time referring to cities inland from the East Coast) and "a considerable portion of the polit-ical news which the country read during [the 1860 presidential campaign] was supplied by the young immigrant who had not yet turned his twenty-sixth birthday."[5]

A friend of Abraham Lincoln, Horace Greeley, and other key players in mid-nineteenth-century America, Villard was perhaps the most reputable war correspondent during the Civil War. He accompanied Union armies in Virginia and the West, and his reports appeared in the *New York Herald* and the *New York Tribune*. After the war he worked as a correspondent in the United States and Europe for a news agency that he and another journalist had formed to compete with the New York Associated Press.

In 1868 Villard became secretary of the American Social Science Association in Boston; in that role he became involved in the movement for civil service reform, but he also studied public and corporate financing, including that of railways.

He spent the early 1870s in Germany to restore his health and met bondholders of the Oregon and California Railroad Company, who in 1874 sent him to Oregon as their representative, launching his career as a railroad financier and developer, as well as introducing him to the Oregon country he came to love.

Initially Villard hoped to control the rail business into Portland by laying track along the south side of the Columbia River. But the financier Jay Cooke, building the Northern Pacific Railroad westward from Minneapolis, had a different destination in mind: Puget Sound, about two hundred miles to the north. When Villard was unable to persuade Cooke to work with him, he decided to buy the Northern Pacific, asking about fifty friends and business acquaintances to subscribe toward a fund of eight million dollars, without telling them why. So great was his reputation by then for integrity and competence that he raised the money easily, and the "Blind Pool," as the fund became known, has been called one of the "notable achievements in the annals of railway finance."[6]

Villard's next step was to organize a holding company, the Oregon and Transcontinental, and on September 15, 1881, he became president of the Northern Pacific Railroad. He also controlled the Oregon and California Railroad, the Oregon Railway and Navigation Company, and the Oregon Improvement Company, among other interests in the region.

The Oregon Railway and Navigation Company laid rails on the south side of the Columbia River from Portland to Wallula, a river port in eastern Oregon, as part of Villard's effort to have the Northern Pacific terminate in Portland, not Puget Sound. In 1883 he drove a gold spike at Independence Creek west of Helena, Montana, linking the sections building from east and west.

Even Villard, however, found the pressures of building a railroad too much; he had a nervous breakdown, left the presidency of the Northern Pacific, and went to Germany to convalesce. The push to terminate the Northern Pacific at Puget Sound resumed under new leadership, and in May 1888 a tunnel under Stampede Pass in the Cascade Mountains allowed the first train directly through to the Sound.

Although there is no direct evidence that Villard funded western newspapers with a view to getting their backing for his project, he did use his own journalistic skills to write advertisements and pamphlets describing Oregon. Although relatively enlightened for his time, Villard was no environmentalist. In 1876 he wrote in a promotional pamphlet of the "wonderful changes" that had taken place since his first visit to Oregon: instead of enormous herds of buffaloes roaming the plains, the animal was now "entirely extinct."[7]

Villard's railroad work made him a wealthy man, and in 1881 he acquired a controlling interest in the *New York Evening Post,* a newspaper founded in 1801 by Alexander Hamilton and in the early twenty-first century owned by the Australian Rupert Murdoch. Villard appointed as editors three men known for their journalistic integrity—Horace White, E. L. Godkin, and Carl Schurz—and gave them independence in editorial decision making. Villard wrote a memoir but otherwise had little to do with journalism later in life. He had married the only daughter of abolitionist William Lloyd Garrison, and their son, Oswald Garrison Villard, eventually became publisher of the *Post.*

JAMES J. HILL

Meanwhile, the Canadian-born James J. Hill was building the Great Northern Railway. A Minneapolis entrepreneur, Hill started buying short railroad lines in 1873 with the purchase of the St. Paul and Pacific Railroad (later renamed the St. Paul, Minneapolis, and Manitoba line), along the Red River north to Winnipeg. He helped build the Canadian Pacific Railway to the Pacific Ocean, but he left the company in 1882 after deciding to build his own transcontinental railroad, the Great Northern Railway. Unlike the other American transcontinental railroad builders, Hill had no government loans or land grants, a fact that led his project to become known as "Hill's Folly."[8] How could you possibly build something as massive as a railroad without government financing?

Hill achieved this by incorporating numerous existing short lines, such as the Montana Central Railroad between Great Falls and Helena, with the laying of new rails, a fact that not only gave him ready-made track but also ensured that his line would reach existing business while also creating new customers. He also punished those who stood in his way. When the town fathers of Benton, Montana, refused his request for right-of-way through town, he built around the town, leaving it cut off a mile from the line.[9] The Great Northern reached Puget Sound in 1893.

Hill's association with newspapers in connection with his railroad building is unclear. His biographer, Albro Martin, said the railroad builder had "poured money, time, and energy" into the *Fargo Argus*.[10] Martin also wrote that the politically minded Hill thought St. Paul needed a "strong Democratic newspaper" and that a like-minded friend bought the *St. Paul Globe* with a view to providing such a voice for St. Paul. In 1893 Hill put twenty-five thousand dollars into the *New York Times,* three years later telling his company treasurer, E. T. Nichols, "I have no objection if you donate the *Times* interest to Mr. Ochs."[11] (Adolph Ochs acquired the ailing newspaper in 1896.) Hill ignored an opportunity to buy the *Minneapolis Tribune* and eventually purchased the *St. Paul Globe* from his friend.[12] After losing half a million dollars, he sold the *Globe* in 1905, but kept the editor, Joseph G. Pyle, as his personal editor at five hundred dollars a month. Martin said Hill turned down invitations to write for various publications, so just what Pyle edited for him in this period is not recorded.

Just as Hill showed Benton, Montana, who was boss, Villard's Northern Pacific played hardball in a similar way with Yakima in central Washington. When the railroad and the town could not agree on the location of railroad facilities, the Northern Pacific rerouted its line to the north of the existing community and platted a new town. This left what became known as "old Yakima" high and dry as far as railroad transportation was concerned. A few decades after most of its residents moved to

North Yakima, "old Yakima" became Union Gap, and North Yakima became simply Yakima.[13]

The story of railroad building of that era is peppered with accounts of bankruptcy. The nationwide financial panics of 1873 and 1893, coupled with the railroad's enormous building costs, brought the Northern Pacific into bankruptcy more than once before the line was completed. Hill's business acumen helped him avoid financial disaster, and in 1896 he absorbed the Northern Pacific into the Great Northern.

RAILROADS AND NEWSPAPERS

Railroad moguls, in their efforts to promote settlement and commerce along their routes, were keenly aware of the role of the booster press. Rumors flew around the West during the railroad-building era that more than one newspaper was actually owned by a railroad and that many more were at least partially funded by them. Certainly a number of newspapers were strong rail-road supporters, and many were started in anticipation of the arrival of the railroad, but as previously noted, those who estab-lished western newspapers understood they needed growth to survive, and what better harbinger of growth than a railroad?

One of the most blatant railroad advocates was the *Kalama Beacon,* in Washington Territory, established in 1871 by M. L. and M. H. Money, a husband-wife team from Jefferson, Iowa, who chose for their front-page logo the headlight of an oncoming locomotive. Mrs. Money was the writer; Mr. Money was the printer. Not shy about practicing self-promotion, Mrs. Money introduced herself with several quotations from Midwest news-papers, including this from the *Iowa State Register:* "Mrs. Money, in particular, is universally conceded to be one of the best paragraphists in the State, and to rank with the best female writers in the West."[14]

Kalama is the Columbia River town, on the Washington side of the river, that at one point expected to be the terminus for the Northern Pacific Railroad. The Moneys promised that "the great and important enterprise inaugurated and already in rapid process of construction by the North Pacific Railroad Company, will receive from us the attention the magnitude of the undertaking demands."[15] The Moneys attacked those who criticized the railroad, and when the Northern Pacific finally designated Tacoma as its terminus, they moved to that city planning to start the *Northern Pacific Headlight*. There is no indication that they actually published anything under that title, but their names were connected with other Tacoma newspapers, and one of their employees, a man named Pickett, published a prospectus for the *Western Terminus*. Nor did that newspaper appear, but in August 1877, Pickett or possibly the Moneys or both brought out the *North Pacific Times,* which a rival newspaper said was published in compliance with the wishes of the Oregon Steam Navigation, Northern Pacific, and Tacoma Land companies, which "infused the first filthy breath of life into the disreputable sheet."[16]

The extent to which the Northern Pacific involved itself in the *Kalama Beacon* remains debatable. As mentioned earlier, Henry Villard, then leading the push to lay rails to the Pacific, or at least to Kalama, said nothing about starting a newspaper to ensure support for his enterprise. Two reputable Washington Territory historians agree only that the Northern Pacific was, indeed, involved. Edmund Meany, who wrote extensively about the Washington Territory press, cites Hubert Howe Bancroft when he says the railroad owned the *Beacon;* Charles Prosch, an editor of that period who also recorded press history, says the Moneys were heavily in debt to the railroad.[17] Neither

Meany nor Prosch connects Hill and the Great Northern with any Pacific Northwest newspaper, but given frontier publishers' unending need for financial help, the possibility remains that the railroad backed one or more frontier newspapers.

Evidence is also strong that Ben Holladay, the Oregon transportation king before Henry Villard arrived on the scene, started the *Oregon Bulletin* in 1870, putting some two hundred thousand dollars into it in five years.[18]

When the Northern Pacific selected Tacoma as its terminus on Puget Sound, the city attracted newspapers as the gold rush had in its day. Thomas Prosch, one of the editor-publishers who was quick to move to the new railroad-center-to-be, wrote, "It was a time of wild excitement. Visions of vast wealth and great population in the new city were seen by all."[19] He was no friend of the railroad, an attitude which, together with the financial panic of 1873, may have created extra challenges when he tried to publish in a new town. Prosch hung on in Tacoma until 1875, when he moved the *Pacific Tribune* to Seattle. Three years later it merged with the *Intelligencer,* the forerunner of the *Post-Intelligencer.*

Prosch's *Pacific Tribune* was a reincarnation of two of his father Charles's earlier newspapers: the *Puget Sound Herald,* an 1858 booster paper in Steilacoom at the south end of the Sound, and the *Pacific Tribune,* a descendant of the *Overland Press,* a newspaper established in Olympia in 1861. The elder Prosch bought the *Tribune* in 1868, but by 1873 it was foundering and would be sold by the sheriff to pay its debts. Twenty-three-year-old Thomas, who had learned the family trade from his father, had saved enough while working as a printer to buy the newspaper himself, and quickly moved it to the new railroad terminus.

The announcement of Tacoma as the Northern Pacific's western terminus attracted other publishers to the city. Clarence

Bagley, publisher of the *Puget Sound Courier* in Olympia, helped finance James Power, who chose as his location the old gold-rush town of Whatcom, at the north end of the Sound, on the assumption the railroad would choose a second terminus and it would likely be Whatcom.[20] When after two years the rail-road had come no closer, Power asked Bagley about prospects in Tacoma. "It's a good place for news," Power commented of Tacoma, "but how is it for money?"[21] Bagley's response was not encouraging, and Power stayed in Whatcom. However, four years later, the closure of coal mines in the area made the like-lihood of the railroad's arrival even more remote, and Power moved his newspaper to nearby LaConner, after obtaining assurance from county authorities that he would get the county printing contract. LaConner was lively enough to host a district court session and ship some grain and produce through its port, creating at least some prospects for growth. Power published in the area for a dozen years and was one of the few newspapermen who fellow editor and press historian Charles Prosch said actually made money.[22]

Anacortes was another northern Sound city that saw itself—or at least its editors did—as a potential terminus of the Northern Pacific. Alfred D. Bowen and F. M. Walsh started the *Northwest Enterprise* as a booster organ in hopes of attracting the railroad.[23]

While the question of the Northern Pacific's terminus attracted the most attention, towns and their newspapers devel-oped elsewhere along the railroad's route. Francis Henry Cook already had a newspaper in Tacoma—the *Herald*—when he decided to investigate potential sites in eastern Washington. He liked the village at Spokane Falls, and when the Northern Pacific announced that its route into the territory would run through Spokane, Cook started the *Spokane Times*.[24]

No fan of the railroad—except for the business he might gain from it—Cook wanted to prevent the railroad from meddling with local politics. He complained that the Northern Pacific was not building fast enough and that the line's involvement with Tacoma politics and newspapers made it difficult for him to operate the *Herald*.[25] He was the editor who attacked the Moneys' effort to start a newspaper in Tacoma, and when the *North Pacific Times* folded in 1879, Cook wrote in his *Tacoma Herald,* referring to the Moneys and their editor Pickett:

> There is no act too low, too unjust, or too pusillanimous for them to engage in, if it promises in any manner to aid their vile schemes. Their newspaper venture has been a signal failure.[26]

There is some irony that this railroad foe rented the bottom floor of his Spokane newspaper's office building to the Northern Pacific.[27]

The Northern Pacific was also responsible for the sudden growth of the eastern Washington community of Sprague and its newspaper, the *Sprague Herald,* when the railroad designated the town as the headquarters of its Pend d'Oreille division. Nearby, George W. Mattice thought the railroad would build a spur to Medical Lake, long known by the Indians for its curative salts, so he started the *Medical Lake Press* in 1882.[28]

Another western railroad town, this one starting in the early twentieth century, was Las Vegas, Nevada. Senator William A. Clark, a Montana copper king turned railroad baron, sought to connect the Union Pacific main line in Utah—already linked to his Montana copper mines—with southern California ports. He acquired property in the Las Vegas Valley because it was about halfway between Salt Lake City and Los Angeles, and because it had water. The railroad was completed on January

30, 1905, and a land auction was held in May.[29] Word of plans
for the new town spread rapidly. Two years before the auction,
an Oregon editor queried Clark about the need for a newspaper in the "proposed new town on the S[alt] L[ake and] L[os]
A[ngeles] R[ailwa]y." Clark responded, confirming that he had
indeed purchased property in southern Nevada but did "not
think there will be any field there for a newspaper."[30] Clark, who
was part-owner of the *Butte Miner,* may have wanted to keep
the field for himself. While his reply apparently deterred the
Oregon man from moving to the desert, several other would-
be publishers decided to try their luck, and even before Clark's
company conducted a land auction in the Las Vegas Valley, the
future town had three weekly newspapers, the *Las Vegas Times,*
the *Advance,* and the *Las Vegas Age;* all were started within two
weeks of one another.[31] The proprietors of the *Times* had gone to
Las Vegas from Butte, Montana, where they likely had worked
on Clark's *Butte Miner.* Whether he had anything to do with
their proposed enterprise in his new town has not been learned,
but they did not stay long. Both the *Times* and the *Advance* were
suspended the following year, and the *Times* owners headed
for Greenwater at the southern end of Death Valley, where the
discovery of copper had raised hopes of prosperity.[32] Had they
remembered why Clark chose Las Vegas for his railroad town—
the availability of water—the Montanans might have avoided
the notoriously dry Death Valley. Their Greenwater enterprise
was short-lived.

The *Age* had the field to itself for a time, survived the Great
Depression, and was the forerunner of today's *Las Vegas Review-
Journal,* now owned by the Stephens Group, successor to Donrey
Media.[33] Charles P. "Pop" Squires bought the *Age* in 1908 and
remained with it until its suspension nearly forty years later.[34]

Except perhaps for the Moneys, these newspaper starts appear to have been individual efforts on the part of their publishers—and the Moneys' railroad connections may have been exaggerated. Railroad histories suggest that railroad builders well knew the value of newspaper support but preferred to cultivate publishers and editors with passes and advertising, rather than start their own newspapers. Railroad passes were freely given to editors; publishers, their staffs, and their families were treated to excursions. Those attending the inaugural Montana Press Association meeting in Butte in 1885 also received theater tickets and other hospitality from their host, Clark of the *Butte Miner*.[35]

As a general rule, the railroads had little need initially to own their own newspapers to get favorable coverage. Townspeople—including newspaper publishers—were excited by the prospect of railroad service and saw it as a major economic boon. In Montana, when the Union Pacific planned a branch line and was debating whether its terminus would be Butte or Helena, Clark's *Butte Miner* claimed that Helena's merchants were willing to bribe the railroad to come to Helena because they realized Butte had a far better case.[36] Helena was so desperate to become the terminus that Samuel Hauser, president of the First National Bank of Helena, reportedly paid George F. Cope, editor of the *Montanian* in Virginia City, up to one hundred dollars a month to tout the railroad's benefits. Cope said that when he argued in his columns for a subsidy for the line, he lost seventy-five subscribers who did not agree with him.[37]

Railroad construction, while valuable in the long term to communities seeking to grow, also brought immediate rewards in employment and contracts for supply. In his history of the Union Pacific, Robert Athearn quotes the *Weekly Standard* in Portland, Oregon, "Are not the railroads the very instruments through which our Northwest coast is being developed?" arguing that hostility toward such companies would be suicidal for western communities.[38] In Utah the Mormons, who were generally so cool to the idea of Gentiles (non-Mormons) in their midst that the *Deseret News* published editorials deprecating mining as an unsuitable activity for nice people, nevertheless eventually welcomed the railroad. Though at first fearing the competition that the railroad would introduce to their homegrown businesses, the Mormons later saw it as a way to get their agricultural products to markets. They also liked the fact that when the Union Pacific came to the Salt Lake Valley, it contracted with Mormon workers and suppliers, helping minimize the impact of a potential influx of new, non-Mormon businessmen and workers.[39] The *Deseret News* voiced approval of the railroad on behalf of the church hierarchy.[40]

Later the Union Pacific failed to pay its Mormon contractors, and the tone changed. The *Deseret News* "declared editorial war on the Union Pacific in an effort to strengthen the hand of Utah claimants."[41] Like merchants and other citizens, many newspapers, initially enthralled by the prospect of a railroad coming to town, became disillusioned at the slowness of the laying of the rails. To the extent that they had worked to make their towns attractive to the railroad through subsidies or other benefits, they felt the railroad had taken unfair advantage of them by not giving their project its full attention and resources. Newspapers, especially those in California, turned on the railroad editorially.

PRESS ON WHEELS

One of the more curious railroad-newspaper connections was that forged by Legh Freeman with what became known as his "press on wheels." The Virginia-born Freeman published in at least sixteen different locations between the Civil War and his death in 1915, many of them located on the Union Pacific's transcontinental route. No formal connection between Freeman and the railroad or the Overland Telegraph has been determined, but though he was free with criticism of many of the economic miscreants of his day, the Union Pacific generally escaped his wrath.

Freeman's biographer, Thomas Heuterman, says that Legh and his family lived in a fantasy world, but Heuterman manages to extract facts at least as interesting as the fictions that Freeman created about himself.[42]

A soldier in the Confederate Army during the Civil War and a telegraph operator at Fort Kearny soon afterward, the twenty-three-year-old Freeman purchased the fort's printing equipment and learned how to set type and pull pages from the press. When he started his newspaper career, Fort Kearny residents, veterans and civilians alike, were awaiting the arrival of the Union Pacific, which was then laying track westward as part of the transcontinental railroad. From Fort Kearny, in the Nebraska Territory, in December 1865 to the completion of the line in 1869, Freeman, aided by his brother Frederick, moved his newspaper nine times, staying just ahead of the lengthening track of the railroad.[43]

Leaving his brother to run the newspaper and take advantage of local economic and political opportunities, Legh Freeman went exploring. He was one of the first to send newspaper articles about the geysers of Yellowstone Park. Meanwhile, in a Republican county in Nebraska, Frederick made the *Kearney Herald* a voice for Democrats and got himself elected to the Nebraska Territorial Council, defeating another interesting individual of the frontier, George Francis Train.[44] When the railroad moved beyond Kearney, it became clear that economic opportunity would be better at the end of the line, and Frederick moved the newspaper to North Platte, where he also speculated in real estate.[45] He also renamed the newspaper the *Frontier Index*.

Legh Freeman signed the frequent articles he sent to the *Frontier Index* "General Horatio Vattel." This alter ego gave Freeman the opportunity to indulge his imagination. As Heuterman explains: "Freeman wrote as the factual frontier journalist. Freeman-as-Vattel, 'Lightning Scout of the Mountains,' wrote of a West larger and more heroic than life."[46] The dual personality was much like that of Samuel Clemens/Mark Twain. "Clemens" felt restricted to the facts; writing as Mark Twain, he could give his imagination free rein. Better known than Freeman, "Vattel" was called "that great western genius whose genuine witticisms, peculiarly expressed prophesies, sensible profundities and wise sayings generally, are so extensively copied and quoted throughout this western country and California."[47]

Heuterman says that Freeman "undoubtedly borrowed from staple frontier lore," noting similarities between some of Freeman's tales and those of Mark Twain and Jim Bridger. Sir Walter Scott also provided ideas for Freeman's writing, which sometimes was in verse.[48] Regardless of the sources for his inspiration, Freeman clearly had a gift for colorful writing. Describing a location in Arizona where he hoped to build Freemansburg, about seventy miles east of modern Las Vegas, Nevada, he wrote about the heat, "The sky is ever brassy, and the birds dare not exert themselves to a song, after spring is gone, until the cool breezes of fall again bring the myriads of water fowl from the north to winter here!"[49]

However colorful and amusing Freeman may have been, he was also racist and intolerant, characteristics that repeatedly brought him trouble. Both he and Frederick also criticized the military in whose forts they frequently headquartered their newspapers until forced out by an angry general.[50] They opposed Ulysses S. Grant's bid for the presidency, accusing him of—among other things—trying to prevent "conservative white men" from controlling Wyoming. Their attacks on Grant led opponents to label the *Index,* then in Green River City, "that filthy rebel sheet."[51] The brothers soon moved their newspaper to Bear River City, in Wyoming Territory, where they were followed by a lawless element of railroad workers they had inspired at a previous stop. They disavowed these rowdies, in part, at least, because the brothers needed peace in town to further their land speculations, and they did not support the vigilantes who arose in an effort to keep that peace by using public hangings as an example for the populace.

On November 20, 1868, events got out of hand and railroad workers burned a temporary jail that vigilantes had built to contain several prisoners. The angry workers then headed for the office of the *Frontier Index,* accusing Legh of heading the vigilantes. Freeman managed to get away from the mob, infuriating them even more, and he headed for Fort Bridger to bring troops back to stem the violence. Details of the rest of the story differ, depending on which newspaper one reads, but dozens were killed or wounded and the *Index* office destroyed.[52]

The Freemans' relationship with the Union Pacific Railroad, then deeply involved in the double-dipping contracting that characterized the Credit Mobilier scandal, was never entirely clear. Years later, Legh Freeman took credit for single-handedly destroying the Credit Mobilier—"that hydra-headed monster"— and for giving Wyoming its name.[53] Heuterman believes this claim was based on hindsight because, prior to the riot, there had been no overt friction between the Freemans and the Union Pacific. When the railroad appointed a land agent in Laramie six months beforehand, the *Frontier Index* welcomed him cordially. Heuterman speculates that the fact that the agent advertised in the newspaper helped smooth the way and notes that had there been conflict between the Freemans and the Union Pacific, it would have been obvious because neither of the Freemans was at all reticent about criticizing or expressing his opinion.

Bear River City was the seventh community in which the Freemans published the *Frontier Index* in 1868; they moved on to the Pacific Northwest, where they continued to publish the newspaper in various towns for another thirty years, but their moves were less frequent, and the later locations had little to do with the railroad. Legh eventually married and with his wife published in Ogden, Utah, the town nearest the site for the ceremonial joining of the east and west legs of the transcontinental railroad, but this newspaper came almost a decade later—from 1879 to 1884—long after the driving of the golden spike connected the Union Pacific with the Central Pacific.

CALIFORNIA NEWSPAPERS AND THE RAILROADS

California newspapers, like their brethren around the region, were early supporters of the iron horse, but they had turned on it even before the golden spike was driven. By 1867 the *Sacramento Union* was criticizing the route and delays in getting tracks laid through the Sierras, surely one of the most difficult places to build a railroad.[54]

The *Union* was a big thorn in the Central Pacific's side, leading Collis P. Huntington to declare to David Colton, "The

Sacramento [*Union*] hurts us very much. . . . If I owned the paper I would control it or burn it."[55] The railroad magnate also complained about the lack of control over the Associated Press in San Francisco. "The matters that hurt the C[entral] P[acific] and S[outhern] P[acific] most here are the dispatches that come from S.F.," he wrote from his position as a lobbyist in Washington, D.C.[56]

The *Bulletin* and *Examiner* in San Francisco joined in the criticism. "California papers hostile to the railroad made much of the discomforts and dangers of the Sierra crossing," writes Oscar Lewis in *The Big Four*. They ignored the protests of railroad officials and gave details of wrecks. "From the middle '80s onward, the *Examiner*'s ridicule of Central and Southern Pacific trains and the manner of their operation was so damaging that Huntington gave his personal attention to the matter of how the paper might be silenced. Nothing could be done, the young man who owned the *Examiner* [William Randolph Hearst] had the backing of a multimillionaire mother, and arguments that had proved effective elsewhere were there found to be useless."[57]

The Southern Pacific, owner of the Central Pacific and often called "the Octopus" in California because it had a hand in so many aspects of California's economy and life, was infamous for "buying" editors. On at least one occasion, Huntington and one of his partners, Leland Stanford, quarreled, putting editors on edge as to which side of the controversy they should take. "Most of them played safe and either ignored the situation or quoted minor railroad officials as deprecating the unfortunate misunderstanding."[58]

Hearst was one of the few editors who remained independent of the railroad. One of his biographers, W. A. Swanberg, writes,

"Considering his financial dependence on his father, his decision to fight the S.P. was downright daring. With the publisher's
approval, the *Examiner* carried the acerbic comments of Ambrose
Bierce who wrote on one occasion that the trains were so often
late that 'the passenger is exposed to the perils of senility.'"[59]
Bierce also blasted the unsafe and uncomfortable travel conditions
on the railroad. "The Overland arrived at midnight last night,
more than nine hours late, and twenty passengers descended
from the snow-covered cars. All were frozen and half-starved,
but thankful they had escaped with their lives."[60] The *Examiner*
thought that passengers should have a chance for survival "at
least equal to that of a soldier on the battlefield."[61]

Hearst, who later in life was thought of as a sour old megaloma-
niac, at this point in his career was considered a man of the people.
He used both news and editorial columns to attack the Southern
Pacific, whose owners, wealthy men like Collis P. Huntington
and Leland Stanford, were crying poor and trying to persuade
the federal government to forgive, or at least extend the time for
payment of, the loans given the railroad builders. The *Examiner*
pointed out the hypocrisy inherent in Stanford spending millions
on racehorses, paintings, and his California estate and endowing a
university in memory of his son while refusing to accept responsibility for a loan that had helped him garner those millions.[62]

HEARST'S LONGEST CRUSADE

The railroad was only one of many Hearst crusades for the "little
people," but it was the longest and hardest one he fought. Hearst
no doubt would have loved to have the power over California
that the Southern Pacific Railroad had.

As he did with so many things, Hearst put the family fortune where his mouth was. He sent Bierce to Washington, D.C., to keep an eye on the Southern Pacific's lobbying efforts. In 1897 Congress was considering giving the railroad moguls what they wanted: the chance to spread their repayments over eighty-eight years. *Examiner* cartoons depicted Huntington, the Southern Pacific's lobbyist, with his hand in the public's pocket, and Bierce sent dispatches that "dripped with ridicule of the railroad's declared inability to pay."[63] The furious Huntington looked for some way to get back at Hearst.

His staff finally found a contract the Southern Pacific had made with the *Examiner* for thirty thousand dollars' worth of advertising, written with the understanding—on the railroad's part, anyway—that the *Examiner* would desist from attacking the monopoly. The Southern Pacific claimed that Hearst continued to attack the railroad because it would not pay him any more money.[64] The railroad finally canceled the contract when they still owed eight thousand dollars on it. Hearst and Huntington invited each other to sue for libel; neither ever did. Rumors continued, however, that Hearst had sold out and was going easy on the Southern Pacific.

Biographer Swanberg, however, concluded, "If the road paid for gentle treatment, it failed to get it."[65] Swanberg got Ronald A. Bergman of the University of California to conduct a content analysis of *Examiner* stories before and after the alleged contract. Bergman's work showed that the newspaper was as critical after the contract as before.[66]

It was a case of what Hearst knew about the advertising contract and when he knew it. Given his reaction when one of his editors told him of an attempted bribe from the Spring Valley Water Company when it was trying to quiet a Hearst attack, Hearst might well have realized that the railroad thought it was bribing him. In the water company case, after the editor told the company's emissary to leave, Hearst is supposed to have said, "You're a fool! Why didn't you take the money and keep up the fight just the same? He would never have dared to say a word about it."[67] He may have applied this philosophy to the railroad advertising contract.

Hearst on the California stage is, in many ways, more interesting than the later Hearst—congressman; would-be candidate for president; influential media mogul; lord of San Simeon, his castle on the California coast; and subject of the Orson Welles film *Citizen Kane*. The early Hearst loved what he was doing; by the time he died, the later Hearst appeared to be a bitter old man, reviled by many for his journalism, his excesses, and his wealth.[68]

Never careful about money because the family pocketbook seemed bottomless, Hearst kept spending until, in the 1930s, his advisors reined him in; at that point he owed so much that he went to a Los Angeles bank and took out a six-hundred-thousand-dollar loan. He was unaware that he had actually mortgaged his property to a major rival, Harry Chandler, publisher of the *Los Angeles Times*.[69] Careful management saved the company, but it was never the same after that; nor was Hearst.

Hearst also took on anti-Communism as a cause, and Hearst reporters went undercover to get interviews with suspected radicals. Swanberg includes this comment from a Hearst reporter interviewing Professor George S. Counts of Teachers' College, Columbia University, in the early 1930s: "Mr. Hearst is engaged at present in conducting a Red Scare. . . . You realize of course that because of my assignment I will have to select the most sensational statements from the interview in order to make out a good case. That is what Mr. Hearst is expecting," the reporter told the professor.[70] Hearst blamed the creation of the American Newspaper Guild and its organizing of employees and subsequent strike at the *Seattle Post-Intelligencer,* which Hearst purchased in 1921, on Communism and swore that despite the cost, he was "enlisted for the duration of the war" against Communism.[71]

In 1937 the Hearst Corporation, deeply in debt thanks to the Chief's profligate spending, asked the Securities and Exchange Commission (SEC) for permission to float a total of $35.5 million in debentures. The SEC decided the company could not handle that much more debt and allowed it to withdraw the request.[72] The company, instead, proceeded to sell some of the art, furniture, and architecture that Hearst had acquired over the years, including a half-million-dollar Spanish monastery, the stones of which occupied 10,700 crates in a warehouse in the Bronx.[73]

Swanberg describes Hearst as two men, not just the young and the old Hearst, but as an individual who might be "cynical one moment and dead serious the next. Being two men, he outraged the logicians and defied the analysts."[74] As he grew even older—into his seventies—Swanberg says, "old age, unpopularity, humiliation and disaster had softened instead of embittered him."[75] When Arthur Brisbane, Hearst's top editor, died, his column *To-Day* died with him. In 1940 Hearst decided to write a regular column and, Swanberg claims, he "could write rings around Brisbane."[76] The biographer describes a warmth and humanity in Hearst, an "indomitable courage and greatness of heart" that made his column so interesting that it quickly spread from the *Examiner* to all of his chain.[77]

Citizen Kane, the 1941 RKO-Orson Welles film openly based on Hearst's life, raised a furor in the Hearst organization, which tried to stop its distribution. Louella Parsons, a

Hearst Hollywood columnist, even called Nelson Rockefeller to tell him it should not be shown at Rockefeller Center, and the Hearst press refused to review the film.[78] The Hearst papers also blackballed all other RKO films, and Orson Welles knew he need not expect an invitation to Hearst's San Simeon estate. The film paralleled Hearst's life, showing some of the genius the young man had exhibited, as well as the ruthlessness of his later years. Charles Foster Kane had his San Simeon–like castle (Xanadu), his Marion Davies–like mistress (a singer in Kane's case rather than an actress), and his newspaper empire. "It was said that angry as he was at the portrayal of himself, he [Hearst] was more incensed at the unflattering characterization of the young woman the public would surely take to represent Miss Davies."[79]

Hearst remained the "Chief" to the end of his days. By the time he died in 1951 at the age of eighty-eight, he had moved from San Simeon to live with Marion Davies in a relatively modest home in Los Angeles. A few days before his death, he told his editor at the *Los Angeles Examiner* to give good play to a story about the Pasadena Playhouse, and on August 12 he dictated letters. He died on August 14. His body lay in state at Grace Episcopal Cathedral on Nob Hill in San Francisco for a day and a half and was buried in the family mausoleum at Cypress Lawn Cemetery at Colma, south of the city.[80]

SIX

FOSTERING POLITICAL DISCOURSE

Politically, western journalism strongly resembles what some have called the "Dark Ages of American journalism," that period in the early nineteenth century when editors chose sides and used their newspapers to promote their particular partisan democratic ideals.

The salutatories—the first editorial in which new publishers introduced themselves—of most western newspapers make it clear that their proprietors started their newspapers because they expected to profit from them. Some entered the business for political influence and power, but most initially declared themselves neutral in politics. Although proprietors of western newspapers were not necessarily *good* businessmen, they usually put business first, at least when they started their papers. They fully understood what modern newspaper editors know: if you become too partisan, you can lose half your audience. And unlike today, when the cost of starting a newspaper is high enough to keep competitors at bay, in frontier days, a town was wide open for someone to buy a printing press, hire a couple of printers, and start another newspaper to set forth the political views of those not represented by an existing sheet.

Many—but by no means all—salutatories carried statements of neutrality. This was particularly true for the first newspaper to be started in a town. When Thomas Jefferson Dryer, publisher of the Portland *Oregonian,* sent two staffers, Thornton F. McElroy and James Wiley, to Olympia in Washington Territory to start a new newspaper, he advised them to avoid partisanship. First of all, McElroy, a Whig like Dryer, and Wiley, a Democrat, needed to get along if their new paper, the *Columbian,* was to be operated successfully. The advice also made sense for a newspaper seeking to grow in a sparsely settled area, a district whose fortunes would be controlled by the Democratic administration in Washington, D.C. Why alienate half of the hands that feed you?

Typically, a newspaper would insist that it was "Independent," defining this not as neutral *in* or independent *of* politics, but as independent *in* politics. That is, the editor felt free to present a partisan viewpoint, but he did not intend to let a politician tell him what he could or could not publish.

PARTISANSHIP TAKES OVER

However, neutrality commonly disappeared when the first election came around, and this was borne out in Olympia. When the *Columbian* failed to produce the revenue Dryer wanted, he sold the paper to a group of Olympia residents, including editor Wiley, who were glad to have an organ they could use to further their political position in the new Washington Territory. They

changed the paper's name to *Pioneer and Democrat* and declared it
to be a "straight out, radical democratic journal." [1]

Throughout the West, partisan newspapers that initially had a
monopoly in their towns found themselves challenged by publications espousing an opposing political view. In a region where
people lived far apart, the newspaper thus served as a forum for
the development of political ideas. This forum often crossed the
line into incivility. Mudslinging was common, and the vitriol
spewed by Oregon editors in the mid-nineteenth century was
so great that neighboring editors labeled it the "Oregon style"
of political discourse.

In 1869 the Democratic members of the California legislature raised money to start the *Daily Standard* in Sacramento
because they did not like the political positions of the *Sacramento
Union.* A number of the *Union*'s writers shifted to the *Standard*
almost immediately when legislators also "offered a resolution
appropriating $1,000 from the contingent fund to pay Messrs.
Cutter and Somner for their services." [2] Cutter and Somner
were *Union* reporters assigned to cover the legislature and "had
made careful reports and been obliging otherwise," as far as
the leaders of the legislature were concerned. [3] Their employers
opposed the action, saying it was not proper for the state to pay
the newspaper's employees, so many of the *Union*'s staff moved
to its competitor, the *Standard,* which raised no objections to
someone else paying its reporters. The proposal initially passed
the legislature, but after the *Union*'s editorial complaints, the
move the newspaper called an "extraordinary proposition" was
rescinded. [4] The *Union* accused the *Standard* of planting the idea
in legislators' heads to benefit themselves—the *Standard* might
not have had to pay its reporters if the legislature took care of

it. The *Standard* denied any involvement.[5] In Nevada, too, the legislature sought to show its appreciation to helpful reporters by paying them a bonus for covering it. This amounted to three dollars a day in 1861 and six dollars a day the following year.[6]

A partisan newspaper breeds more partisanship, and another newspaper quickly emerged in Olympia to balance the *Pioneer and Democrat*. Newspapers started only for partisan purposes often closed after the votes were counted, especially if their advocacy had proved futile. And the *Puget Sound Courier,* in the nearby town of Steilacoom, was close to form. In its initial incarnation, it lasted barely a year before the territory's Indian wars and too few Whigs to make up a satisfactory subscriber and advertiser base led to its collapse.[7]

The *Courier* was avowedly Whig, in accordance with the political ideology of its backer, Lafayette Balch, the founder of Steilacoom. Balch, owner of a profitable shipping trade between the Pacific Northwest and San Francisco, found himself cut out of commercial opportunities in Olympia, so he built his own town, Steilacoom. He had helped support the start of the *Columbian* in Olympia and saw its benefits for that town, so he no doubt had dual motives in importing two printers and a press to Steilacoom. The *Courier* could play a booster role, as well as satisfy his need to see his politics represented. Balch brought in an editor, Charles Prosch, who, although a Republican, as most Whigs became in the late 1850s, followed a middle-of-the-road political policy that was not much help to his party.

Regardless of Prosch's efforts to appeal to a wide variety of voters, as had been expected, the Democrats dominated the new Washington Territory, and the *Courier* could not get enough subscribers. It was not until the Whigs—now Republicans—put Abraham Lincoln in the White House in 1860 that Washington

Territory got a successful Republican newspaper, the *Washington Standard* in Olympia. Oddly enough in those days of keen partisanship, the *Standard* could have easily been a Democratic newspaper because its founder, John Miller Murphy, was more interested in obtaining the public printing contract from the territorial government than he was in politics. But because of Prosch's neutrality, the entrepreneurial Murphy, anticipating the change in political temper, saw a void to be filled when the Republicans would come to power. His decision gained him enough Republican support that he won the public printing contract for a short period, but after the Civil War he returned to his partisan roots and moved the *Standard* into the Democratic camp.

"LUCRATIVE" PUBLIC PRINTING CONTRACTS

For partisan newspaper publishers there was more at stake in an election than simply the satisfaction of seeing one's political party hold the reins of power. If a newspaper's party won the election, the editor was in a prime position to win a lucrative public printing contract from the state or territorial government. Just as News Corporation owner Rupert Murdoch has averred that owning a newspaper is like owning a press to print money, pioneer printers were convinced that, as California's Jonas Winchester wrote his wife Susan, in 1850, "It is on the State work that we shall coin gold."[8]

The publisher who got the public printing for his job shop would not only be paid by the government for his work, but he could also print additional copies of the laws to sell for his own profit. Winchester estimated that he could sell about one thousand copies of California's new laws in the state, plus almost as many to people in other states, bringing him a profit of seventy thousand dollars. He urged Susan to move to California to help him "count the money."[9]

Unfortunately, despite legislative good intentions, the state and territorial governments were not always able to hold up their end of the printing contract by paying what was owed the printer in a timely manner. Winchester also soon discovered that he was sharing the public printing with other job shops, and he had to borrow fifteen thousand dollars to complete the Spanish-language edition of the laws because the state had not collected the taxes that would pay his bill. Ever the optimistic and loyal Democrat, Winchester was devastated when he realized that he would be paid in warrants that fluctuated in value and that he might not even make enough money to cover his expenses. (Similarly, a Washington man got caught up in currency depreciation problems when he discovered that a dollar of government currency in the East would fetch only fifty cents on the West Coast.)

Winchester's litany of problems did not end with currency problems. He had a fire, then a flood, and some of the volumes of laws were damaged. Then the legislature rewrote some of the laws, leaving him with a stock of unsold law books with no market. He would have been better off in Washington Territory, where Governor Alvan Flanders, seeking to save the territory's money, vetoed a series of laws that would have required a new printing of the legislation.[10]

Although on the surface, public printing appeared to be a certain gold mine, publishers who did their calculations carefully did not always bid for the contract. Alfred Doten of Gold Hill, Nevada, won the contracts for federal laws in 1872 and 1874, but in 1873 he did not even bid because he figured he would lose money.[11] In the early years the term *bid* was used loosely; local political leaders appointed by the party in control of the federal government were in a position to award the contract. Later a real bid system was established in some territories. Sometimes the favored printing company was too small to actually carry out the contract, so publishers joined forces, or they subcontracted the work. Rarely was the public printing for the state of Nevada done in the state until about 1881; similarly, the Oregon public printing was done in New York in the early days.

Printers maneuvered among themselves in an attempt to obtain the printing contract. If one publisher knew he would not be welcomed by the particular officers who would make the decision because he had not boosted the party hard enough or in some way had earned their dislike, he would take as a partner someone who was in the good graces of the party leaders. Printers also made deals with the public officers, offering them a share of the profits—bribes, kickbacks, and extortion all seemed to occur as printers sought the steady income the public printing contracts were supposed to provide.

For example, when Elwood Evans served as secretary of the Washington Territory in the 1860s, he appointed Thornton F. McElroy as public printer. After leaving the *Columbian* in the hands of the Democrats, McElroy operated a job printing office in Olympia. Fellow publisher Elisha Gunn was known to be one of McElroy's partners in the job shop. A competitor for the public printing, Charles Prosch, publisher of the *Pacific Tribune* in Olympia, claimed that Evans was also one of McElroy's partners.[12] Neither McElroy nor Evans challenged Prosch's allegation. Since McElroy was a Republican and Evans a Democrat,

Prosch's suspicion that the secretary was getting a portion of the profits seems well founded. McElroy also went on to become one of the richest men in the territory.[13]

Prosch, so quick to criticize McElroy and Evans for their deal, was also quick to admit to a similar arrangement he made for himself. His admission came not, however, as a result of a guilty conscience, but because he felt his ethical compromise had been for naught. In 1867, with a new territorial governor and a new secretary of the territory, Prosch received the public printing contract. Four years later in the *Pacific Tribune,* then published by his son Thomas in Tacoma, Prosch wrote:

> We are indebted to Mr. Smith [the new territorial secretary]. He appointed us public printer, charged us over $2,000 for the boon, got his pay at the start, and so laid the foundation for his present prosperity. We have not yet been paid for our labor.[14]

John Miller Murphy, publisher of the *Washington Standard* in Olympia and another seeker for entrée to the public purse, laid the blame at the feet of the politicians, not the publishers. To Prosch and his fellow printers, such arrangements were political and just part of the way of doing business.[15]

Printers, however, were not always the reliable, honest providers of service that the taxpayer expected. The printing contracts prescribed type size and other requirements of the job, but printers sometimes used larger type and cheaper paper, colluded to boost the price of the job, and then shared the benefits, paying kickbacks to those who sent the contracts their way.[16] Alternatively, they used smaller type to get as much on a page as possible in order to save paper. In 1883 the Arizona legislature resolved that publishers should either use large type or provide a magnifying glass.[17] In the intensely partisan decades of the 1870s and 1880s in Arizona, publishers who fought for the public printing contract accused one another of everything from an excess of typographical errors in the printed laws to outright theft and tax evasion.[18]

In 1859 the *Sacramento Union* reprinted comments from the *San Francisco Bulletin* about the state printer: "It is an office where there has been more partisan stealing, in proportion to the services rendered, than any office in the state."[19] The fact that the *Bulletin* was having a bad experience with the city printing contract—and claimed to be doing it for nothing—may have soured the publisher on all public printing. The *Bulletin* and the *San Francisco Times* argued back and forth for several months about the issue because the *Times* contended the *Bulletin* was being paid, while the later insisted, "We scorn to defend ourselves further against assaults from such a source. The effort would be fruitless; for the long practice of our contemporary enables him to coin twenty new falsehoods for each one that we explode."[20]

EDITORS AS POLITICIANS

If a loyal partisan publisher did not win the public printing contract, his party might help him win an election. Republican John Watson started Seattle's first newspaper, the *Seattle Gazette,* in 1863. After his election to the territorial legislature, Watson sold the paper to Ike M. Hall, who changed its name to the *Puget Sound Weekly* and used it to further the cause of the Union Republicans during the territorial election campaign of 1867. Hall was rewarded for his party loyalty by election as county auditor. With a regular income assured, he sold the weekly to William Maxwell, who renamed it the *Weekly Intelligencer,* the ancestor of the *Seattle Post-Intelligencer.*[21]

Another Washington Territory editor, Clarence Bagley, showed little interest in running for office but great enthusiasm for politics. He attached himself to politician Selucius Garfielde, a former Democrat and surveyor-general of the territory, who had become a Republican. Bagley and his father, an influential Seattle minister, became active Republicans in the Garfielde camp as the latter sought the position of territorial delegate to the U.S. Congress. Eventually the Republicans backed the younger Bagley—then twenty-five years old—in publishing their own newspaper, the *Republican,* renamed the *Commercial Age.* While many partisan editors supported their favorite party on the strength of a handshake, Bagley had a written contract with Garfielde and the Republican Party which read, in part:

> [The *Commercial Age* was to be] published in the interests of the party known and generally styled "Republican Party," and to advocate the claims of Selucius Garfielde, and his only, for next Delegate to Congress from the Territory, until the nomination by the next Republican Territorial Convention of its candidate, and should the said Selucius Garfielde receive such nomination at the hands of said convention for Delegate to Congress, to continue such advocacy until after the ensuing election in the year 1870.[22]

Garfielde won the election and kept a close watch on his young editor. When he ran for reelection two years later, he told Bagley to send five hundred copies of the newspaper "into the nooks and corners, and out of the way, and needful places."[23]

He also tried to get back into the good graces of sawmill owner Marshall Blinn, whom he had alienated and who sponsored an opposing Republican voice, the *Olympia Transcript.* Garfielde warned Bagley to treat Blinn well. "Don't let any of our papers abuse the mill men," he wrote his editor in 1870.[24] Bagley played his role ably and was rewarded with a public printing contract as well as whatever profit he could make from the newspaper.

After Garfielde lost in 1872, he also lost interest in supporting the newspaper, by then renamed the *Courier.* Taken over by Elisha Ferry, two-term territorial governor and the first governor of the state of Washington, the political machine that Garfielde created continued to dominate state politics, and Bagley did the public printing for a decade.[25]

THE ARIZONA EXAMPLE

Politically connected editors could be found in all parts of the West, but Arizona may well be a special case. Arizona journalism historian William Lyon argues that politics provided the primary reason for the establishment of Arizona newspapers. The first Arizona newspaper, the *Arizonian,* founded in the mining camp of Tubac in 1859, was political, but not overtly partisan. Local mining companies were unhappy about having to go all the way to the (New Mexico) territorial capital of Santa Fe to deal with government business, and they sought the creation of the Arizona Territory. Like the Washington Territory businesspeople and politicians earlier that decade, Arizonans thought that having a newspaper would help advance their cause.[26] Unlike the Washington crowd, the Arizonans were not excited about territorial status per se; they wanted a judicial district that would be apolitical, and low-cost enough that it would not require much in taxes.

The mine owners were Republicans, whereas, according to Lyon, "most Arizonians were Southern Democrats." The *Arizonian* failed during the Civil War, but it had achieved its goal of creating a new territory, and the new territorial officials brought printing materials with them to Prescott, the site of the new government. One of the principals in the new government, Territorial Secretary Richard C. McCormick, also brought to the desert extensive experience as a journalist. McCormick had served as a newspaper correspondent at Sevastopol during the Crimean War in 1854–55, was the editor of *Young Men's Magazine* in New York from 1857 to 1859, and was a correspondent for the *New York Evening Post* and the *New York Commercial Advertiser* during the Civil War.[27]

The thirty-two-year-old McCormick set up his press in the Prescott area upon his appointment as secretary in 1864, and he soon founded the *Miner* as a "creature of the territorial government," according to Lyon.[28] Three years later McCormick, now territorial governor, moved the capital to Tucson and sold the *Miner* to former prospector John Marion, who said the *Miner* would be the "Organ of the White People of Arizona."[29] A Democrat who felt betrayed by McCormick's move of the capital because it had upset his plans to get a public printing contract, Marion blasted the Republican governor with all the fervor his Democratic political soul could muster. He accused the governor—later territorial delegate—of fraud and Republican editors of being lackeys of the governor.[30] McCormick eventually returned to his native New York, which elected him to Congress in 1895. He also served as first assistant secretary of the Treasury in 1877. He died in 1901.[31]

When he founded his "creature of the territorial government," McCormick eschewed partisan politics in its columns, as had the mining companies that published in Tubac. After reviving the *Arizonian* in the late 1860s, McCormick eventually turned it over to Pierson W. Dooner, a save-the-world editor who not only avoided politics in the columns of the newspaper but condemned partisanship and political parties. Closely aligned with McCormick and other Republicans, however, Dooner could hardly be called neutral. In 1870 Dooner became a Democrat, so McCormick and his partner collected the printing press they still owned, leaving Dooner to resurrect an even older press so he could continue to produce the *Arizonian*.[32] Then the man who had excessively praised McCormick and his fellow Republicans showed he could be equally excessive in attacking them.

Marion, at the *Miner* in Prescott, disliked Dooner, but now anyone who attacked McCormick was a friend of Marion's. Marion turned his vitriol toward John Wasson, editor of the *Tucson Citizen,* which was, in Marion's view, McCormick's "new valet, lackey, and a vile wretch."[33] Nevertheless, McCormick was reelected delegate to Congress. In 1871 Dooner gave up the fight, put away his composing stick, and moved to California.[34]

In 1882, with the territorial capital now back in Prescott, politically minded editors were concerned about "the refusal of carpetbag governors to cooperate with the established party papers and their propensity to set up their own sheets."[35] Two years later they had a major example when President Grover Cleveland appointed Conrad Meyer Zulick governor of the Arizona Territory. Zulick and his secretary became cozy with Democrat Marion, who had started a new newspaper, the *Prescott Courier,* as a rival to the *Arizonian,* which had been secretly purchased by a prominent Republican.[36] Marion's loyalty to the Democrats earned him the position of territorial treasurer.

Meanwhile, back in Tucson, Louis C. Hughes had founded the *Tucson Star,* which rivaled Marion's publications in Democratic enthusiasm. Hughes, who believed hardworking political editors like himself had a right to some of the spoils of office, hoped to benefit from Zulick, but the new governor passed him over in making appointments, earning Hughes's enmity. Hughes took his case to the national stage and, after nominating Cleveland for his second term, was rewarded with the territorial governorship for himself.

The Republicans were back in control in 1888 and returned the capital to Tucson, where the *Tucson Citizen* expected to benefit. When President Benjamin Harrison appointed Lewis Wolfley governor of Arizona Territory, Wasson at the *Citizen* thought he would be called upon to support the new administration, but Wolfley ignored him and moved the capital to Phoenix, where, with fellow politicians, he started his own organ, the *Arizona Republican.*[37]

An Idaho editor, Frank S. Kenyon at the *Lewiston Golden Age,* experienced similar disappointments at the hands of maneuvering politicians. In 1860 Lewiston was the Idaho territorial capital, and Kenyon obtained the public printing contract. Lewiston had only 359 people, however, so Kenyon expected the capital to be moved to Boise, and he made plans to move there as well.[38] The new territorial governor wanted a strong Union paper in Lewiston, so he promised Kenyon he would continue to get the public printing and offered him an appointment as census taker if he would stay in Lewiston. Kenyon's press was on a wagon heading for Boise, but he called it back. The capital was moved to Boise anyway, angering the citizens of Lewiston who took some of their ire out on Kenyon, boycotting his newspaper.[39]

The emphasis on partisanship, Lyon says, sometimes backfired. In some communities, such as Tucson, a party had so many voices that the voters became confused by the cacophony, making it easier for the other party. Tombstone, probably Arizona's most famous frontier town, boasted a population during its boom years in the 1880s of about fifteen thousand with as many as a dozen newspapers at one point.[40]

Several factors brought politicians and newspapermen together—when they were not already one and the same, as in the case of Arizona's Richard McCormick. Sometimes the tie was strictly political; other times economics was the stronger force. A New Mexico journalism historian says that frontier journalists in New Mexico Territory were too poor to stand up to politicians and were thus "forced to submit to [their] will."[41] Lyon makes a similar argument about the Arizona editors he studied: "Newspapering was such a precarious enterprise, and political factionalism such a pervasive force, that editors were too overwhelmed with practical problems to promote very many high ideals."[42]

It is likely that the New Mexico and Arizona journalists were indeed poor and overwhelmed, and that some discarded their partisan principles in the interests of economic survival. But editors then, as now, lived for politics. It exaggerates their condition to say they were "forced" to submit to the will of the politicians. Even the struggling ones loved the give-and-take of politics.

SEVEN

PLENTIFUL VOICES

Thus far, we have been looking at the role of what are typically called "mainstream" newspapers, publications intended for
everyman and everywoman. The reader well acquainted with
the history of the colonial press in the United States will no
doubt have observed the parallels evidenced in the western press:
editors wearing many hats in their communities and in their
businesses because of a dearth of labor and newspapers bridging
distance to provide channels for the social and political discourse
that brings citizens into communities and political structures.

The far western frontier was not and is not a homoge-
neous region. The lush forests of the Pacific Northwest, Idaho,
and northern California contrast vividly with the deserts and
canyons of the Great Basin and the Southwest. Its people, too,
reflected this diversity, both in terms of those who inhabited the
land when the immigrants arrived and within the immigrating
parties themselves. It is to be expected, then, that their press will
reflect the same diversity, and indeed it does.

The mainstream press, or what the U.S. census described as
having a "news and politics" orientation in English, is only part

of the story of western journalism. Again, like its forebears on the East Coast, the western press proliferated to serve a multitude of interests and needs, but it did so in a fraction of the time the development had required earlier. In 1732, twenty-eight years after the start of the first successful colonial newspaper, the *Boston News-Letter,* Benjamin Franklin introduced the *Philadelphische Zeitung* to the German immigrants in his hometown. Franklin's paper soon folded, but in 1739 a German immigrant printer, Christopher Sauer, started the more enduring *Der Hoch-Deutsch Pennsylvanische Geschichts-Schreiber* (*High German Pennsylvania Analyst*). The French-speaking residents of the United States followed fifty years later with their own newspapers. Ulf Jonas Bjork, writing about the ethnic press for the *History of the Mass Media in the United States,* says that some three hundred foreign-language publications, mostly in German and French, had been started by 1860, but he calls the American ethnic press "primarily a phenomenon of the era of mass migration from Europe to the United States between the 1880s and the 1920s."[1]

FOREIGN-LANGUAGE AND ETHNIC NEWSPAPERS

In fact, the first foreign-language newspapers on the West Coast predated by several decades the mass migration press to which Bjork refers. Another historian, William Huntzicker, estimates that of those three hundred or so nineteenth-century foreign-language newspapers, more than a hundred of them were started in California.[2] Whereas German-speaking residents in the eastern United States had to wait about three *decades* after the *Boston News-Letter* for the first newspaper in their own language, Germans in California were reading the *California Demokrat* only six *years* after the *Californian* first appeared.[3] Regardless of their language and origins, westerners were eager to re-create the lives they had left behind and saw a newspaper as one way to do it.

California was the heart of the foreign-language press in the nineteenth century, as it remains today. Kemble lists *Le Californien,* started on January 21, 1850, as the first French newspaper in San Francisco, "a curious looking print," lithographed because the publisher could not get French-accented type.[4] Kemble could not determine how long it existed, so it almost certainly failed quickly. By 1880, San Francisco alone listed twenty-six foreign-language periodicals—including a German humor magazine—among its 125 publications.[5] In 1996 ethnic media leaders lunched at a San Francisco Chinese restaurant to talk about increasing cooperation and sharing news stories. The result was an organization called New California Media. "California is ground zero," said Sandy Close, executive director of New California Media. "The ethnic media really took off here ten years ago and have been growing ever since."[6] In recognition of how the rest of the nation has echoed the growth of ethnic media in the West, the organization now calls itself New America Media, has more than seven hundred members across the continent, according to its Web site, and operates an Ethnic Media Network as a vehicle for the exchange of news.[7]

The western ethnic press, again like its eastern counterparts, was centered in the cities. The foreign-born residents who frequented the mining camps seldom concentrated enough members from one ethnic group in one place to justify the establishment of a newspaper in their native languages, and even though the census shows a high percentage of foreign-born residents in western mining camps, this does not mean that the mainstream newspapers failed to serve them. Given the generally high level of literacy and foreigners' need to be able to use English in their business affairs, they probably read the *Territorial Enterprise* and other English-language camp papers without difficulty, while also subscribing to the San Francisco periodicals printed in their native tongues.

SPANISH-LANGUAGE NEWSPAPERS

Contemporary treatments of the newspapers of two ethnic or racial groups, Hispanics and African Americans, focus largely on their role in the civil rights movements of the mid-twentieth century. However, both groups had newspapers in the frontier West. The first Spanish-language newspaper in the United States is believed to be *El Misisipí* in New Orleans in 1808.[8] Other early Spanish-language newspapers appeared in Louisiana, which was an important seaport for trade between the United States and Latin America. Texas, too, fielded a Spanish-language newspaper as early as 1813, but of the states and territories discussed in this book, New Mexico has the best claim to the first Spanish-language press with *El Crepúsculo de la Libertad,* an election sheet published four times in 1834. A total of 136 Spanish-language newspapers appeared in New Mexico during the nineteenth century, most of them weekly.[9]

Communities with large Hispanic populations often experimented with offering bilingual newspapers. For example, the equipment that eventually gave California its first newspaper was delivered to Monterey by the Spaniards a dozen years after *El Crepúsculo* was established, but even though the *Californian* that eventually came from its type was bilingual, it was intended primarily for the Anglos, so it is generally not included in the list of early Hispanic newspapers.[10]

The first West Coast newspaper entirely in the Spanish language was *El Clamor Público* in Los Angeles, which grew out of another bilingual newspaper. Seventeen-year-old Francisco Ramírez had edited *La Estrella,* the Spanish section of the *Los Angeles Star.* Félix Gutiérrez writes that Ramírez took moderate positions in the *Star,* but after he started *El Clamor Público* in 1855, he began attacking Anglos ("the pirate instinct of the Anglo-Saxons is still alive"), insisting that in "six years of armed violence, Vigilante raids and lynchings against Chicanos, 'the criminals have always escaped,'" and urging Chicanos to move to northern Mexico.[11]

In all, Californios—residents with Spanish ancestry—and other Spanish-speaking and reading residents were served by forty-six Spanish-language newspapers in the nineteenth century. Twenty-two of these were in San Francisco, nineteen in Los Angeles, and the remainder in a scattering of other towns. Nine of the papers were bilingual, including the *Californian* in Monterey and the *Star* in Los Angeles.[12]

Historian Victoria Goff notes that the early Spanish-language press in California should not be considered a "Mexican-American" press because the Spanish, not the Mexicans, influenced California society at that time.[13] Goff suggests that the Spanish-language press helped both Californios and Hispanic immigrants adapt to American life, just as elsewhere in the nation the foreign-language press aided other immigrant groups to assimilate into Anglo culture.

THE CHINESE PRESS

The early press of another large ethnic population in the West, the Chinese, had religious connections. In 1851 the Reverend

William Speer, corresponding secretary of the Presbyterian Board of Education and a former missionary in China and California, published a one-sheet religious tract that is sometimes called the first Chinese newspaper in America, no doubt because of the "news" in its name: variously, *Gold Hill News, Golden Hill News,* or *Golden Mountain News.* Four years later Speer helped another Presbyterian missionary, Lai Sam, issue the *Oriental,*[14] which was printed in English on one side and lithographed in Chinese on the other. The cost of the lithography was supported by the Six Companies, "a powerful interest group that controlled Chinese immigrants" and obviously saw the newspaper as a way to develop the kind of community the group wanted.[15]

San Francisco had other Chinese-language newspapers in the nineteenth century, including at least one devoted to business news. Chinese-language newspapers, like other ethnic publications, showed a keen awareness of the racism that existed on the frontier. The mainstream press generally reflected its readers' discomfort with people who looked and behaved differently from the dominant population. The *Owyhee Avalanche* in southwestern Idaho was probably typical in its distaste for the Chinese, mocking their worship, referring to it as "tomfoolery," their women—"She don't wear waterfalls nor 'tilting hoops'—don't think she is refined enough for either," and overall appearance, which it termed "more unsightly than even the Indian race."[16]

The Chinese, who were brought to the West as cheap labor for the mines and the railroads, were the subject of a major anti-Chinese campaign in Seattle in 1885 by the Knights of Labor, who believed the Asians were displacing white workers. The wealthy in the Washington city liked being able to hire the Chinese as servants, but the middle class worried about Washington's depressed economy and a flood of new people competing for work when the railroad construction was completed. The *Seattle Call,* operated by two young men, the son and nephew of a Seattle lawyer and a utopian community mother, Ike and Laura Hall, served as spokespaper for the Knights and repeatedly printed the mantra: "The Chinese Must Go!" in its ads and news columns. Before things quieted down, the city experienced violence, martial law, and the indictment of fifteen people, including a distant cousin of Laura Hall, Peter Peyto Good, a labor organizer from New York.[17] A conservative Seattle editor classed Laura Hall with "every socialist and anarchist who could walk or steal a ride to Seattle. . . . Long-haired men and short-haired women were noticeable by their numbers and their noise."[18] But it should be noted that Hall was really only a supporter of the white workingman.

AFRICAN AMERICAN NEWSPAPERS

The West's oldest surviving African American newspaper, the *California Eagle,* started in Los Angeles in 1879.[19] Owner John Neimore apparently neglected to respond to S. N. D. North's survey for his special census report in 1880 because the paper is not listed. The *Eagle* was preceded by the *Mirror of the Times,* in San Francisco, listed by Kemble as a Negro newspaper and lasting perhaps two years from its start in 1856.[20] Other early black newspapers included the *Elevator* and the *Pacific Appeal,* published in San Francisco from 1865 to 1898 and 1862 to 1880, respectively, and the *Vindicator,* 1887–89, also in San Francisco; the *Seattle Republican,* 1894–1915; the *Portland New Age,* 1899–1907; and the *BroadAx* in Salt Lake City, 1895–99. Of the latter, Alter records, "A country onlooker observes: 'The editors of the

BroadAx and the Salt Lake Herald are indulging in the pastime of calling each other . . . pet names,'" and credits the *Wasatch Wave* in Heber City with this observation: "The capital city has two weekly papers, edited by colored gentlemen, who have been saying . . . unpleasant things of each other."[21] However, Alter's compilation of information about individual newspapers in Utah gives no other indication that the *Salt Lake Herald* was a black newspaper.[22]

At the turn of the century, African Americans became more active in western journalism, starting additional newspapers in Colorado and Oregon.[23] As in the modern era, these newspapers were started to remedy the neglect of African Americans by the mainstream media.

CHARLOTTA SPEARS BASS AND THE *CALIFORNIA EAGLE*

A woman who became an icon in the black newspaper publishing field in Los Angeles arrived soon after the turn of the twentieth century and eventually took over a newspaper started some twenty years earlier. A diminutive woman whose size belied her strength, Charlotta Spears Bass edited the *California Eagle* from 1912 to 1951.

Like most African American editors, she used her newspaper as a forum to advance the cause of her community. With a circulation smaller than the *Chicago Defender,* which topped one hundred thousand in its prime, the *Eagle*'s voice nonetheless resounded throughout southern California and the West and reached across the nation. One historian of women journalists has written that although Bass focused on race issues, she also addressed gender stereotypes, and her experiences "reflect the intersection between race and gender discussed in the works of many prominent historians who have examined this nexus."[24]

The details of Charlotta Spears's childhood are fuzzy; in her autobiography she says she was born in Little Compton, Rhode Island, but she does not say when. The birth year on her 1969 death certificate is 1874, which means she was thirty-six when she arrived in southern California, apparently seeking a warmer, drier climate on the advice of a physician.[25] Before long she decided she needed a job, and having worked for the *Providence Watchman* in her native state, newspapering had a natural attraction for her, so she took a position in the circulation department of the *California Eagle*.[26]

When *Eagle* owner Neimore decided to take a vacation to try to regain his health, he left Spears in charge, and just before he died two years later, he asked her to continue to operate the newspaper. With the paper $150 in debt and with only $10 in the bank, Spears agreed reluctantly. She existed on crackers and milk for several months, but she held on.[27]

In addition to racism, Spears had to deal with a sexist business community that did not expect her to be able to keep the paper alive.[28] She persevered and in 1913 hired an experienced newspaperman, Joseph Bass, the man who would become her husband. The marriage, notes historian Kathleen Cairns, who examines the challenges of sexism as well as racism that Spears had to face, "brought her legitimacy as a female publisher," and gave the enterprise the benefit of Bass's experience.[29]

However much she may have done to remedy sexism, it is for her advocacy of African American causes that she is remembered. Not long after she married Bass, filmmaker D. W. Griffith sought to use the streets of Los Angeles for the filming of *Birth of a Nation,* a motion picture that was anathema to the black community because it glorified the Ku Klux Klan. Bass's newspaper stories and personal efforts in lobbying the Los Angeles City Council initially persuaded the council not to give Griffith the permit he wanted, although later efforts by the filmmaker and the film industry got him the permit anyway. With Griffith also trying to hire African Americans as extras for the film, Bass campaigned to get black actors to boycott it. Afterward, although unsuccessful in stopping the production, Bass took credit for getting Griffith "to cut some of the most vicious attacks against the morals of the Negro people."[30]

Bass also fought to get the Los Angeles County Hospital to hire African American nurses and nurse's aides, and to increase civil service opportunities for African American women.[31] In the Depression, when she discovered that no African Americans were employed on one of the Southwest's major public construction projects, the building of Boulder (Hoover) Dam on the Colorado River, because there was no segregated housing available, she first worked to get a dormitory built for blacks and then for black men to have an equal opportunity for the jobs on the project.

In the 1920s she turned the tables on the Ku Klux Klan by publishing a letter from a Klan leader discussing how to get rid of the black leaders in Watts. The Klan claimed the letter was a fake, but she was acquitted in the subsequent libel suit. Bass was fearless, walking Watts streets alone and working late alone in her office. She kept a gun in her desk, but claimed she did not really know how to use it. An exchange with her husband has been reprinted in many accounts of her life: Joseph Bass: "Mrs.

Bass, one of these days you're going to get me killed." Mrs. Bass: "Mr. Bass, it will be in a good cause."

Joseph Bass died in 1934 and Charlotta continued to publish the *Eagle,* trying to build community awareness among the growing number of African Americans in Los Angeles. She also traveled widely and became a popular lecturer. She joined African Americans around the country—and the Communist Party—in condemning the decision in the Scottsboro case, fought and bested the Southern California Telephone Company by getting blacks to cancel their telephone service until the company agreed to hire African Americans, and exposed an employment agency that was exploiting black women.[32]

During World War II, when some 120,000 people of Japanese ancestry were "evacuated" to what many have called "concentration camps," the *Eagle* encouraged southern California's African Americans to consider buying the farms the Japanese were forced to relinquish. In an editorial the editor wrote:

> "Today, Negroes once again are faced with a tremendous agricultural opportunity, and once again these columns throb with the old cry, "Back to the Farm!"
>
> Today's opportunity may be seen on the front page of your morning newspaper: "U.S. (to) Remove Aliens From West Coast Area." It is well known that the Japanese people have become masters of the soil throughout our great state. With unflagging industry and determination, these people have built here an [agr]arian empire that is tremendous. If it must be lost to them, why shouldn't it fall into our hands.[33]

Six weeks later, apparently having had little positive response to the editorial, the *Eagle* repeated the "back to the farm" encour-

agement in a second editorial.[34] Although this would seem to
show Bass as unsympathetic to the plight of other ethnic groups,
James Phillip Jeter, in his research on the black press's response
to Executive Order 9066 which led to the internment, found
that the *Eagle* published many stories about the issue, in addition to the two editorials, and he argues that the *Eagle*'s position
was not simply one of a "black land/property grab." Prior to the
issuance of the order, but after Pearl Harbor, the *Eagle* noted that
the Japanese-American Citizens League of Southern California
had pledged loyalty to the United States. At the end of the story,
the *Eagle* urged "an attitude of friendliness, sympathy and cour-
tesy toward all Japanese." Jeter concludes that the *Eagle* had
not been among those calling for the Japanese evacuation and
internment. After the executive order, he suggests, Bass "apparently viewed the Japanese relocation as a 'fait accompli' . . . and
attempted to offer a plan for blacks to benefit from the misfor-
tune of the Japanese."[35]

Bass became increasingly radical, especially after World War
II, connecting the fight for civil rights with the fight against
Hitler. In 1947 she helped create the Independent Progressive
Party of California, and the following year she campaigned for
Henry Wallace, the Progressive Party candidate for president.
These activities brought her to the notice of the FBI and gained
her the label "Communist sympathizer." By 1951 the FBI's atten-
tion was hurting the *Eagle,* so she sold it. She ran for mayor of
Los Angeles and for a seat in the House of Representatives, and
in 1952 singer Paul Robeson nominated Bass for vice president
on the Progressive ticket headed by Vincent Hallinan. W. E. B.
DuBois seconded the nomination.[36] The *Eagle* ceased publishing
in 1964. Bass died five years later, but is remembered as a "radical
precursor of the Black Power Movement."[37]

RELIGIOUS PUBLICATIONS

At the top of any discussion of religious publications in the West sits the Latter-day Saints Church's *Deseret News,* although it could fit well into the mainstream newspaper category because it did much more than preach church doctrine to its readers. The *Deseret News* had, one historian has commented, "all the appearance and aspiration of a regular newspaper." [38] One of the inland West's earliest publications, the *Deseret News* started publication in 1850, only four years after Walter Colton and Robert Semple issued the first *Californian* and only four years after the Mormons arrived in the Salt Lake Valley. The Mormons have a history with strong newspaper links. At each of the locations where they tried to build a colony, they started newspapers. They arrived in Utah in 1846, and they considered communication so important that, initially, youth groups throughout the area produced manuscript newspapers for their communities. [39] San Francisco's Brannan published a church-sponsored newspaper in New York before heading west with his party of Mormon colonists. Mormons issued the *Times and Seasons* in Nauvoo, Illinois, and had a press in Independence, Missouri, that was thrown into the river by one of the many angry mobs that attacked them as they sought a place to call their own. That press, by the way, was the one subsequently rescued by John L. Merrick, who took it to Colorado, where he lost the competition to print the first newspaper in what would become Denver. [40]

The church's attitude toward the press was expressed in a note Brigham Young and his council gave to William W. Phelps when they instructed him to make a trip to Nauvoo and bring a printing press back to Salt Lake City. They wrote: "This people cannot live without intelligence, for it is through obedience to that principle they are to receive their exaltation; and if the intelligence cannot be had, justice has no claim on obedience, and their exaltation must be decreased."[41] Small in format (approximately seven by ten inches), the eight-page first issue of the *Deseret News* devoted eleven of its twenty-four columns to news of Congress. Wendell J. Ashton, author of a history of the *Deseret News,* said that much of the out-of-town copy actually came from Horace Greeley's weekly *New York Tribune.*[42] New York newspapers commonly prepared weekly summaries of their daily news for circulation across the nation, and western newspapers used these alongside the exchanges as their news services.

Paper shortages, not a supply of news, hindered the development of the *Deseret News.* Almost immediately after its first issue, editor W. Richards changed the paper from weekly to biweekly to conserve paper. The pages of early issues of newspapers are replete with pleas to readers to save their rags with a view to eventual construction of a paper mill. Mormon bishops told their flocks that contributions of rags could count toward their tithe to the church, but the Utah pioneers tended to be so poor they needed even the worn cloth for themselves.

The *Deseret News* has been described as one of the few frontier newspapers that did not have serious financial worries, thanks to the backing of the church. One historian has noted that while many church employees were not paid, *News* employees were—although not always in cash. Part of the newspaper's key to success, like that of its church, was a willingness and ability to barter. The *News* frequently told its readers they could pay for their subscriptions with farm produce: "Wanted at our office, flour, corn meal, butter, cheese, tallow and pork in exchange for the News."[43] On other occasions the newspaper asked for cash because suppliers of ink and other press materials were not interested in chickens, but said it would nevertheless continue to accept food, supplies, skins, and furs—anything for home and garden.[44]

Despite the church's efforts to resolve the paper problem by building a paper mill, it was two years before the newspaper appeared on homemade paper. A papermaker named Thomas Howard got Brigham Young's approval to use the construction plan brought to Utah for a sugar mill—but never successfully used—to make paper instead. The rags were ground in the beet grinder (it would have made beet sugar) and dried in the sun. In addition to thick, gray newsprint, the mill produced wrapping paper and cardboard for boxes and sunbonnet brim stiffeners.[45]

The 1880 census identified only one other Mormon newspaper in Utah, the *Ogden Junction,* located a few miles north of Salt Lake City and close to the juncture of the transcontinental railroad, but there probably were others. In the *Junction's* first issue, January 1, 1870, Charles W. Penrose was listed as associate editor, but he soon moved to the top position. Cecil Alter's *Early Utah Journalism* does not list the *Junction* as a church-sponsored newspaper, although it describes Penrose as "Elder" Penrose and a temporary editor as "Bishop" Johnson, titles used by the Mormons, suggesting a church connection.[46] Being a church elder did not save the handsome Penrose from a caning on a Salt Lake City street in 1872 by a "pettifogging lawyer, named W. R. Keithly." Penrose received a gash on his head in the confrontation, and Keithly was fined one hundred dollars for his actions.[47]

The church recognized Penrose's editorial talents and loyalty and brought him to Salt Lake City to edit the *Deseret News* in 1877, just in time to battle a growing anti-Mormon, anti-polygamy campaign waged by the federal government and the other Salt Lake City newspapers.[48] Although Penrose's approach to the polygamy issue was scholarly, he nevertheless was forced into exile; John Nicholson, who took over the editorial duties in 1885, also expected to go to jail for his support of multiple marriage.[49] While Penrose was in exile, Brigham Young sent him to Washington, D.C., to assist Young's son, John W., in lobbying for statehood for Utah Territory. Both men operated under pseudonyms: Penrose used C. Williams; Young was "Embargo." Penrose's primary assignment apparently was to determine which eastern newspapers were friendly to their cause and how much it would cost to ensure favorable press reports.[50] By the time Utah achieved statehood in 1896, Penrose had returned to—and retired from—the *Deseret News*. In 1899 he heeded the call of the church again and served another eight years as editor. During this time he was also called to the church's top governing body, the Council of Twelve.[51]

Other religious periodicals were scattered around the West, primarily in the cities because of access to resources, but with the purpose of reaching out into the hinterland.[52] The early publications encountered the same challenges as the mainstream newspapers: problems with financing, fires, floods, poor management, and the departure of staff for the mines whenever a promising new ore find was announced. Like their mainstream counterparts, religious publishers had trouble getting readers to pay their subscription bills. The Methodist Episcopalians were more systematic than most denominations. They required local pastors to act as agents for the publication and to collect for the subscriptions. In exchange, the pastors got a modest commission and their own subscription free.[53]

More than a third of religious periodicals failed within a year—mainstream newspapers often lasted a bit longer.[54] Twenty-six western religious publications of various frequencies responded to the 1880 census survey, twelve of them in San Francisco, including one called *Light for All,* serving spiritualists. These periodicals and many of the other specialized journals published in the West offered more opportunities than the mainstream press did to women who wanted to write and edit.

CULTURAL NEWSPAPERS

It may be overstating the case to call the *Daily Dramatic Chronicle* an example of the "cultural" press. It did, of course, tell early San Franciscans what they could expect to find on the stages of the city, but the two young brothers who started the paper, Michel and Charles De Young, put income from advertisers far ahead of advising theatergoers where they would get the best entertainment. In fact, as part of their promotion of the early issues of the *Chronicle,* the teenagers played on the common practice of newspapers acknowledging newcomers by printing a bogus welcome from the "Daily Halter" criticizing their paper for printing interesting items that might take attention from its advertisers, something the "Daily Halter" would never do.[55] Within a few months, however, the De Youngs quickly learned that news, too, could pay. The *Chronicle* took a major step toward its future as a real newspaper in April 1865. When news of President Lincoln's assassination reached San Francisco, the alert young publishers rushed an extra onto the streets and briefly captured the news-hungry market. They never looked back, and the *Chronicle* developed into one of the West's leading mainstream newspapers.

San Francisco, the cultural hub of the West and the main supplier to miners, soon became home to several literary publications, which provided both an outlet and reading material for the literate miners scratching poems and stories in candlelit cabins in the remote canyons of the Sierra Nevada and other mountains. They also brought nationally famous writers to the attention of western readers. Many of these periodicals, which were listed by Kemble in his history of California newspapers, were more like today's magazines, both in dimensions and content.

The *Golden Era* led the field; its first issue as a weekly Sunday literary newspaper was delivered to readers in 1852. It was still publishing at the end of the decade when Kemble did his survey, and he noted, "A number of similar papers have been started in the State, but this is the only one which has proved permanent. It has now a quarto form, and has a large circulation among the miners, to whose tastes it is more especially adapted."[56]

The *Contra Costa,* edited across the bay in Oakland by Sarah Moore Clarke each week for about a year starting in 1854, was printed in San Francisco because no one had yet established a press in Oakland.[57] Clarke's plan for the newspaper is not known; Kemble considered it a woman's paper, but its only surviving issue is full of literary material amid news items, much like the general weeklies of its day.

The *Athenaeum* was initially published semimonthly. Cora Anna Weekes and her husband brought out the first issue in 1858, but after three issues they took off for Australia.[58] That same year the *Hesperian,* the next literary effort, lasted considerably longer, but two owners and five years later it became the *Pacific Monthly* to avoid being branded a "woman's magazine," even then an approbation sure to limit circulation.[59]

MEDICAL AND SCIENTIFIC PERIODICALS

Perhaps surprisingly for the time, medical publications provided another venue for women writers and editors. San Francisco's first such periodical, the *Pacific Medical Journal,* had men at its helm when it was started in January 1858, but the *Medico-Literary Journal* of 1878–86 was edited by Mrs. M. P. Sawtelle and perhaps—given its hybrid title—should be classed with the cultural journals.[60]

Carrie Fisher Young started the *Women's Pacific Coast Journal* in May 1870, changing its name to *Pacific Journal of Health* two years later. Young, who had campaigned against slavery and lectured on temperance before moving to the West Coast, continued lecturing even while editing the *Journal,* expanding her repertoire to include physiology and health, particularly for women and children. She further supported women's causes by employing women printers and engravers who had formed associations in San Francisco.[61] Early on she protested against the suffix *ess* to signify the female form of an occupation. "We protest against being called an *editress,* or a *lecturess,* and object to having it said of us that because we are a *hard workeress,* we are a hearty *eateress,* and a sound *sleeperess.*"[62]

In Utah two women, plural wives Ellis Reynolds Shipp and Margaret (Maggie) Curtis Shipp, joined their husband in the establishment of the *Salt Lake Sanitorium.* In 1873 Mormon leader Brigham Young had started sending students to eastern schools to study medicine, in order to ensure adequate medical help for his flock. Maggie was in the 1875 contingent, studying at the Woman's Medical College of Pennsylvania, but she quickly became homesick, so Ellis replaced her. She received her medical degree three years later, practiced medicine in Utah for ten years, and then went east for postgraduate work. When she returned to Utah, Maggie tried medical school again and this time stayed the course, receiving her degree in 1883.[63]

Their husband Bard decided medicine looked more promising than the law he had been studying, and he got his medical degree from the Jefferson Medical College of Philadelphia, also in 1883. In 1888 the three Drs. Shipp decided that the faithful needed a health and medical journal. All three contributed to the journal, and historian Sherilyn Cox Bennion speculates that Ellis, who published poetry elsewhere, added a special literary touch. The *Salt Lake Sanitorium* generally lived up to its promise of spreading the understanding of physiology, illness, and treatments. Ellis and Bard wrote regular columns, and they selected from a wide range of medical exchanges.[64] In 1889, during the government's anti-polygamy campaign, Bard Shipp was jailed for ten weeks for having more than one wife.

The Shipps' articles in the *Salt Lake Sanitorium* attacked unhealthy clothing, such as the body-squeezing corset, and provided useful information for new mothers, but when the professionalization of medicine resulted in jargon-heavy articles unsuitable for a general readership, they no longer had good sources to draw upon and closed the journal.[65]

UTOPIAN NEWSPAPERS

The Mormons were not the only group seeking refuge in the West from people who disagreed with them. Scattered around the West were a number of utopian communities, and most of them had newspapers to help build community awareness and proselytize. For example, the Puget Sound area near

Seattle attracted at least eight such communitarian colonies. The oldest, the Puget Sound Cooperative Colony, started in Seattle but eventually moved to a settlement near Port Angeles on the Olympic Peninsula. Three months after the colony was formed in 1886, its newspaper, *Model Commonwealth,* made its appearance.[66]

The communitarian colonies of the late nineteenth century have been described as a reaction to the strains of industrialization. Many of them were accused of being hotbeds for anarchism, free love, and other seemingly antisocial activities. Certainly the founders of the Puget Sound Cooperative Colony were in the midst of an immigration conflict, much like that of the early twenty-first century, only this time the Chinese, not Mexicans, were at the center of the controversy.

In the mid-1880s the Washington Territory was on the verge of statehood and was experiencing major growth. Both the Northern Pacific and the Great Northern railroads were about to complete their lines to Puget Sound, and their Chinese building crews would soon flood the local job market. At the same time, sensing a receptive audience for their activities, the Knights of Labor sent representatives to organize the white workers. These labor issues eventually resulted in martial law in Seattle, but while the workers marched in torchlight parades, several communitarian idealists met to talk about how to improve the lot of the white workingman. Among them was a woman named Laura Crane Hall, whose son and nephews edited the *Seattle Daily Call,* one of the loudest anti-Chinese voices. Although her son and her ex-husband, Ike Hall, were all in newspapers, Laura apparently had no direct newspaper experience before being appointed to start the *Model Commonwealth* for the new colony.

Editing a newspaper on the frontier did not require great reporting or writing skills because so much of it was done by reprinting articles from other publications. Thus, Hall filled her columns with Knights of Labor organizing materials, official colony documents, treatises from other leaders of the colony, and news taken from newspapers in other, like-minded colonies. And like other booster newspapers in the West, the *Model Commonwealth* included stories about the good life the colonists experienced in Port Angeles. In 1887, after a colony uprising that nearly led to the replacement of most of its leaders, Hall resigned as the newspaper's editor. Thus she was not in charge when news of the hanging of the anarchists convicted in the Haymarket Riots in Chicago reached the West Coast. The paper's new editor, Venier Voldo, "turned the rules," the printer's traditional way of showing mourning by placing thick, black borders around the paper's pages.[67] He declared that free speech and a free press had died at Chicago that November, a position that offended many observers of the colony. Although the *Model Commonwealth* did not lose its mailing privileges, a common way of controlling publications outside the political or social mainstream, the incident hurt the paper and the colony financially. The next year several colony members tried to operate the newspaper but could not make a profit, and they sold the plant to A. H. Howells. He changed the paper's name to *Times,* and it eventually became the *Port Angeles Evening News,* a mainstream newspaper for the town of Port Angeles. The public's perception of the Puget Sound Cooperative Colony's connection with violent anarchists, plus accusations that the colonists practiced free love, pushed the already shaky organization over the edge. Its leaders were replaced and soon the organization fell apart.

To the north end of the Sound, the Equality Colony in Skagit County, sponsored by the Brotherhood of the Cooperative Commonwealth, published the *Coming Nation.*[68] When some members who became dissatisfied with the Equality Colony's rules and who sought more freedom formed the Freeland Colony on Whidbey Island, they relied on the efforts of DeForest and Ethel Brooke Sanford, who started the *Whidby* [*sic*] *Islander* in 1900. DeForest Sanford had written for a number of newspapers, as well as for the Knights of Labor and the Socialist Party, and dreamed of starting his own Socialist newspaper in the Far West. Wrote Sanford in his salutatory: "Upon labor depends the progress of the world, and an unjust distribution of the products tends to devastate mankind physically, morally and socially. An equal distribution of labor's product would equalize dignity and bring mankind to a higher stage generally."[69]

The longest-lived of Puget Sound's utopian newspapers was the *Co-operator,* the newspaper of the Burley Colony. Cyrus Field Willard, who helped establish the colony, published the newspaper for eight years.

At the Home Colony, founded in 1898, the newspaper went through a series of incarnations, starting as the *New Era* while the colony was still being organized, soon becoming *Discontent: Mother of Progress,* turning into the *Demonstrator* in 1903, and finally, in 1910, being issued as the *Agitator.* The *Agitator* was finally shut down when its editor, Jay Fox, was jailed for an editorial, titled "Nudes and Prudes," that essentially defended the colony's practice of swimming in the nude. He was charged with advocating disrespect for the law.

The *Tacoma Daily Ledger,* which had harassed the colony for years, calling it a "nest of vipers" and an "unclean den of infamy" when it welcomed speakers such as Emma Goldman and other avowed anarchists, seemed sympathetic to Fox in the nude swimming incident, although his troubles gave the Tacoma paper the opportunity to poke fun at colonists when it wrote that the Home Colony was "being well advertised as a community in which people frequently take baths."[70]

THE WOMEN'S SUFFRAGE PRESS

Western states were well in advance of their eastern neighbors in accepting women's right to vote. Wyoming approved women's suffrage as early as 1869, Utah was next in 1870, and by 1914 all women west of the Rocky Mountains could vote, even though the national amendment granting women the right to vote was not approved until 1920.[71] At least seven suffrage periodicals were published in the West prior to 1900.[72] "These publications were founded because the suffragists, considered outsiders by the conventional press and denied access by those who controlled it, resorted to establishing their own," says historian Bennion.[73]

For example, in Portland, Abigail Scott Duniway and her brother Harvey Scott, publisher of the Portland *Oregonian,* disagreed about women's suffrage. Nevertheless, Scott helped Duniway publish her own newspaper, *New Northwest,* which she did weekly for sixteen years.[74]

The earliest of the western suffrage publications was started in 1869 in San Francisco by Emily A. Pitts, a schoolteacher from New York. Pitts bought a half interest in the *Sunday Mercury,* renamed it the *Pioneer,* and said it would be "devoted to the promotion of human rights: liberty, justice, fraternity." She said she used *fraternity* because no word expressed the brotherhood and sisterhood of the race. "We defend the rights of women fearlessly and to the best of our ability," she wrote in her salutatory. "We shall insist upon woman's independence—her elevation, socially and politically, to the platform now solely occupied by man." [75]

In Colorado, the *Queen Bee* referred to both the newspaper and its editor, Caroline Churchill. The masthead claimed it to be "the only paper in the State advocating Woman's Political Equality and Individuality." Churchill said she took as her feminist model the journalist Jane Grey Swissholm. [76]

Other suffrage papers were the *Alki* in Seattle, the *Nevada Citizen* in Reno, and the *Woman's Exponent* in Utah, and Duniway had a second newspaper, the *Pacific Empire.* Louisa Lula Greene Richards edited the *Woman's Exponent,* a publication for Mormon women. Both of Richards's grandmothers were sisters of Brigham Young, and the family was part of the early Mormon migration to Utah, arriving in Smithfield, Utah, in 1852. Early in her life Greene started to write poetry, and she participated in the production of one of the many handwritten newspapers produced by Mormon youth groups in Utah communities lacking a printing press. [77]

Greene became a teacher, and in the fall of 1871 she needed money to get from her school job in Salt Lake City to her home in Smithfield because of a family illness, so she "sat up all night writing poetry." She took it to Edward L. Sloan, editor of the *Salt Lake Daily Herald,* who paid her $7.50, the amount she needed for her travel. A few days later, she received a letter from him asking if she would be interested in editing a publication for Mormon women. She would later write that "he had contemplated giving her work on the *Herald* but, since other staff protested, conceived the idea of the women's paper." [78] True to her faith, she first asked Brigham Young's permission via a letter to Eliza R. Snow, the most influential woman in the church. Both Snow and Young approved, so planning went ahead. In 1872 the first issue of the *Exponent* was printed in the *Herald* plant.[79] Greene told readers the paper would discuss

> every subject interesting and valuable to women. It will contain a brief and graphic summary of current news, local and general; household hints, educational matters, articles on health and dress, correspondence, editorials on leading topics of interest suitable to its columns, and miscellaneous reading.[80]

She initially listed herself as L. L. Greene, but she did not like getting letters addressed to "Mr. L. L. Greene" or "Dear Sir" and soon began using her full name. During the five years she edited the *Exponent* she also married and bore two daughters, both of whom died in infancy. When she resigned in 1877, turning the paper over to Emmeline B. Wells, who had been assisting her with the publication, she again made sure that her action had the church leader's approval. She wrote Brigham Young that she did not have sufficient energy to be a wife, mother, and editor. She continued to contribute to the paper, wrote for other Mormon publications, and penned poetry and song lyrics for special occasions.[81]

Western readers were treated to periodicals on many other topics. For example, the 1880 census listed several collegiate, temperance, agricultural, science, and humor newspapers, among others. Financial newspapers, including some specializing in mining and hotels, also enlightened readers. Most were centered in the cities, but the occasional periodical found a home in a small, remote district, such as the *Rocky Mountain Husbandman,* which was issued weekly from White Sulphur

Springs in Meagher County, Montana, population 2,743, starting in 1875.[82]

This variety and multiplicity of publications helped create communities of interest across the expansive West in the same way the mainstream press linked the broader communities with their special roots. These specialized publications also educated westerners on numerous subjects, introduced new ideas, and offered outlets for the creativity and knowledge of westerners.

EIGHT

◇

OBLITERATING
THE FRONTIER

In 1890, the U.S. Bureau of the Census added up the total population of the United States and declared that the frontier was no more. A Wisconsin professor, Frederick Jackson Turner, subsequently built a reputation for his "frontier thesis," stressing the importance of free land and its influence on development both of the nation and of character. At the time, the nation contained 17.8 people for every square mile of area, a 25.5 percent increase over 1880.[1]

As noted in chapter 1, the struggle to define *frontier* continues, but as also noted, whether *frontier* is properly applied to newspapers is questionable; some parts of definitions apply—distance from major centers, for example—but others, such as self-sufficiency, do not. However far they were from major population centers, western newspapers relied upon cities for both production resources and content.

If anyone was committed to obliterating the frontier it was the newspaperman. From the day he, or sometimes she, opened an office in a mining camp or rural town, the primary goal was to bring civilization to the community.

Recent scholarship challenges the long-held notion that Euro-Americans settled a land whose peoples were "uncivilized."[2] Nevertheless, the Euro-Americans who were part of the westward movement defined *civilization* in terms of the familiar. As we have seen, a legitimate community had a newspaper, which, along with churches and schools, ensured that a town would have a chance of creating a civilization that was like the one its residents had left behind.

In chapter 1 we saw how residents welcomed the advent of their newspapers, and we read statements from the press that showed newspapermen's awareness of their importance to their communities.[3]

In June 1879 the editors of the *Los Angeles Star* told their readers:

> The newspaper is emphatically a poor man's lyceum, his library, and his best instructor. The newspaper brings to him a vast treasure of information, which he cannot read without being a wiser and better man. It has aptly been said that a newspaper is as good as a lesson to the thoughtful. Where newspapers are seen on the table in a family circle, there will be found intelligence and virtue.

In a region where the newspaper sometimes preceded schools, libraries, and even churches, this claim is not as inflated as it might seem today, when these institutions are taken for granted. It may be hard to swallow notions of intelligence and virtue in the present day, when journalists are often held in low repute, but *Star* readers almost certainly nodded their agreement as they perused the newspaper.

The typical frontier newspaper was generally devoid of illustrations, except in its advertising columns and on its front-page nameplate, or flag. The halftone, a process which enables the printing of shades of gray, not just black and white, was not available to the nation's press until the 1890s, and its expense prevented most small-town newspapers from using it. That did not stop newspapers from using woodcuts or engraved line drawings. Services provided sets of small woodcuts—much like today's clip art—that could be used to break up the monotony of columns of type or draw attention to an advertisement. These sets contained pictures of such things as steamers, hotel fronts, plows, barrels, false teeth, medicine bottles, hats, horses, and houses, as well as arrows, stars, and other useful artistic devices. Printers were flexible. In one issue of the *San Joaquin Republican* in 1853 in Stockton, California, a tiny woodcut of a house represented the White House, the California capitol at Sacramento, and the palace of the Russian czar.[4]

Printers also used type creatively to make their pages more pleasing to the eye, particularly in advertisements. Learning from their eastern brothers in the craft, they built pyramids and other shapes of words and letters. For example, the *Oregonian* ran this advertisement for a dry goods merchant in 1873:

A man

when about

to buy always

looks around for

a place where he can

purchase goods at very

low prices, and of good quality.

Recollect, that for clothing and

gentlemen's furnishing goods you get

bargains at Fishel & Roberts' establishment.[5]

The frontier press provided its readers with short stories and serialized books, and it served as an outlet for local poets. Most of the poetry was not particularly good, but to the poet and his or her friends and family, it was undoubtedly great literature.

Modern readers may wonder, too, about how well the content of nineteenth-century western newspapers served the local community. After all, many of these newspapers were clearly established to "boost" their local communities. Like the land developer of today, they tried to put the best face possible on their locale and its attributes. Does that mean, as some have suggested, that the booster newspapers carried only the good news about their towns? What happened to journalism in this context?

In the first place, journalism as we know it in the twenty-first century did not exist when most of these newspapers first published. We've seen that the frontier newspaperman wore many hats—reporter, editor, scissors-wielder (to deal with the exchanges), typesetter, advertising salesman, bookkeeper, and pressman. The departmentalization of the American newspaper business was just beginning in the major cities when the McElroys, Kembles, Dotens, and Dryers set up their presses in embryo towns and cities. For these men, "journalism education" was largely at the type case. They may have done apprenticeships in print shops to learn to set type, but preparation for the editorial and business aspects of the newspaper was informal. Then, as now, being a journalist required no specific training or professional licensing.

Although they rarely talked specifically about freedom of the press in their columns, frontier newspapermen appreciated the responsibility that freedom implied. Truth—at least as they perceived it—was important to them. They also understood the value of being first with the news. The minute-by-minute competition to be first in Denver appears to have been an isolated effort, but the *Sacramento Daily Union* said in its salutatory on March 19, 1851, that it would provide "first news in the best style and at the lowest prices." The proprietors vowed that Sacramento and its newspaper were friends of California and would boost California but would also tell the truth.[6]

Frontier newspapermen assumed that their readers wanted their news as fresh as possible, and "extras" were frequent. In some communities prior to the completion of the telegraph, the arrival of the stage or the Pony Express with a bundle of exchange newspapers occasioned an extra. Sometimes a local connection to a regional story precipitated an extra, as when a distinguished local citizen died in a train crash. Foreign wars, elections, and, in 1865, the assassination of President Lincoln created a demand for immediate news and, thus, extras in most frontier communities. The *Deseret News* issued a forty-eight-page pamphlet on polygamy as an "extra," but newspapers' extras were usually a single sheet, sometimes printed on the publisher's job press instead of the newspaper press and therefore quite small.[7] An Oregon editor tried increasing the frequency of his newspaper when he discovered he was producing extras with great regularity. Since that meant an increased subscription fee as well, readers showed they preferred to pay a little at a time, rather than all at once, and his experiment failed.[8]

The unreliability of the mails on which most editors relied for much of their content, either from letters or from the exchanges, provided grounds for many complaints. We've seen Thornton McElroy's complaints to his wife about how the weather hindered the delivery of mail. In Prescott the *Arizona*

Miner grumbled, "Again we are compelled to issue our paper without news. . . . It is over forty days since we received a mail of any account. This is an intolerable state of things."[9]

Taking seriously their responsibilities to be first, editors frequently passed along news with the caveat to readers that they had not had time to check the story personally. In its second issue, for example, the *Sacramento Daily Union* told readers that a report about a meeting to form a fire department had come from one of the meeting's organizers, not from personal observation, but the editors believed that man to be reliable.

The *Reese River Reveille* in Austin, Nevada, commented that "it was reported in Winnemucca, on Tuesday, that eight white men had been killed by Indians, forty miles south of Battle Mountain. Guess it's not so, or we should have heard of it." During the Indian wars, after a story alleging that soldiers had stolen property from a man, the *Reveille* asked for proof. The editor said he did not like printing false claims and wanted to ensure justice "to the military, to the public and to ourselves."[10]

On August 7, 1852, the *Oregon Statesman* reported a "fiendish murder." A man was accused of killing his young wife and running off. At the end of the brief story, the *Statesman* added: "Later.– Just as we were going to press we were informed that Wimple had been taken and was in irons in Polk County. We do not know whether the report is correct or not."

The *Oakland Tribune* (at the time, known as the *Evening Tribune*), in California, chided its rival, the *Oakland Transcript,* for inaccuracies. The *Tribune* quoted the *Transcript:* "On Sunday steamer *Whipple* made three fast trips between San Francisco and the city wharf," and added, "With the exception that the *Whipple* didn't leave the dock in San Francisco at all on Sunday last, the Transcript's statement is unusually accurate."[11]

Thomas Jefferson Dryer, whose *Oregonian* had published the ditty about rain quoted in chapter 1, held the view that his should be a newspaper of record. He wrote, "We understand it to be not only the right but the duty of all public journalists to be faithful chroniclers of events, whether good or evil. We have always regarded the newspaper as a mirror in which all may look and see the events of the day as they pass, and as a journal in which are to be recorded for future reference the public acts and deeds of men; with marginal note of approval or disapprobation." [12]

Across the Willamette River in Oregon City, the *Oregon Statesman* told readers on September 18, 1852, that it would not run marriage notices received in the mail unsigned. "Malicious, mischievous persons are sometimes in the habit of sending the names of persons to the press who have never been married."

M. H. Abbott at the *Oregon Herald* said his paper would carry telegraphic news but would not guarantee "that these will always be correct, as we shall be dependent on persons hundreds, and sometimes thousands of miles distant, for statements which they may, from day to day, embody. We will give them to our readers as we get them. Our telegraphic reports will cost us not less than One Hundred Dollars per week, and it will be no fault of ours if at times they will be incorrect." [13] The *Herald* published for seven years.

This is not to say that all western newspapers held themselves to journalistic standards with which we might be familiar in the twenty-first century. There is no question that some editors could be bought. The story of political journalism on the frontier is replete with editors being supported by a politician or political party in exchange for favorable treatment and access to a channel through which they could transmit their partisan message. [14]

Most editors took the view that telling their readers about the arrival of new goods and services in town was news, hence the plugs in the "locals" columns for theatrical events, restaurants, and hotels. To be sure, theater promoters freely distributed tickets to newspapermen, restaurants did not always charge them for meals, and a hotel might give a journalist a place to sleep off his binge.

Asahel Bush at the *Oregon Statesman* moved from Oregon City to Salem, however, determined to protect his news columns. "We insert nothing in the editorial columns for pay, and receive no price for anything inserted there," he wrote, explaining that a businessman from another town had sent payment seeking an item in the news columns. "The eagle we return," Bush wrote, "and respectfully decline all such requests."[15] The *Idaho Avalanche* in Silver City, Idaho, took a similar perspective. "Some men seem to have a sort of stupid idea that because they pay us the princely sum of $5 a year in support of their local newspaper and get the fullest kind of return on their investment, that it is our bounden duty to puff them 'from July to eternity,' especially if they are before the public."[16]

Market reports were common news in western newspapers whose readers wanted to know the price of gold, silver, coal, or whatever they were mining. Aware that use of the exchanges was a two-way process, the publishers of the *Avalanche* refused to publish a weekly market report. They feared it would mislead readers in other parts of the country because the quoted dollar prices in Silver City were inflated, and delays in delivery could result in significant price differences.[17]

Most western towns escaped the level of violence commonly portrayed in motion pictures and television, but like other towns, they had their murders and fights. Although ignoring these might help the long-term prospects of a town and its newspaper, paying the bills was easier if a newspaper kept the local subscribers happy, and as the success of the "Penny Press" in New York showed, sensationalism sells; a drunk found with a bullet in his head would get his name in the paper. Technological limitations prevented most weeklies from extensive coverage of most events—they had neither the space nor the time to cover a big story—so a murder might get only a paragraph. The dailies in western cities, on the other hand, carried the more spectacular trials in considerable detail.

Newspapers also reflected the prejudices of their communities. Whether it was the "Chinese must go!" statements in both news columns and advertising that ran in the *Seattle Daily Call* in 1885, or the general indifference to the welfare of the Chinese as evidenced by their openly lackluster coverage of offenses against the Chinese, western editors basically reinforced their readers' attitudes.[18] For example, the *Sonora Union Democrat* in Tuolumne County, California, reported:

> Killed and Flung in the Bushes.—The body of a Chinaman was found Sunday a short distance from Chinese Camp on the Jacksonville Road. A deep gash was cut on one side of the neck severing the arteries and a mark cut entirely around the neck. The wrists looked as if they had been tied. He was murdered and the body carried to the place where it was found. Little trouble was taken to ascertain the particulars as he was a bummer Chinaman.[19]

On another occasion, however, the *Union Democrat* suggested there should be some recourse for Chinese who were ill-treated. "We candidly confess that the law of evidence, in criminal cases at least, should be so modified as to open the door to the testimony of Chinamen in cases where there is no other evidence. There certainly ought to be some way adopted to protect them in the right and to redress their wrongs and injuries." [20]

Frontier newspapers did relatively little to challenge growing corruption in their midst. And in some cases they fed it. The example of the *Los Angeles Times'* role in the Owens River water scandal of the early twentieth century, described in chapter 10, is a case in point, and chapter 5 discussed newspapers' interaction with the railroads. Although Hearst's *Examiner* survived the counterattacks from the railroad faction, the *Sacramento Union* was not so lucky. In 1875 newspapers reported the sale of the *Union*. One newspaper observed:

> The *Union* was a power in the land and wielded an influence second to no journal on the Pacific Coast. Its power was felt by the Central Pacific Railroad Company, and it was said that its persistent attacks upon that company had at one time nearly ruined its credit in Europe. . . . It had been the leading organ of the dominant party of California, and in its efforts to expose the fraud and corruption of that party it has fallen at the feet of the Central Pacific Railroad Company. It exposed the frauds of the most corrupt political rings ever organized on the Pacific Coast—these rings, too, were of its own political faith and creed. . . . The *Union* will be missed at home and abroad; it was a newspaper in every sense of the word. [21]

Journalism historian Jack A. Nelson says the frontier press lacked a social conscience. [22] He challenges the "idealistic picture of a noble editor building a better society." [23] Although most salutatories expressed concern about justice, as Nelson notes, that concern "apparently . . . did not extend to those of other races."[24] He recounts several examples of particularly callous reports about the condition of the Chinese, the Native Americans, and the African Americans on the frontier, as well as the general meanness with which some editors approached their work.

"The vindictiveness and venality with which some editors took to their tasks can barely be imagined," Nelson wrote in 1982, citing the *Territorial Enterprise*'s retaliation against *Frank Leslie's Illustrated Weekly* in 1877 for its derogatory comments about Virginia City, Nevada.[25] Mrs. Leslie had written that the town was "dreary, desolate, homeless, uncomfortable, wicked and Godforsaken."[26] She had also described the female population as of the worst possible type and lacking in virtue. About a month later the editor of the *Enterprise* responded with an "exposé of the personal character, sex life, and scurrilous past of both Mr. and Mrs. Frank Leslie."[27]

Nelson also recalls the time when the *Territorial Enterprise* feuded with the owner of Maguire's Opera House in Virginia City. Maguire moved his advertising and printing business to the *Virginia Evening Bulletin,* so the *Enterprise* editor at the time, Joe Goodman,

> ordered his reporters to mention Maguire or any of his shows only unfavorably from then on. By that time Virginia City had grown in size and prestige to become one of the best theater towns in the country, and rave notices from the *Enterprise* carried all the prestige of the New York drama reviews. Within a short time Maguire had trouble booking the best shows because favorable reviews were impossible there. Eventually, faced with economic ruin, Maguire gave in and restored his advertising

and printing to Goodman's newspaper. In addition, there was [*sic*] the usual reserved seats in the front row for the *Enterprise* staff on opening nights, complete with champagne.[28]

One question is whether editors really intended to build a "better society." For most of them, building a society like the one they had left behind was enough of a goal. The "better" society for the frontier editor more than likely was one in which he made a comfortable living and exercised considerable influence on the political affairs of his town. Journalism had not yet started to engage in muckraking or even the stunt journalism of the late nineteenth century that exposed terrible conditions in hospitals, asylums, and prisons.

Journalists were not, however, without sensitivity. In the 1850s the *San Francisco Bulletin* engaged in a crusade on behalf of California womanhood. A member of the California State Medical Society issued a report on obstetrics and diseases of women in which he had incautiously attributed "every species of immorality to unmarried females." To many in California this constituted an uncalled-for slur on the virtue of California women by suggesting they were all prostitutes with venereal disease. The *Bulletin* covered the controversy in detail for several weeks until the physician finally retracted his original statement.[29]

However outraged Nelson might be at the vindictiveness of the *Enterprise,* he enjoyed the humor that it and other frontier newspapers published. In a separate paper, one on frontier newspaper humor, he cites some of the laughs provided as fillers (i.e., short items used to space out a column of type). For example, "Rhode Island was struck by lightning the other day, causing wide-spread devastation in the adjoining states."[30]

Another example: William J. Forbes of the *Humboldt Register* in Unionville commented about the poor lumber available, "Half of it is just what it is cracked up to be. Half of it is knot." [31]

It does not seem to bother Nelson that writers like Twain and Dan DeQuille indulged "the frontier propensity for exaggeration and the tall tale." [32] He continues: "At the same time, they were true of the spirit of their place and time, for in a sense the whole westward movement was built on the fantasy that there was a bountiful new world waiting for those who would travel over the next hill to claim it." [33]

Frontier newspapermen reflected their times and society. These editors were mortal, and while we might wish for greater honesty, idealism, and courage on their part, as we wish for it in today's journalism, we have to acknowledge the frailty of human nature. Overall, frontier editors met their goals of serving their communities with news and literature and making the connection with the worlds that had been left behind. The goal they generally did not meet was their plan to make their fortunes. They suffered through the boom-and-bust conditions that left many western towns poor and depopulated, and they were forced to cope with the general idiosyncrasies endemic in a rapidly changing society and with their own inept management, through which they usually got themselves so deeply in debt they could not pay their bills.

───────────◇───────────

NINE

THE LEGACY OF
FRONTIER JOURNALISM

Usually a "legacy" comes from someone older, not young in the way the American West is young. But like young Lochinvar, several things have come out of the West: Mark Twain, William Randolph Hearst, and the Chandler family at the *Los Angeles Times,* for starters.[1] Regardless of one's overall opinion of Hearst, he helped make newspapers better looking and more readable, increased pay for newspaper employees, introduced "sob sister" journalism, and ramped up the crusading style and participatory or "stunt" journalism that Joseph Pulitzer favored in New York City. The latter two "achievements" no doubt offend serious journalists, but they delighted readers, and still increase readership. Otis Chandler proved that good journalism could be profitable—in the days before television and the Internet, at least. Alden Blethen in Seattle and E. W. Scripps in several western cities showed that profitable newspapers could also benefit the community.

All of these newspapermen's lives and work straddled the late nineteenth and twentieth centuries. While the nineteenth century had brief episodes of economic hardship, the next century brought particularly harsh economic challenges to the press of the West, as it did to newspapers in all parts of the nation. The Great Depression of the 1930s led to declines in circulation and advertising and put a number of newspapers on the rack. The subsequent rise of competing news media—first radio and then television—hurt newspaper circulation and profits, as did the increasing pace of American life, which reduced people's time for newspaper reading. Early evening television news programs cut into leisurely after-work newspaper perusal, creating a general shift in favor of morning newspapers.

THE JOINT OPERATING AGREEMENT

Several western newspapers found an unusual way to address the problem of declining circulation and increased costs: the joint operating agreement (JOA). Though not unique to the region today, the JOA first appeared in Albuquerque, New Mexico, where the *Albuquerque Journal* and the *Albuquerque Tribune* combined business operations in 1933 during the Depression. As the JOA model developed, two newspapers, one believed likely to close if conditions continued, agreed to combine all non-journalistic functions—advertising, printing, circulation, and other business-related activities—thus benefiting from economies of scale, as in the purchase of newsprint and ink, and from eliminating duplication of production and sales efforts. The combination also usually created a monopoly situation in which the company could raise advertising and subscription rates without fear of competition. The rationale given for JOAs, particularly after they were exempted from antitrust laws by the Newspaper Preservation Act (1970), was that they ensured that a community had more than one source of news so that the marketplace of ideas would work.

Although the Supreme Court eventually ruled that the antitrust laws—the Sherman Act and the Clayton Act—applied to newspapers, the Justice Department paid little attention to the Albuquerque papers' joint venture.[2] A similar joint operating agreement was established in 1940 between two newspapers in neighboring Arizona, the *Arizona Star* and the *Tucson Citizen,* but a buyer eventually turned up for the dominant *Star.* To prevent the buyer from getting the *Star,* the Citizen Publishing Company, which had been formed to operate the JOA, proceeded to acquire it, and published both newspapers through a holding company. At this juncture, the Justice Department's antitrust division stepped in, charging that the arrangement violated the Sherman and Clayton acts. A federal district court agreed, pointing to the price fixing, profit pooling, and market allocation it said occurred thanks to the agreement as illegal under the antitrust laws.[3] The court did not object to the combined printing and advertising departments. Citizen Publishing appealed to the Supreme Court, which affirmed that the Tucson JOA violated antitrust laws. The Court noted further that the "failing company" defense, often used in buyouts and mergers that diminished competition, did not apply in this case. The *Star* was, after all, the dominant newspaper.[4]

By this time, newspapers in twenty-two cities had formed JOAs. The newspaper industry's lobbyists went to work, and in 1970 Congress passed the Newspaper Preservation Act, grandfathering in existing JOAs.[5] Congress was persuaded that maintaining editorial diversity in a community was more important than strict interpretation of the antitrust laws, and it gave the newspaper industry a specific exemption from the laws. The act does, however, require a strict interpretation of the "failing industry" idea—one of the newspapers in a combination must be shown to be in a "downward spiral" with no one interested in acquiring it.

Over time, all of the major West Coast newspapers except the *Los Angeles Times* have participated in joint operating agreements. As of 2007, the *Salt Lake City Tribune* and the *Deseret News* continue a JOA that is due to expire in 2012. The *Tribune*'s circulation is approximately twice that of the *News*. The *Arizona Star* and *Tucson Citizen* remain in a JOA that expires in 2015, and the *Star* has about twice the number of readers as its partner. The Albuquerque papers' agreement runs to 2022; the family-owned *Albuquerque Journal* has a circulation of 113,694; its partner, the Scripps-owned *Tribune,* has one of 25,061.[6]

The two Seattle papers in a JOA, the Blethen family's *Seattle Times* and the Hearst Corporation's *Post-Intelligencer,* are close in circulation and have been in court a number of times over whether there is a failing newspaper here at all. Their agreement runs to 2083. In one of the West's other major cities, Denver, the *Denver Post* and the *Rocky Mountain News* also have comparable circulations of more than 350,000 each, but are in a JOA that expires in 2050.

Western newspapers no longer in JOAs include the *Anchorage Daily News* and *Anchorage Times,* which ended their JOA in 1978; the once-dominant *Times* folded in 1992. The *San Francisco Chronicle* and the *San Francisco Examiner* ended their JOA in 1999; both still publish, albeit under different ownership. In 2000 the *Honolulu Star-Bulletin* and the *Honolulu Advertiser* dissolved their agreement; the papers still publish. Another pair of newspapers, the *Las Vegas Sun* and the *Las Vegas Review-Journal,* modified their fifteen-year-old agreement in 2005. The Greenspun family continues to publish the *Sun* with a separate editorial staff, but it appears as a daily section in the *Review-Journal,* owned by the Stephens Group, instead of as a separate newspaper.[7]

While the *Los Angeles Times* has not entered into a joint operating agreement, it has engaged in business practices that have caught the attention of antitrust enforcers. In the 1960s, while JOAs were under attack as violations of antitrust, the Times-Mirror Company, publisher of the *Los Angeles Times,* bought the Sun Company, publisher of newspapers in neighboring San Bernardino County, where the *Times* already had significant circulation. The Justice Department charged that the acquisition would "substantially lessen competition" and thus violate section 7 of the Clayton Act.[8] Times-Mirror was ordered to sell the Sun Company.[9]

LAS VEGAS, NEVADA

As noted, the two newspapers in Las Vegas have a joint operating agreement. The fastest-growing city in the nation at the turn of the twenty-first century, the self-styled "Entertainment Capital of the World" has made several noteworthy contributions to western journalism history. For one thing, as late as 1980 it could boast not just two competing daily newspapers, but three. Elsewhere in the nation, newspaper competition had already dwindled significantly, especially in smaller cities. At that time the Las Vegas Valley claimed about a half million residents who could subscribe to the dominant *Las Vegas Review-Journal,* owned by multimillionaire Donald W. Reynolds from Arkansas; the *Las Vegas Sun,* owned by Hank M. Greenspun, an attorney turned publisher and real estate developer; and the *Valley Times,* owned by Robert L. Brown, a former wire service correspondent who had edited newspapers for Reynolds.

THE *VALLEY TIMES*

According to historian Michael Green, the frailest of the three 1980 Las Vegas dailies, the *Valley Times,* "has a place among Nevada's most controversial and important newspapers."[10] It began as a weekly, the *North Las Vegas and Moapa Valley Times,* on March 26, 1959. Its founder, Adam Yacenda, had been the *Las Vegas Sun*'s managing editor for most of the 1950s. Prior to moving to Las Vegas, Yacenda worked at the *New York World-Telegram.* During World War II he moved to California for his health and took a job publishing the *Beverly Hills Bulletin* for Will Rogers Jr. Yacenda indulged his bent for politics by serving as Representative Richard Nixon's press secretary in his 1950 U.S. Senate campaign. The search for an even warmer climate drew Yacenda to Las Vegas after the election, and he first sought a position with the *Las Vegas Review-Journal,* then owned by Reynolds and edited by John Cahlan. Cahlan's apparent indifference at his interview led Yacenda to apply at the new *Las Vegas Sun.* Two years later, owner Greenspun promoted him to editor.[11]

Yacenda returned to politics in 1954 to help Republican Charles Russell become Nevada's governor. After the election he spent four more years at the *Sun,* and historian Green suggests he "may have been the only editor who ever was able to stand up to [publisher Hank Greenspun]."[12] Yacenda lived in North Las Vegas and believed it was growing fast enough to support its own newspaper. So did Greenspun, with whom Yacenda feuded over politics. Greenspun already owned the weekly *North Las Vegas News.*[13]

On March 26, 1959, Yacenda produced the first issue of the weekly *North Las Vegas and Moapa Valley Times.*[14] He published the newspaper for nearly fifteen years, in 1973 selling it to Robert L. Brown, whose experience and abilities paralleled Yacenda's—

Brown had held positions on Las Vegas and other newspapers, had a keen sense of politics, and was a "business maneuverer, and a conservative in the good sense of the word."[15] Brown had been a foreign correspondent with the United Press wire service prior to 1958, when he became an editor and manager for Reynolds, first in Arkansas and later in Alaska. In 1961 Reynolds brought him to Las Vegas to edit the *Review-Journal*. Until that time, Green records, the morning *Sun* had been increasing in circulation faster than the evening *Review-Journal*, a common story in the newspaper industry in that period. Brown skillfully reversed the trend and soon raised the readership of the *Review-Journal*, which traces its roots to one of Las Vegas's first newspapers, the *Las Vegas Age*.[16]

Brown operated the *Valley Times* from 1973 until his death in 1984. During those years, the *Valley Times* and its editor gained respect statewide, giving it status well above the typical suburban newspaper. Brown hired first-rate journalists, including a street-savvy reporter named Ned Day whose exposés of fraud and "the mob" became legendary in Las Vegas journalism.

When Brown died, his newspaper was closed, but the *Review-Journal* and the *Sun* engaged in a rivalry that continued into 2007 with the two publishers—one the corporate Stephens Media Group, the other Hank Greenspun's family, particularly his eldest son, Brian—joined at the hip in a joint operating agreement but still sniping at each other in their respective editorial columns.

Although some subscribers rail at being exposed to the *Sun* in their morning *Review-Journal*, the new arrangement allows the *Sun* staff to focus on in-depth stories instead of scrabbling for the same day-to-day hard news. The *Sun* has thus been active in digging into the scandals relating to Nevada governor Jim Gibbons, who was elected in 2006. The *Sun* section has its own editorials and columns, as well as background stories.[17]

HANK GREENSPUN

In the second half of the twentieth century, Hank Greenspun was one of the few remaining practitioners of "personal journalism" in the nation. Greenspun took a personal interest in what went into the *Las Vegas Sun,* and employees tell numerous stories of Hank coming through the newspaper office in the evening and overriding the desk staff's decision about what would be the banner headline for the next day.

Herman (Hank) Greenspun, the son of a Talmudic scholar, grew up in New Haven, Connecticut, down the road from the Winchester Repeating Arms Company where his father worked more "as a patriotic gesture to his adopted country" than for the money.[18] Descended from Polish Jews by way of London and Canada, Greenspun wrote that he "knew every wrinkle on the painted face of Theodor Herzl, founder of the Zionist movement, before I could even identify a picture of George Washington."[19] His mother taught him not to tolerate anti-Semitic insults. On one occasion after such an insult she told him, "You let him insult you? . . . And you didn't even insult him back? What's the matter with you?"[20] Throughout his life, Greenspun lived by her warning: "When you let people walk over you, you might as well be dead."[21]

The family moved to New York, and Greenspun worked at a variety of jobs while attending evening high school. In 1928 he entered St. John's University to study law, a career the family had determined for him. He completed his law degree, served in the army in World War II, and married an Irish bride. Upon his discharge in 1945 he met a racetrack promoter, Joe Smoot, who wanted to build a track in Las Vegas, Nevada, and invited Greenspun to join him in investigating the city's prospects. They drove across the country to the desert oasis, which had been kept alive primarily by the construction of Boulder (Hoover) Dam in the 1930s, and which now had ambitious plans for tourism. One sign of the latter was a "six-million-dollar concrete-and-steel fantasy" on a bare stretch of U.S. Highway 91. "The man behind the incomplete building, a smirking, quick-tempered hoodlum named Benjamin ('Bugsy') Siegel, liked to call it 'the fabulous Flamingo.'" [22]

Greenspun says it was love at first sight upon arrival in Las Vegas, where he entered a "perfect paradise of majestic mountains, infinite skies, and balmy air that looked and felt like warm, breathable crystal." He told Barbara (his Irish bride) to come right away: "Pack everything, baby, and come on out! We won't be going back." [23] While Smoot was working his deals with the Las Vegans, Greenspun talked with an old friend from law school, at the time a reporter between jobs. They and another journalist decided to publish a semimonthly magazine devoted to Las Vegas nightlife. Greenspun also briefly worked for Siegel and the Flamingo, writing publicity releases and dreaming up promotional stunts until the mobster was gunned down at his home in Beverly Hills. No longer able to fund the magazine, Greenspun shifted the bulk of his capital to Wilbur Clark, who was planning to build the Desert Inn. He invested the remainder in a project to set up a new Las Vegas radio station.

His next enterprise had nothing to do with Las Vegas or journalism. Committed to the success of the new nation of Israel, he joined an effort to smuggle guns to the new country, which was established amidst conflict and controversy when the United Nations partitioned Palestine and voted for the establishment of a Jewish state. When he returned to Las Vegas after a Robert Ludlum–like adventure, he found that Clark had teamed with some Cleveland "investors" in order to complete financing for his new hotel. By the time the Clevelanders were finished with "negotiations," Clark's interest in the project was down to 26 percent. Greenspun's share of the Desert Inn project was reduced from 15 percent to 1 percent, plus a salary for his service as head of publicity and promotion. Then, in 1949, Greenspun was indicted by the U.S. government for his gun-running activities. Found innocent in the first trial, a year later he was indicted for violating the Neutrality Act.

While awaiting trial on the second charge, Greenspun organized publicity for the opening of the Desert Inn. As part of the package, he bought advertising space in the *Free Press,* a three-times-a-week newspaper published by striking International Typographical Union members who had been locked out by the *Las Vegas Review-Journal.* Greenspun not only sought publicity for the opening, but he wrote that he also wanted to make a point about the *Review-Journal's* local monopoly by buying space in the competing publication.[24] The *Review-Journal* felt the snub and complained to Moe Dalitz, the Clevelander brought in to run the Desert Inn. The *Review-Journal's* owner, Donald Reynolds, notorious for his anti-union positions, demanded that the new casino spend all of its advertising budget with his newspaper. Dalitz jumped on Greenspun, who refused to boycott the union's newspaper. Soon the locked-out printers were suggesting to Greenspun that he take over the *Free Press.* He liked the paper's prospects, and it gave him a way to get out from under Dalitz, as well as offering a challenge to the monopoly of the *Review-Journal.*[25]

Paying one thousand dollars down, Greenspun took control of the newspaper, expanded it to five days a week, and changed its name to the *Las Vegas Morning Sun.*[26] In response to a *Review-Journal* column by its managing director, Al Cahlan, called "From Where I Sit," Greenspun started a column called

"Where I Stand" in which he frequently attacked Nevada political boss and senator Patrick McCarran and later Wisconsin senator Joseph McCarthy, the demagogue engaged in an anti-Communist witch hunt. Greenspun's attacks on McCarran led to an attempted advertising boycott by the senator's casino-owning friends, such as the Desert Inn's Dalitz.[27] Greenspun told Dalitz he expected the problem to be solved in twenty-four hours; when it was not, he exposed the boycott in his *Sun* column. He also successfully sued McCarran for conspiracy to drive the *Sun* out of business.[28] The conflict gained national attention and considerable press sympathy for Greenspun.

Greenspun's attack on Senator Joseph McCarthy included not only criticism in his column, but a face-to-face encounter when McCarthy visited Las Vegas on a speaking tour and told his audience the *Sun* should be called the *Daily Worker*. Greenspun challenged McCarthy to prove his statements and eventually got most of the crowd, which McCarthy had mesmerized, on his side. In fact, as he tells it in his autobiography, *Where I Stand,*

> As I finished, there were loud cheers, whistles, and applause. The sound of it drove me to weary rage.
>
> "Don't cheer me!" I shouted. "Twenty minutes ago you were a lynch mob!"
>
> The crowd refused to listen, cheering on.[29]

Greenspun was by no means the only newspaperman to challenge McCarthy. In his famous "See It Now" broadcast exposing the senator, Edward R. Murrow shows a stack of newspapers that he said criticized the Red-baiter, but the Nevada publisher may have been one of the most aggressive of McCarthy's critics. After the encounter, Greenspun continued the attack, questioning

McCarthy's integrity, loyalty, sanity, honesty, and sexuality. Nevada historian Eugene Moehring comments, "At a time when both McCarthy and McCarran were at the height of their power, any challenge by a small-time Nevada editor was nothing short of heroic." [30]

Greenspun was famous for supporting his friends. When the Department of Justice investigated U.S. District Judge Harry Claiborne, who was subsequently impeached after conviction for tax evasion, Greenspun stood by him. [31] He also went after local corruption, organizing a sting operation to catch the local sheriff suspected of protecting Roxie's Club, a brothel. [32] His biggest campaign may have been his fight against the nuclear waste dump proposed for Yucca Mountain, about fifty miles north of Las Vegas. The *Sun* continues the battle against the depository today.

MAINTAINING HIS VOICE

Fire, that nemesis of many a frontier editor, destroyed the *Sun*'s printing plant in 1963, and the newspaper never quite recovered. For two decades its circulation declined while the city and the *Review-Journal* grew. [33] By the 1980s the situation had become serious, and Greenspun started thinking about the desirability of a joint operating agreement with the *Review-Journal*. Reynolds wasn't interested, however, until the Greenspuns were willing to include some stock in the local cable company that Reynolds wanted. Greenspun died in 1989, and in 1990 a fifty-year JOA was concluded with a new company managed by the *Review-Journal* to be responsible for the advertising, circulation, and mechanical aspects of the newspapers, but with the two newsrooms separate and competitive. Profits were to be split, with 90 percent going to the *Review-Journal* (now part of the Stephens Media Group, formerly the Donrey Media Group) and 10 percent to the Greenspuns. The two papers would combine on the weekends, the *Sun* getting a separate page in the *Review-Journal* on Saturday and its own section in the Sunday newspaper. The weekday *Sun* was also moved to the afternoon slot, a move that appeared to lead to certain death for the newspaper. Sure enough, the *Sun*'s circulation continued to slide, and by 2005 it had dropped to twenty-eight thousand subscribers.[34] However, rather than take the kind of action that had terminated several JOAs, that is, kill the weaker paper, the Greenspuns and the Stephens Group agreed to a novel solution. Instead of its own section just on Sundays, the *Sun* now has a separate section every day of the week, usually eight advertising-free pages, which it fills with in-depth stories, features, and opinion. Hank's son Brian, now the editor of the newspaper, says this puts the *Sun* "back where it belongs—in the morning with the largest circulation in the state."[35] Reportedly, the Greenspuns were to get an unannounced fixed payment, instead of a percentage, as their financial share of the agreement. Locals speculated about why the *Review-Journal* did not find a way to end the JOA and shut down the *Sun*. One view was that the Stephens Group calculated that they could save a fortune by not having to publish the *Sun* in the afternoon. Another view stressed their fear that the disappearance of the *Sun* would attract competitors. Or perhaps the JOA did not contain the same kind of escape clause that has allowed other pairs of newspapers to terminate the weaker one. The current JOA runs to 2040.

The Greenspuns do not appear to need the money. Hank had the foresight to buy a large parcel of land in the southern part of the Las Vegas Valley that has since become a master-planned community, Green Valley—actually within the city limits of the bedroom community of Henderson—and has significantly helped the family's bank account.[36] Like newspaper families in other cities, appreciation of the founder's legacy seems to keep them determined to continue the *Sun.*

Despite the continued competitive spirit, it is interesting to note that both Las Vegas papers have been in the position of following up revelations by the *Los Angeles Times* and the *Wall Street Journal* about problems within the county's court system and questionable actions on the part of Nevada's governor, former congressman Jim Gibbons, respectively.

DONALD W. REYNOLDS

The man Hank Greenspun challenged and almost conquered for newspaper supremacy in Las Vegas, Donald Worthington Reynolds, hailed originally from Texas and spent his early life in Oklahoma City. He got into the newspaper business early, as so many do, as a newsboy. At the University of Missouri, his family's poverty marked him as "the boy with patches on his pants."[37] Graduating in 1927, Reynolds failed at his first two newspaper jobs because, he said, he did not sell enough advertising. "He was determined not to fail again," says Jake Highton, University of Nevada, Reno, journalism professor. Indeed, he did not fail, and he proceeded to build a major newspaper empire and become one of the nation's richest men, regularly appearing near the top of *Forbes* magazine's list of the four hundred wealthiest people in the United States.

Much as he had systematically worked his way through school, Reynolds applied himself with great deliberation to the newspaper business. By 1940 he owned three newspapers, the start of the Donrey Media Group. He took time out from acquiring more newspaper properties to serve in World War II. He was put in charge of *Yank* magazine published in Australia and later earned a Bronze Star while serving in the European theater of operations as well.[38] In 1945, at the age of thirty-eight, Reynolds was able to return to newspapering. He slowly acquired additional newspapers and in 1949, with a Las Vegas partner, bought the *Las Vegas Review-Journal.* He soon became sole owner. He installed automatic typesetting machines that led to a printers' strike. In response, the International Typographical Union started its own newspaper, the *Free Press,* the newspaper that Greenspun later bought and transformed into the *Las Vegas Sun.*

Known for his hands-off approach to operating newspapers, Reynolds usually supported the autonomy of local editors. Occasionally a decree would land on an editor's desk, ordering the endorsement of a particular—conservative—political candidate, but former editors said he rarely told them what to publish.[39] Even with that freedom, at least one of his former editors had little positive to say about him. John Cahlan, who had been associated with the paper since 1929, asserted that Reynolds had no other god but money. "I tried to work for Reynolds," he said in an oral history, "and I just found it impossible . . . I worked for a lot of bastards. But I just couldn't work for Reynolds."[40] Cahlan claimed that Reynolds liked to keep employees in a "constant state of confusion so that they wouldn't squawk about the low wage scale he paid."[41]

Cahlan also called the editorial battle between the *Review-Journal* and the *Sun* "the liveliest and most vitriolic editorial duel witnessed in Nevada in some eighty years."[42] He said he thought that Greenspun would have "done a tremendous lot more good had he not had so much bitterness in his heart for the *Review-*

Journal. It was an economic matter, entirely, because he was fighting for his life in the *Sun*." [43]

Reynolds died in 1993, having fulfilled his determination to rise out of poverty. He left millions to the Donald W. Reynolds Foundation, which in turn has given millions to a number of journalism schools, including his alma mater, the University of Missouri. [44] The Donrey Media Group became the Stephens Media Group after Reynolds's death. Former *Review-Journal* publisher Sherman Frederick is chief executive officer of the Stephens Group, which now has its headquarters in Las Vegas and publishes thirty newspapers in eight states.

Although both of the founders of Las Vegas media companies are gone, the competition continues. Both the Greenspun Media Group and the Stephens Media Group continue to expand their enterprises in Las Vegas, with magazines, alternative weeklies, and Internet sites. Brian Greenspun, executive editor of the *Sun,* still writes the "Where I Stand" column and regularly refers to the *Review-Journal* as the "Little Paper Down the Street." *Review-Journal* publisher Sherman Frederick returns the attention in kind in his Sunday column. Gifts from both companies have helped establish journalism schools in Nevada: the Donald W. Reynolds School at the University of Nevada, Reno, and the Hank Greenspun School at the University of Nevada, Las Vegas.

TEN

THE NEW FRONTIER

The West's major newspapers in the twenty-first century can all trace their roots to nineteenth-century frontier newspapers. Names may have changed—probably several times—and in most cases today's publishers are not related to the founders. Like much of the West's business, the newspaper industry has been gobbled up by companies listed on the New York Stock Exchange. But while the conventional wisdom about frontier newspapers—that thousands of small papers were offered to the public but most of them failed—is basically accurate, a handful have celebrated their centennials and continue to publish into the twenty-first century.

Although the roots of the *Los Angeles Times* do not go back as far as some other survivors of the frontier, it still has a direct lineage from a newspaper of the same name in the 1880s. And despite spending its first twenty years in the nineteenth century, the *Times'* significance is as a newspaper of the twentieth century, not of the early frontier.

LOS ANGELES

During the frontier period, the now-great city of Los Angeles was a sleepy enclave of a few thousand original Californians, or Californios, as the original Hispanic settlers are sometimes called to distinguish them from Anglo residents of the state. Although Captain John C. Frémont made Los Angeles his capital when he was appointed military governor of California after the territory was wrenched from the Mexicans, "civilization" as the Anglos knew it was slow to take hold in the old Mexican capital. Kemble reported that Los Angeles was "the favorite resort of the native Californians of the South for leagues around," including "gamblers and desperate characters thither from Mexico and Texas," and he noted "the frequent disorders growing out of their presence."[1]

Nevertheless, where people go—even antisocial ones—the printing press follows, and in 1850 San Francisco newspapers carried a prospectus for a newspaper to be published in Los Angeles. In early 1851 the *Alta California* reported that the would-be publishers had not been able to acquire a press and printing materials. Says Kemble, "This somewhat discouraging want appears to have been left unsupplied, for we do not hear of the paper being started."[2]

A few weeks later, however, a pair of men who had also circulated a prospectus managed to get equipment and materials for a print shop together, and on May 17, 1851, John A. Lewis and Edward Gould Buffum issued the *Los Angeles Star*. Lewis, a Boston reporter and forty-niner, had followed a relative to the Sonora mines and then to San Francisco before going to Los Angeles.[3] Buffum had subbed for Kemble as editor of the *Alta California* while the latter made one of his European trips, and for a time Buffum edited the *San Francisco Citizen* prior to his move

to the southern part of the state. They may have been encouraged to try their luck in Los Angeles after a fire in early May
destroyed the printing offices of many of San Francisco's newspapers, putting many printers temporarily out of work. The *Alta*'s
buildings were destroyed, too, but Kemble and his staff saved
the printing materials and continued publishing.[4] In any case,
despite Buffum's early interest in the *Star,* he pulled out at the last
minute and New Yorker John McElroy joined the enterprise.[5]

The *Star* obviously filled a need for the business community
in Los Angeles. In the second issue, the editor wrote, "Several
articles intended for this week's paper have been crowded out
by the lengthy county advertisements, which will be found as
interesting as any matter we could place before our readers."[6]

The *Star* prospered, but in the fashion typical of western
newspapers, several changes of ownership occurred. In 1856
the English-born Henry Hamilton, described by Kemble as
having a "long and successful career in S. Calif and Hawaiian
publishing," acquired the paper.[7] Originally bilingual, the *Star*
can take some credit for the establishment of *El Clamor Público,*
the first fully Spanish-language newspaper in California, because
a former *Star* staffer decided the Californios deserved their own
newspaper, not just a Spanish-language section in the *Star.*[8]

By the time Kemble wrote his history in the late 1850s, three
other publishers had tried appealing to Los Angeles readers. The
Southern Californian published for about two years, according to
Kemble, trying to further the cause of splitting the state. The
Southern Vineyard and the *News* had started in 1858, just in time
to respond to Kemble's survey.[9] Both eventually joined the
graveyard of western newspapers.

Nevertheless, by the 1880 census, Los Angeles boasted three
morning daily newspapers, one evening daily, four general weeklies (including one in Spanish and one in German), a semiweekly

in French, and two weekly temperance newspapers, one of which was the *Los Angeles Weekly Mirror,* born in 1873. Of these, only the *Mirror*'s name endured into the twentieth century. The newspaper that put Los Angeles on the journalism map was yet to come, but in the late 1870s, like the greatly anticipated arrival of the railroad and the boom times it was expected to bring, the *Los Angeles Times* was about to make its appearance.

THE *LOS ANGELES TIMES*

The two men who actually founded the *Los Angeles Daily Times,* Nathan Cole Jr. and Thomas Gardiner, have largely disappeared from historical writing about the newspaper. Dennis McDougal says, in *Privileged Son,* that the first issue of the *Times,* December 4, 1881, was "awash in advertisements," but an examination of a copy shows the newspaper was typical of frontier newspapers, with about half of its pages devoted to ads.[10] That was not enough to ensure survival. Within a year Cole and Gardiner could no longer pay the Mirror Printing Company to produce their newspaper. The printers took over the failing daily and hired Harrison Gray Otis, a former Union Army officer, to edit it. Lieutenant Colonel Otis soon bought a share of the *Times* and by 1884 controlled both the newspaper and the printing company, renaming it the Times-Mirror Company.[11]

Like George Hearst (William Randolph's father) to the north, Otis had perfect financial timing. The Southern Pacific had recently completed its southern route, and in its first year the railroad's immigration efforts had doubled the population of Los Angeles to ten thousand people. In 1883 the Southern Pacific linked up with the Atchison, Topeka, and Santa Fe Railway to form a southern transcontinental line, and the rivalry of the rail-road companies accelerated the population boom.[12] The south was on its way to match the San Francisco Bay area in impor-tance to the state with its own newspaper dynasty.

The "colonel"—a rank conferred on Otis for "gallant and meritorious service" in the Civil War—was the youngest of sixteen children of an Ohio farm family. He was named for a cousin who had been a distinguished Massachusetts politician, but the colonel was too bombastic and impatient to deal with the politics of the eastern establishment. Nor did he have the Ivy League education generally required for political success. Otis's education came mostly at the printer's type case, although during a brief foray into formal schooling he met his future wife, Eliza Ann Wetherby.[13] They married in 1859 without the blessing of her father, and thus without much of a dowry. In *Privileged Son,* McDougal describes them both as dreamers as they moved from place to place trying to cobble together a satis-factory existence.[14]

Lack of the right connections did not stop Otis from attempting to develop a political role for himself, and he was at the 1860 Republican National Convention in Chicago that nominated Abraham Lincoln for president, a fact of which he was particu-larly proud. When the Civil War started, Otis enlisted in the 12th Regiment, Ohio Volunteer Infantry, on June 25, 1861, and served until July 26, 1865, with gallantry and merit, as already noted.[15] Afterward he returned to his family in Ohio, where he published the *Washington County News* in Marietta. He held a number of government positions over the next decade while also working as a correspondent for the *Ohio State Journal* and as managing editor of the *Grand Army Journal,* a Union soldiers' newspaper.[16]

Ever watchful for ways to improve his situation, "Otis skimmed the back pages of magazines and newspaper classifieds for that main-chance business opportunity that would free him from the shackles of daily drudgery and make him independently wealthy." He thought he had found it when he read about Angora goats, and he even made a trip west to look into the prospects of a goat farm on Guadalupe Island off the shore of Baja California. He decided goats were not for him, but he liked what he saw of California, and in 1876 he moved his family to Santa Barbara, where a friend from Ohio offered to back him as publisher of the *Santa Barbara Press.*[17]

In Santa Barbara, Otis found a challenge that enabled him to indulge his political inclinations because the other Santa Barbara newspaper, the *Daily News,* was as firmly Democratic as the colonel was Republican. "With a bellicose prose style that blended politics and passion with half-truths and full-blown fiction, Harrison Gray Otis jammed his personal point of view into every inch of his staunchly Republican newspaper."[18] After two years Otis had Santa Barbara's journalism stage to himself, having acquired the *Daily News,* the *Advertiser,* and the *Index.* He had not acquired any significant wealth, however, so he appealed to Republican president Rutherford B. Hayes, hoping for some of the patronage "spoils" that go to partisans after a victory. It was a case of "be careful what you ask for." Named the government's official representative in Alaska's Seal Islands, a place with a climate drastically different from Santa Barbara's, Otis had to police poaching and prevent alcohol from getting into the hands of the Indians who lived on the islands.[19] It paid well, however, and at the end of his three-year appointment, Eliza had saved his salary and sold the Santa Barbara newspaper, giving them a nest egg for future investing. Even so, when the opportunity arose to buy a piece of the Los Angeles newspaper, the *Times,* they had to call upon another old Ohio friend, A. W. Francisco, to help them with financing.[20]

Ostensibly, responsibilities were divided among the partners, but the Otises appear to have done all the work, from selling advertising to getting the paper distributed by 6:00 A.M. each day. Eliza—"Lizzie" to her husband—gave the newspaper its long-standing motto, "Stand Fast, Stand Firm, Stand Sure, Stand True." She also wrote and edited almost everything except front-page news and editorials. Her aggressive spouse handled the latter, writing "some of the most vitriolic and libelous personal opinions ever printed anywhere," according to McDougal.[21]

Otis alternated between castigating those with different political opinions and boosting Los Angeles. The onetime union member became a union hater and baiter, and the *Times'* stance on the union would eventually lead to the 1910 bombing of its offices and Otis's home. Twenty-one people were killed, twenty of them *Times* employees. The men subsequently charged in the case, brothers James B. and John McNamara, said the *Times* bombings and several others in Los Angeles at the same time were intended to intimidate, not kill, but they had not counted on the explosion setting off the gas lines.[22]

ENTER HARRY CHANDLER

Meanwhile, the Otises had been joined by the man whose name would be even more closely associated with the newspaper than theirs over the coming century, Harry Chandler. On a doctor's advice, Chandler dropped out of Dartmouth University and came west for his health in 1882, at first working on a farm while he recovered his well-being and accumulated savings through some side deals with farm produce. His health restored, he returned to Dartmouth, but the cold soon had him coughing blood again, so he boarded another train to the West Coast.[23]

His first job at the *Times* was in circulation. Each morning he loaded wagons with bundles of the newspaper for distribution. Soon he had advanced to chief of collections, then mail-order manager, and using his savings from his farmwork, he became an independent contractor with the *Times,* as well as one of its clerks. He purchased the *Times'* subscriber lists, as well as those of other local newspapers and the *San Diego Union,* sometimes personally delivering newspapers if someone in his delivery crew failed to show up for work. He also managed a crew of newsboys under the typical arrangement that allowed him to keep a percentage of each sale.[24] At the same time, he learned the value of real estate in the Los Angeles area and started to acquire a substantial share of it.

Chandler earned Otis's favor in the late 1890s by helping him drive one of his competitors, the *Los Angeles Tribune,* into bankruptcy. When the *Tribune* went on the auction block, Otis tried to buy it, but the farsighted Chandler got there first, paying five cents on the dollar. Otis made Chandler his business manager. Chandler's first wife, whom he married in 1891, died after bearing their second daughter in 1892, and he went on to court the boss's daughter. Four years later Harry Chandler and Emma Marian Otis were married. Lizzie supervised the wedding story in the *Times.*[25]

Los Angeles continued to grow. After the arrival of the railroads, starting in the 1870s, Los Angeles approximately doubled in population every decade, surpassing one hundred thousand by 1900. The *Times* prospered with the city. Even Otis's conflicts with the International Typographical Union failed to slow the Otis-Chandler newspaper juggernaut.

In 1903 Los Angeles officials realized the city needed more water if growth was to continue. Mayor Fred Eaton figured out how to do it when he got interested in retiring to a ranch in the Owens Valley on the eastern border of the state and decided it had water to spare. While Eaton helped the new U.S. Bureau of Reclamation obtain water rights in the valley—rights that would be transferred to Los Angeles—Otis and Chandler acquired adjacent San Fernando Valley land that they planned to develop when the Owens River water reached southern California. McDougal calls the plan, made public in 1905, "a textbook study in mob manipulation, utilitarian theft, and winner-take-all water politics in the arid American West."[26] The behind-the-scenes intrigues in which the two newspapermen participated formed the basis for the Roman Polansky film *Chinatown*.

About the same time, Otis and Chandler faced increased newspaper competition. William Randolph Hearst came south from San Francisco. On December 12, 1903, he published the first issue of the *Los Angeles Examiner*. Otis's anti-union stance led Los Angeles unions to guarantee Hearst a substantial number of subscribers if he would make Los Angeles his next conquest, rather than invade Boston as he had planned.[27] At first it appeared the unions' ploy would be successful in undercutting the *Times,* but even after the *Examiner* exposed Otis's interest in the San Fernando Valley land and water deal, the *Times* maintained its premier position in the city's journalism.

Supporters of the *Times* feared the 1910 bombing would undermine its influence and result in the election of a Socialist mayor out of labor's sympathy for the two bombers. When attorney Clarence Darrow had them plead guilty, however, the anti-union *Times* was once again vindicated.

Otis died in 1917, then a general thanks to his volunteer service in the Spanish-American War. For nearly thirty years Harry Chandler, real estate salesman par excellence, controlled the *Times*—and he who controlled the *Times* largely controlled Los Angeles. Chandler had little of Otis's personality or ideology, however. He shared his father-in-law's interest in boosting Los Angeles and doing whatever it took to sell the parcels of land he had accumulated. While Otis saw Los Angeles as populated by "first-class men in almost any line of business," Chandler was less idealistic.[28] "Without the greedy, the superficial, the venal, and the shiftless as customers, newsman Harry Chandler would probably have enjoyed minimal success in his true vocation: selling real estate," writes McDougal.[29]

Never publicly flamboyant like his father-in-law or his northern competitor, Hearst, who in 1919 started construction of his castle in San Simeon on the central California coast, Chandler lived a quiet private life with Marian and their eight children and was active in the Congregational Church and a few other local organizations. They had a home in Hollywood, a ranch in the San Fernando Valley, and another near Pomona—and later others in Mexico (Baja California) and New Mexico—but their social activities were rarely reported in the *Times*.[30]

Always on the lookout for a good investment, Chandler backed Donald Douglas's efforts to bring the aviation industry to southern California in the 1920s.[31] He also helped establish the California Institute of Technology.

Under Chandler's direction, the *Times* continued to boost Los Angeles, but its rhetoric now lacked Otis's passion and bellicosity.

It continued its anti-union position, but its news columns had relatively little to offer except when it came to covering and attacking Communism. Chandler had initially thought he could profit by dealing with the Bolsheviks after the Russian Revolution, but concerns about the Reds led Chandler to open a bureau in Washington, D.C., so he could keep an eye on politicians who disagreed with him. He largely turned the news operations of the *Times* over to Kyle Palmer, the kind of "personally loyal but occasionally fact-bending journalists whom Harry preferred." [32] Under Chandler, the *Times* failed to distinguish itself in any way but profit.

Chandler retired from the newspaper in 1944 and was succeeded by his son, Norman. While Norman ran the *Times,* his wife, Dorothy Buffum Chandler, daughter of a wealthy Los Angeles department store family, made her mark on the city's social and cultural scene. The main concert hall in the Los Angeles Music Center is named for her in recognition of her years of work in funding the center. Norman's stint with the *Times* was not particularly noteworthy, and by the time Norman and Dorothy's son, Otis, took over the newspaper in 1960, the paper had been ranked the nation's second-worst newspaper, second only to the *Chicago Tribune,* which would become its owner some forty years later. [33]

OTIS CHANDLER'S TURN

Otis, however, was determined to raise the *Times'* reputation. Handing new editor Nick Williams a notebook full of what he had identified as the *Times'* deficiencies, the new publisher launched an era that would see the newspaper win four Pulitzer

Prizes in one decade[34] and earn the respect that Otis sought for it.[35] He improved salaries and working conditions to the point that envious observers called the *Times* the "velvet coffin"; its reporters were supposedly so comfortable they wanted to stay forever.

Otis Chandler gained a thorough grounding in the operations of the company, starting at the bottom and moving from department to department, meeting the people and learning the ways of newspapering. The Stanford graduate who had worked his way through college waiting tables and drilling with the Naval ROTC identified numerous shortcomings, particularly in the financial operations of the company, in addition to the newsroom concerns he passed along to editor Williams.

After he became publisher, Otis continued his father's philosophy of economic diversification. Norman Chandler had taken the company into television and paper manufacturing, and he had diversified the board of directors, bringing three local businessmen to the family-run concern.[36] Otis added book publishing and an aviation mapping and information publisher; joined with the *Washington Post* to form a news service; bought General Features Corporation; built a chain of newspapers, including a controlling interest in *Newsday* on Long Island; and, in the face of some family opposition, took the company public. The Times-Mirror Company was listed on the New York Stock Exchange in 1964.[37] Also during the early 1960s, the *Mirror* newspaper ceased to exist.

Otis Chandler ran the *Times* for twenty years. When he stepped down as publisher in 1980, Tom Johnson became the first non–family member to hold the position of publisher. Otis had hired Johnson to run the *Dallas Times Herald* when he bought it in 1973, and named him president and chief operating officer of the Los Angeles paper in 1977. Otis's admonition to Johnson: "Don't just manage it status quo, 'cause if you don't move forward, it will start to slide backwards," seems especially prescient today.[38]

In the early twenty-first century the *Los Angeles Times,* although still better than many other newspapers in the country, started to slide backward. Purchased by the *Chicago Tribune* in 2000—the same newspaper with which it vied for the bottom of the newspaper barrel some forty years previously—the *Times* made national news in 2006 when then-publisher Jeffrey M. Johnson and editor Dean Baquet defied Tribune Company executives and refused to lay off additional staff, having already reduced personnel numbers by eighty-five and whacked costs the previous year.[39] Anticipating that Johnson's and Baquet's jobs were on the line, some 400 of the *Times'* 940-member editorial staff petitioned the Tribune Company in support of their publisher and editor. It did no good. Both were forced out and replaced by *Tribune* people, David D. Hiller and James O'Shea, respectively.[40]

By this time the Tribune Company itself was for sale; its shareholders—many of them Chandlers—were unhappy with declining profits and were demanding more for their money. In Los Angeles a contingent of businesspeople made a bid for the *Times,* following the examples of a group of Philadelphia businessmen who had purchased the *Philadelphia Inquirer* from the Knight Ridder chain earlier in 2006, local investors in Baltimore who sought to buy the *Baltimore Sun,* and a wealthy Connecticut family that showed interest in acquiring the *Hartford Courant.*[41] In November 2006, after the latest change in management, the Tribune Company announced that it would make no decision about selling the company until the first quarter of 2007.

"'We are committed to a complete review process that will yield maximum value for all Tribune shareholders,' William A. Osborn, chairman of a committee set up to review offers, said in a statement."[42]

During the subsequent business debate, members of the Chandler family discussed retaking control of the newspaper but could not agree on how to go about it. Finally, in March 2007, the Tribune board accepted the bid of a Chicago real estate billionaire, Sam Zell, a man who once nicknamed himself the "grave dancer" because of his history of buying troubled businesses.[43]

At the end of 2007, Zell took the Tribune Company private, became its chairman, and promised he would streamline its operations. He emphasized the importance of finding new revenue, rather than slashing costs, but about a month later, in January 2008, Hiller ordered a four-million-dollar cut in the *Los Angeles Times* newsroom budget.[44] When O'Shea resisted, he followed Baquet into the ousted-editor club.

Times staff were uncertain that Zell was behind the cuts, because the new owner has indicated he will give newspapers considerable autonomy, so Hiller may have acted on his own.[45] At the same time, Zell has said he sees opportunity in the newspaper business and that he bought the Tribune Company to make money. "I am probably not as pessimistic about the future of newspapers as others might be," he told the *International Herald Tribune*.[46]

SACRAMENTO AND McCLATCHY

Chandler and Hearst are not the only names with a longtime connection to California newspapers that started the twenty-first century in the news. James McClatchy edited the *Sacramento Bee* in its founding year, 1857, and went on to build a newspaper empire of thirty-two daily newspapers in thirty U.S. markets.[47] McClatchy was associated with the third newspaper started in Sacramento, the *Settlers' and Miners' Tribune,* started on October 30, 1850. It followed the *Placer Times,* which was started by Edward Kemble, by then an owner of the successful *Alta California,* at the behest of Sam Brannan, then a wealthy merchant in town. Kemble relates how he solved the problem of inadequate printing materials by gathering up type from the "little heaps of 'pi'" around the *Alta* office and by appropriating the old California Ramage press used at Monterey to print the *Californian.* These materials were sent up the Sacramento River on the *Dice me Nana* steamer and arrived in Sacramento on March 20, 1850.[48] The first issue of the *Placer Times* appeared in April. In June the publishing company's name was changed from E. C. Kemble and Co. to T. R. Per Lee and Co., but the owners of the *Alta* continued to own the Sacramento newspaper office. Kemble says Theron Rudd Per Lee didn't know anything about the newspaper business and soon left. The owners put Jesse Howard Giles in charge. A former printer for the *New York Tribune,* Giles stayed with the *Placer Times* until April 1850. He returned to the East Coast with, according to Kemble, "a snug competency, one of the very few newspaper publishers who have taken a fortune with them out of the State."[49]

Sacramento's second newspaper, the *Transcript,* first appeared as a triweekly on April 1, 1850. (The *Placer Times* soon increased its frequency to match.) It was immediately popular and respected, with ownership shares trading hands at ever-increasing prices. Kemble suggests the *Boston Transcript* was its model and says "it affected a high order of literary taste, and contained a large amount of editorial" (as opposed to being full of advertising). He adds, "Of course there was much rivalry and not a little ill-feeling between the two journals."[50] The *Transcript* advocated the Democratic Party; with the Democrats in power, the *Transcript* won the state public printing contract, an important financial coup.

The paper that brought James McClatchy to Sacramento, the *Settlers' and Miners' Tribune,* initially published six days a week, but cholera in the mining camp "considerably interfered with the prospects of the new organ."[51] As a daily, the *Tribune* lasted a month; as a weekly, about two months.

With the *Transcript* in the Democratic camp and the *Placer Times* claiming to be neutral but obviously leaning toward the Democrats as well, the Sacramento field was ripe for the entry of a Whig newspaper. Just before Christmas of 1850, the *Sacramento Index* entered the fray. When the *Index* condemned the vigilantes who had lynched a gambler who had been arrested for shooting a citizen, it lost readership and disappeared from the scene the following March.[52]

Two days after the closure of the *Index,* four *Transcript* compositors got together and presented the town with the first issue of the *Sacramento Daily Union.* The *Union* had been in gestation for about a year, but the proprietors had trouble getting the necessary printing materials. In early 1851, while they debated which of two opportunities to acquire printing plants they should take, the *Transcript* attempted to reduce the typesetting pay rate by 25 percent and the compositors decided to strike and start the new newspaper right away. By this time nine printers had signed on to the company, and this "union of practical journeymen printers" gave the newspaper its name.[53] In 1851 the *Placer Times* and the *Transcript* merged into one newspaper that lasted about a year.

The *Sacramento Daily Bee* also started life as an association of practical printers, independent in politics.[54] The Irish-born McClatchy had been in Sacramento a few years before becoming involved with the *Bee*. He had worked in banking in New York after coming to the United States and eventually took a job with the *New York Tribune,* which sent him to California to report on the gold rush in 1849. He tried mining but soon turned back to newspapering, helping start several Sacramento newspapers. He had had an interest in the *Democratic State Journal,* which became the *California Statesman* when the Democrats lost control of the statehouse; and although he was not the "founding editor" of the *Bee,* he was one of the founders.

McClatchy took his time expanding his newspaper interests.[55] In the 1920s the McClatchy Company started *Bee*s in the nearby Central Valley (California) cities of Fresno and Modesto. Fifty years later it ventured farther afield by buying the *Anchorage Daily News* and the *Tri-City Herald* in Kennewick, Washington. In 1986 the *Tacoma (Washington) News Tribune* joined the McClatchy group, and two years later the company went public, although it does not trade its Class B common stock, which controls the majority of shareholder voting power. In 1990 the McClatchy Company went fully national by purchasing three dailies in South Carolina, and in 1995 North Carolina dailies were added to the list, including the *News and Observer* in Raleigh. With this newspaper, the company also acquired what became known as McClatchy Interactive, its World Wide Web presence. Acquisitions continued into the twenty-first century with the purchase of several more Central Valley newspapers and, in 2006, the

Knight Ridder chain of thirty-two dailies, the latter making the McClatchy Company the second-largest newspaper publisher in the United States, after the Gannett Corporation.[56] McClatchy sold a dozen of the Knight Ridder papers because they were not in rapidly growing markets.

DEAN SINGLETON IN DENVER

Still another western media voice with deep pockets being heard in the early twenty-first century was William Dean Singleton, chairman and chief executive officer of the MediaNews Group. Headquartered in Denver, MediaNews operated fifty-four daily newspapers in twelve states.[57]

A controversial figure among newspaper people, Singleton early became known as a cost-cutting publisher who was insensitive to his employees and to good journalism. He had a history of buying ailing newspapers—selecting the sick ones because he did not have the money to buy the healthy ones—and often burying them rather than saving them. Those he saved were noteworthy for their emphasis on local news. In the process this son of a Texas oil field roustabout became very wealthy, earning more than a million dollars a year, owning a mansion in Denver, four cattle ranches in Colorado, and a house on Cape Cod.[58] He also eventually tried to downplay his reputation as "the industry's leading skinflint."[59] In 2003 he was part of a White House– and Kremlin-sponsored summit of media executives that gave advice to Russian publishers about operating within a free-market situation.

Although his empire was nationwide, Singleton long had a particular interest in other western newspapers. He maintained his role as publisher of the *Denver Post,* which is in a joint operating agreement with the Scripps-owned *Rocky Mountain News.* In 1985 he bought a number of suburban San Francisco dailies; in 1992 he bought the *Oakland Tribune* and brought it out of the red ink; and in 1997 he tried to buy the *Inland Valley Daily Bulletin* from the Stephens Group. That deal did not go through, but MediaNews and Stephens formed the California Newspaper Partnership, and Gannett also joined the consortium.[60] The partnership allowed the participants to save money by consolidating production facilities and purchasing and by providing more convenient packaging for advertisers.

MediaNews owned the controlling share in the partnership (55 percent). When MediaNews bought the *San Jose Mercury News* and the *Contra Costa Times,* both in the San Francisco Bay area, from the McClatchy Company in 2006 for nearly one billion dollars, the Hearst Corporation provided financial backing in exchange for a minority share.[61] Hearst's involvement came as a surprise, and the company "stressed that it would keep its financial distance from the MediaNews Bay Area properties" to avoid antitrust complications.[62] MediaNews said in 2006 that it was ready to replace the $263 million it got from Hearst, if required by the government. The difference in the purchase price would come from the newspaper project. The transaction gave MediaNews a circulation of more than seven hundred thousand in the same area in which the rival *San Francisco Chronicle* had not quite four hundred thousand.[63]

Singleton's company also formed the Texas–New Mexico Newspaper Partnership with Gannett in 2003. The partnership was operated by Gannett, which had the controlling financial interest, and was managed by a five-person committee. Observers characterize Singleton as ambitious and eager to enlarge his empire, particularly by acquiring one of the San Francisco newspapers. The full impact he will have on the quality of western journalism remains to be seen, but most observers' forecasts are gloomy. They don't think he has outgrown his old "skinflint" ways.

ELEVEN

MANIFEST DESTINY REALIZED

In 1845, about the time the Mormons started packing their earthly belongings for the move to their new Zion in the largely deserted and desolate Great Basin, the Spaniards hauled a printing press into Mexican California so they could print governmental edicts and other official documents. Earlier the same year, Edgar Allan Poe first published "The Raven" in the *New York Evening Mirror; Scientific American* began publication; and Frederick Douglass published his autobiography, *Narrative of the Life of Frederick Douglass, an American Slave.* And the editor of the six-year-old *United States Magazine and Democratic Review,* John L. O'Sullivan, coined the phrase "manifest destiny." This was at least the second article O'Sullivan had written in which he extolled the nation's destiny. In his magazine's first year, 1839, he wrote about "The Great Nation of Futurity," in which he frequently referred to the nation's destiny but never used the full phrase "manifest destiny." Rejecting the monarchies and aristocracies of antiquity, O'Sullivan declared:

The expansive future is our arena, and for our history. . . . The far-reaching, the boundless future will be the era of American greatness. In its magnificent domain of space and time, the nation of many nations is destined to manifest to mankind the excellence of divine principles, to establish on earth the noblest temple ever dedicated to the worship of the Most High—the Sacred and the True.[1]

It is clear that, in 1839, at least, the destiny O'Sullivan thought would be made manifest in the United States was not unlike the Puritans' "city on a hill," which would serve as a beacon to all that the United States was based on "the Sacred and the True," as O'Sullivan labeled its virtues. In this article O'Sullivan wrote much about freedom and liberty.

The notion of the "city on a hill" was not a foreign one in the West. The *Silver State* in Unionville, Nevada, claimed in its first issue that the people "demanded an organ that their light may be made to shine abroad," and promised to be that organ.[2]

Six years later, the more generally accepted meaning of *manifest destiny,* describing the inevitable expansion of the United States' hegemony across the continent from the Atlantic to the shores of the Pacific, was evident in an article in which O'Sullivan applauded the annexation of Texas. This article evidenced his concern for the "fulfillment of our manifest destiny to overspread the continent allotted by Providence for the free development of our yearly multiplying millions." Indeed, he predicted that California, perhaps all of Spanish America, would come under the umbrella of America, and that even the British Canadas would sever "their present colonial relation to the little island three thousand miles across the Atlantic; soon to be followed by Annexation, and destined to swell the still accumulating momentum of our progress." He further predicted that Europe would be no match for the American millions "destined to gather beneath the flutter of the stripes and stars" a century hence.[3]

"Manifest destiny" is not the only well-known phrase from the nineteenth century attributed to a periodical editor—"Go West, young man, go West," commonly attributed to *New York Tribune* editor Horace Greeley, comes to mind—but because *destiny* is so intertwined in our discussion of the press in the West, it is appropriate to give the phrase from which it comes special attention.[4]

One way to attend to manifest destiny is to look at the way in which it was fulfilled, at least in terms of the frontier press. To what extent was the peopling of the western half of the continent more than the transplanting of excess residents from the eastern half? Was the West any more the "city on a hill" for citizens in nineteenth-century America than towns in the East were?[5] We have asserted in earlier pages that the press of the western frontier was both the same and somehow different from the press of the older, settled regions of the nation.

William H. Lyon, perhaps the most thoughtful of the early historians of the frontier press, said that the prime goal of the frontier publisher was to "obliterate the frontier."[6] We have argued that his prime goal was, at the least, to survive, and better yet, to prosper. It was, of course, by obliterating the frontier, that is, turning dusty frontier towns into thriving villages with businesses-seeking customers, that the publisher himself would thrive.

The frontier publisher viewed his newspaper as a substitute for the gold mine he had hoped to discover when he came west: it was to make his fortune, and the fact that in most cases it did not is a reflection more on his incompetence—or perhaps naïveté—in business matters than on the quality of the ore.

That frontier publishers saw the West as a way to secure their fortunes should not surprise us. "New" western historian Patricia Limerick argues that much of the history of the West reflects a foundation of economics and that issues of profit and loss provide continuity between the earliest days of the frontier and today. An anecdote from the author's college days provides further support for this notion as it relates to newspapers. A highly regarded professor mentioned that he was about to leave for a press association meeting in the Southeast to talk to them about ethics. "Oh," said I, "you must get a lot of such invitations." "Yes," he told me, "but not so many in the West. Western editors seem less interested in the subject."[7]

Western press associations provided early evidence of a commitment to financial success. Their minutes tell of junkets, social events, and sessions on how to treat advertisers and make money; there is little discussion of content. Sometimes they got together in order to set advertising and subscription rates with a view to avoiding price wars. Although ongoing press associations did not become a reality until the 1880s or later, in some areas publishers early on recognized the value of agreeing to standardize rates. California publishers got together as early as 1851, when about sixteen publishers attended a convention and set wage scales, subscription prices, and rates for job printing. In 1870 four publishers in Olympia, Washington, agreed to standardize prices.[8] A fifth protested and said he would not stoop so low as to join in such an agreement, but there is no indication he was invited.

Since most publishers were also printers, some of the earliest associations were designed to protect their role as compositors or pressmen, but it did not take long before newspaper owners saw labor as an adversary.[9] In 1864 two newspapers in San Francisco, the *Argus* and the *Daily American Flag,* tried to get away with paying their printers less than the going rate and were "ratted" by the union.[10]

As the industry became more specialized and even printer-publishers had to hire additional workers, the journalists, too, started to form associations, but they remained the least organized, and their organizations were largely social. The *Journalist,* a national magazine for the trade, reported in 1889 that the San Francisco Press Club held its first benefit.[11] Although many frontier journalists were happy to take handouts from sources, they remained the least financially oriented of the newspaper fraternity.

Amidst all the failures, a considerable number of pioneer publications have celebrated their centennials, and continue to publish. The conventional wisdom, or at least suspicion, is that the thousands of frontier newspapers that did not survive failed because no one wanted to read them. Actually, they failed because their proprietors were poor economic stewards. They borrowed too much money, failed to collect what was due them, and otherwise mismanaged their businesses. The survivors followed good business practices and took advantage of opportunities to buy land, as well as grow their newspaper businesses, and their descendants are with us today.

OUTLIVING THE FRONTIER

The better known of the frontier survivors include the *San Francisco Examiner,* which started as the *Daily Democratic Press,* and became the *Examiner* to hide its anti-Lincoln political position. It was called the *Examiner* when George Hearst acquired it in payment of a debt and then let his son, William, run it, starting a major newspaper empire. The *San Francisco Chronicle* began in 1863 as the *Daily Dramatic Chronicle.* For most of their existence the two newspapers provided San Francisco with independent journalism; then for a period in the twentieth century, the two papers participated in a joint operating agreement. They are separate again and under new owners. The *Chronicle* is now owned by the Hearst Corporation, which sold its longtime flagship newspaper, the *Examiner,* to a local businessman.

The *Seattle Post-Intelligencer* traces its roots to the founding of the *Puget Sound Weekly,* which became the *Weekly Intelligencer* in 1866, and then the *Post-Intelligencer* in 1881.[12] The *Seattle Times* was first published in 1891. The *Deseret News* has a direct lineage to the frontier paper of 1850; the *Salt Lake Tribune* to 1871. Today's *Rocky Mountain News* is a direct descendant of the newspaper William Byers hand-printed on the banks of Cherry Creek in 1859. All of these pairs of newspapers are in joint operating agreements, although the Seattle partnership is still in litigation. Citizen groups fought the original JOA and have come forward again as the two newspapers have proposed modifications of the partnership that would close the *Post-Intelligencer* but continue to give the Hearst Corporation a percentage of the profits. Hearst, meanwhile, is alleging that the *Times* has not been completely fair in its treatment of the *Post-Intelligencer* under the JOA.[13]

The *Las Vegas Review-Journal* traces its roots to one of the city's pioneer papers and celebrated its centennial in 2005, along with the city; the *Santa Cruz Sentinel,* on the California coast south of San Francisco, celebrated 150 years in 2006, and other western papers have hit similar milestones.

The *Los Angeles Times* also continues to publish, and during one period of its existence attained a level of quality met by few other newspapers in the United States. As sophisticated and enterprising as any eastern newspaper, the *Times* was to the West what the *New York Times* was to the East. The controversies over the paper's recent sale suggest that it is not likely to achieve such distinction again soon, although many would argue that it is still the best in the West, and its reporters get more respect from the eastern journalism establishment than do those of other western newspapers.[14]

Novelist Larry McMurtry argues that "the *selling* of the West" often "preceded the *settling*" of it.[15] McMurtry's interest is in the popular images created by the dime novels, Wild West shows, and other artifacts of popular culture. But he might have included the frontier press in his catalog of entities that emphasized the selling of the West. However, he also questions whether anything but lies about the West will find a real audience. Edward Kemble recognized this in a way as well, when he said in 1859 that the history of California newspapers did not hold much interest for the average reader.

I hope I have proven them both in error.

NOTES

PREFACE

1. *Las Vegas Review-Journal,* December 26, 2006, 7B.

CHAPTER ONE

1. Eugene P. Moehring's new study of urban development in the West gives newspapers more credit for their contributions than do most other recent studies. See *Urbanism and Empire in the West, 1840–1890* (Reno: University of Nevada Press, 2004).

2. Oliver Knight, "The Frontier Newspaper as a Catalyst in Social Change," *Pacific Northwest Quarterly* 58, no. 2 (April 1967): 74.

3. Ibid., 77.

4. But see Ray Allen Billington, *America's Frontier Heritage* (Albuquerque: University of New Mexico Press, 1974), 80, where he says that newspapers and magazines served "as a bridge between West and East for adults" and newspapers "were usually the first cultural transplant in each new community."

5. Frank T. Gilbert, *Historic Sketches of Walla Walla, Whitman, Columbia and Garfield Counties, Washington Territory* (Portland, Ore.: A. G. Walling, 1882), 392–93.

6. For more about manuscript newspapers on the frontier, see Roy Alden Atwood, "Handwritten Newspapers on the Iowa Frontier, 1844–1854," *Journalism History* 7, no. 2 (Summer 1980): 56–59.

7. Lawrence Clark Powell, *Philosopher Pickett: The Life and Writings of Charles Edward Pickett Esq. of Virginia, Who Came Overland to the Pacific Coast in 1842–43, and for Fifty Years Waged War with Pen and Pamphlet* (Berkeley: University of California Press, 1942).

8. J. Cecil Alter, *Early Utah Journalism: A Half Century of Forensic Warfare, Waged by the West's Most Militant Press* (1938; reprint, Westport, Conn.: Greenwood, 1970), 90.

9. Ibid., 108.

10. Quoted ibid., 129.

11. Richard E. Lingenfelter and Karen Rix Gash, *The Newspapers of Nevada: A History and Bibliography, 1854–1979* (Reno: University of Nevada Press, 1984), 122. At the time Johntown and all of what is now Nevada were part of Utah Territory.

12. Ibid., 89.

13. Alfred Doten, *The Journals of Alfred Doten, 1849–1903,* 3 vols., ed. Walter Van Tilburg Clark (Reno: University of Nevada Press, 1973), 1:769.

14. Agreement, with list of monetary pledges, between residents of Olympia, Washington, and Thomas Jefferson Dryer, July 8, 1852, McElroy papers, University of Washington Libraries.

15. See William H. Lyon, *The Pioneer Editor in Missouri, 1808–1860* (Columbia: University of Missouri Press, 1965). The other reasons Lyon offers are (1) an outlet for the publication of laws, (2) a place for political parties to disseminate their views, and (3) a way for printers with job shops to use excess production capacity. Since Lyon's work, other reasons have been offered: businessmen wanted to promote business and settlement (the booster press), added by Oliver Knight in his review of Lyon's book in *Journalism Quarterly* 42, no. 3 (Summer 1965): 478–79; and the desire for the community stability that a newspaper represents, proposed by Jerilyn McIntyre in "Communication on a Western Frontier—Some Questions About Context," *Journalism History* 3, no. 2 (Summer 1976): 53–55.

16. Frederic Hudson, *Journalism in the United States* (1873; reprint, Grosse Pointe, Mich.: Scholarly Press, 1968), 593.

17. Alfred McClung Lee, *The Daily Newspaper in America* (New York: Macmillan, 1937), 263. Lee also records that the *Herald* sent ten thousand copies to California with each boat to the isthmus. The *New York Evening Post* also had a western edition (Lee, *Daily Newspaper,* 384).

18. *New York Weekly Tribune,* September 3, 1857.

19. Allan Nevins, Review of *Gold Rush: The Journals, Drawings and Other Papers of J. Goldsborough Bruff 1849–1951,* ed. Georgia Willis Reed and Ruth Gaines, *Saturday Review of Literature* 32 (May 14, 1949): 52.

20. Lee, *Daily Newspaper,* 230.

21. Earl Pomeroy, *The Pacific Slope: A History of California, Oregon, Washington, Idaho, Utah and Nevada* (1965; reprint, Seattle: University of Washington Press, 1973), 42.

22. Barbara Cloud, *The Business of Newspapers on the Western Frontier* (Reno: University of Nevada Press, 1992), 12. In its May 19, 1849, issue, the *Placer Times* in Sacramento sought correspondents in the mines and offered copies of eastern newspapers in payment for their work.

23. Pomeroy, *Pacific Slope,* 26.

24. Ibid.

25. Harriet D. Munnick, "Medard Godard Foisy, Pioneer Printer," *Marion County History* 10 (1969–71): 5.

26. The Spaniards introduced printing into Mexico City in the sixteenth century, and one of the earliest publications was a news broadside telling of the 1541 earthquake that destroyed much of Guatemala. See articles by Al Hester, Félix Gutiérrez, and Ernesto Ballesteros in a special issue of *Journalism History* 6, no. 3 (Autumn 1979): 77–83. See also *Journalism History*'s "Spanish Language Media Issue" 4, no. 2 (Summer 1977).

27. Palace of the Governors, "The Palace Print Shop and Bindery," http://palaceofthegovernors.org/PrintShop/coll.html.

28. Edward C. Kemble, *A History of California Newspapers* (1858), edited with a foreword by Helen Harding Bretnor (Los Gatos, Calif.: Talisman, 1962), 50–66.

29. Ralph S. Kuykendall, "History of Early California Journalism" (M.A. thesis, University of California, Berkeley, 1918), 10.

30. Daniel J. Boorstin, *The Americans: The National Experience* (New York: Vintage Books, 1965), 125.

31. Barbara Cloud, "Start the Presses: The Birth of Journalism in Washington Territory" (Ph.D. diss., University of Washington, 1979), 170.

32. For more about the frontier press generally, see the special issue of *Journalism History* 7, no. 2 (Summer 1980).

33. Clyde A. Milner II, Patricia Nelson Limerick, and Charles E. Rankin, eds., *Trails: Toward a New Western History* (Lawrence: University of Kansas Press, 1991). See also Limerick's *The Legacy of Conquest: The Unbroken Past of the American West* (New York: W. W. Norton, 1987).

34. And, of course, the two states outside "mainland" United States, Alaska and Hawaii, both added in 1959.

35. People per square mile calculated from census data reported in *The World Almanac and Book of Facts, 2005* (New York: World Almanac Books, 2005), 622, profiles of the states, 414–39.

36. A phrase in an 1880 song about a miner's daughter who drowned.

37. Thornton L. McElroy to Sally McElroy, January 11, 1853, McElroy papers, University of Washington Libraries.

38. Biographical sketch written in 1892 by McElroy's son Harry, McElroy papers, University of Washington Libraries.

39. Cloud, *Business of Newspapers,* 22.

40. Cloud, "Start the Presses," 145.

41. See Barbara Cloud, "A Party Press? You Bet, but Not Just Yet! Political Publishing on the Frontier," *Journalism History* 7, no. 2 (Summer 1980): 54–55, 72–73.

42. Thornton L. McElroy to Sally McElroy, January 11, 1853, McElroy papers, University of Washington Libraries.

43. *Esmeralda Star,* May 17, 1862. Aurora is on the California-Nevada border and is generally identified with Nevada, but when the *Star* was established, Mono County, California, claimed the town.

44. *Deseret News,* March 6, 1852.

45. *Idaho Avalanche* (Silver City, Idaho), January 4, 1873. The word in brackets is a guess; the microfilm was damaged.

46. *Los Angeles Star,* May 17, 1851. John McElroy does not appear to be related to Thornton McElroy of the Pacific Northwest. Kemble lists John's home state as New York.

47. Ostensibly, joint operating agreements were intended to preserve competitive news content in a community; I believe they are designed to make publishers wealthier.

48. Geoffrey Blainey, *The Tyranny of Distance* (Melbourne, Australia: Sun Books, 1966).

49. Pomeroy, *Pacific Slope*, 41.

CHAPTER TWO

1. See, for example, David A. Copeland's *The Idea of a Free Press: The Enlightenment and Its Unruly Legacy* (Evanston, Ill.: Northwestern University Press, 2006). Copeland has also written about the press during the French and Indian War, among other themed topics.

2. Max Sugar, *Regional Identity and Behavior* (New York: Kluwer Academic, Plenum, 2002).

3. "A Sense of Place," interview of David Hackett Fischer by William R. Ferris, *Humanities* 20 (July–August 1999): 6.

4. Ibid., 4.

5. I have had to learn to stop trying to grow fuchsias in the dry climate of the desert, for example. They grew splendidly in the Seattle environment in which I resided prior to moving to Las Vegas.

6. Quoted by Frederick C. Leubke in "Regionalism and the Great Plains: Problems of Concept and Method," *Western Historical Quarterly* 15 (1984): 31.

7. Sometimes one wonders what the modern ethos of home ownership is. As a colleague once said to me after moving into a new house, "It's all very fine to talk about home ownership, but all you do is sleep there. You spend your days at Home Depot or Lowes."

8. It will also allow us to explore one of the questions raised in the preface: to what extent did newspapers influence people to move west?

9. S. N. D. North, the compiler of the extensive report on newspapers and periodicals for the 1880 census, did numerous other reports on business and industry for the Census Bureau, and after Congress made the bureau permanent in 1902, he became its first director. In 1910 he was president of the American Statistical Association. Although a Google search (spring 2007) resulted in 922 citations of North and his work, relatively little has been written about him.

10. We know that the *California Eagle* was in existence in 1879, but it is not listed in the report, whereas other newspapers started that year

are. Either North neglected to send the survey or the proprietor chose not to fill it out and return it by whatever deadline North set.

11. One of the problems of census data is inconsistency in categories. For example, in 1880 North's report on the *History and Present Condition of the Newspaper and Periodical Press of the United States* did not include book and job printing, whereas those enterprises—often done by the same plants that published newspapers—are part of the 1890 report.

12. U.S. Bureau of the Census, "Newspapers and Periodicals," in Eleventh U.S. Census, 1890, vol. 6, pt. 3, 649. The 1890 total does not include newspapers and periodical establishments that did no other printing.

13. Table: "Statistics Relating to Daily Publications in 28 Principal Cities: 1890," ibid., 6:658–59. Notes to the table say that two New York daily newspapers with an estimated circulation of 65,000 did not submit reports, increasing New York's ratio. To its credit, the census also points out that cities such as Brooklyn, New York, and Allegheny, Pennsylvania, which had high ratios (Allegheny actually reported no daily newspapers), adjoined New York City and Pittsburgh, in *western* Pennsylvania, respectively.

14. Ibid., 6:660. Curiously, the census report makes a point of noting that the ratio included the population of Indian territory, even though the total population figure given did not.

15. Consisting of Maine, New Hampshire, Vermont, Massachusetts, Rhode Island, Connecticut, New York, New Jersey, and Pennsylvania.

16. Delaware, Maryland, District of Columbia, Virginia, West Virginia, North Carolina, South Carolina, Georgia, and Florida.

17. Ohio, Indiana, Illinois, Michigan, Minnesota, Iowa, Missouri, North Dakota, South Dakota, Nebraska, and Kansas.

18. Kentucky, Tennessee, Alabama, Mississippi, Louisiana, Texas, Oklahoma, and Arkansas.

19. Montana, Wyoming, Colorado, New Mexico, Arizona, Utah, Nevada, Idaho, Washington, Oregon, and California.

20. The 1890 report was a regular part of the census. Unfortu-

nately, the data gathered was not identical in form to that of the 1880 project. On some topics, the census reports in both 1880 and 1890, but even there I question whether the newspapermen answering the questions interpreted them the same way in both decades.

21. See, for example, Las Vegas, Nevada, which now claims a metropolitan area population of nearly two million, but the major newspaper, the *Las Vegas Review-Journal* in a joint operating agreement with the *Las Vegas Sun,* has a circulation of only about two hundred thousand, according to the Audit Bureau of Circulation's Web site.

22. Charles P. Squires, unpublished typescript about his early life, 12. Squires papers, Special Collections, University of Nevada, Las Vegas Lied Library.

23. The inclusion of Raleigh, a state capital and a university town, may not be entirely fair, but Austin matches that description as well.

24. Newspapers throughout the frontier printed this "law" on occasion.

25. In 1964 the *Los Angeles Times* became the first newspaper to publish more than four million classified ads and one hundred million ad lines overall during a single year. Dennis McDougal, *Privileged Son: Otis Chandler and the Rise and Fall of the L.A. Times Dynasty* (Cambridge, Mass.: Perseus, 2001), 260–61.

26. Lee Drutman, writing about the McClatchy Company's purchase of Knight Ridder, notes that the average profit margin for American business generally over the last twenty-five years has been 8.3 percent; the margin for newspapers has been in double digits. Lee Drutman, "Opportunity in Newspaper's Breakup," Common Dreams, March 22, 2006, www.commondreams.org.

27. *Sacramento Union,* editorial, March 20, 1851; agreement, July 22, 1851.

28. See, for example, Ellen Goodman, "Rush, Rush Inevitably Leads to Screw-ups: Blogosphere's Bogus Scoops Only Part of the Problem," *Las Vegas Review-Journal,* April 4, 2007, 11B.

29. See Cloud, *Business of Newspapers,* especially chapter 12, "Success and Failure," 175–91.

CHAPTER THREE

1. JoAnn Levy tells of a number of women miners in *They Saw the Elephant: Women in the California Gold Rush* (Norman: University of Oklahoma Press, 1992); see particularly pages 108–25. See also Ronald M. James and Kenneth H. Fliess, "Women of the Mining Camp West: Virginia City Revisited," in *Comstock Women: The Making of a Mining Community,* ed. Ronald M. James and Elizabeth Raymond (Reno: University of Nevada Press, 1998), 36–37.

2. Showing another newspaper office would limit the number of saloons on the movie set, and every movie mining camp had to have a lot of saloons.

3. Ray Allen Billington, *The Far Western Frontier: 1830–1860* (New York: Harper, 1956), 240.

4. Barbara Cloud, "Photographic Technology," in *History of the Mass Media in the United States: An Encyclopedia,* ed. Margaret A. Blanchard (Chicago: Fitzroy, Dearborn, 1998), 510, 512.

5. See Cloud, *Business of Newspapers,* 41–48.

6. See Sherilyn Cox Bennion, *Equal to the Occasion: Women Editors of the Nineteenth-Century West* (Reno: University of Nevada Press, 1990), for a discussion of women in frontier journalism.

7. Alter, *Early Utah Journalism,* 24.

8. Most successful mining camps exaggerated their numbers.

9. Mark Twain, *Roughing It,* 2 vols. (1871; reprint, New York: Books, Inc., 1913).

10. Ibid., 2:6.

11. Ibid., 2:7.

12. A Washington Territory printer, Urban Hicks, claimed to have taught Clemens to set type. I have been unable to find any evidence of this connection.

13. Russell R. Elliott, *History of Nevada* (Lincoln: University of Nebraska Press, 1973), 100.

14. Lingenfelter and Gash, *Newspapers of Nevada,* 5.

15. Ibid.

16. Twain, *Roughing It,* 2:4.

17. See, for example, Twain's *Roughing It* and Paul Fatout, *Mark Twain in Virginia City* (Bloomington: Indiana University Press, 1964), which relies heavily on Twain's own words.

18. See, for example, Doten, *Journals of Alfred Doten.* Twain's good friend Dan DeQuille was also engaged in writing fiction and appears to have been an early model for Twain.

19. Hazel Dicken-Garcia, "News Manufacturing in Late Nineteenth-Century America," paper presented at the American Journalism Historians Association conference, Wichita, Kans., October 2006.

20. Vivian Paladin, "Henry N. Blake: Proper Bostonian, Purposeful Pioneer," *Montana: The Magazine of Western History* 14 (August 1974): 38.

21. "Joseph Thompson Goodman," in *American National Biography* (New York: Oxford University Press, 1999), 9:244.

22. Ibid., 9:245.

23. Lingenfelter and Gash, *Newspapers of Nevada,* 254.

24. *American National Biography,* 9:245.

25. The *Palouse Gazette* in eastern Washington, September 29, 1877, announced that wedding notices would be accepted and their length would be in proportion to the liberality of the bridegroom or the amount of cake conferred on the newspaper office.

26. Miners measured their wealth in terms of the length of the vein of ore; the width did not matter. See Walter Blair, ed., *Mark Twain's West: The Author's Memoirs About His Boyhood, Riverboats and Western Adventures* (Chicago: Lakeside, 1983), 302–3.

27. Wells Drury, *An Editor on the Comstock Lode* (New York: Farrar and Rinehart, 1936), 5.

28. Henry Nash Smith, ed., *Mark Twain of the Enterprise* (Berkeley: University of California Press, 1957), 211–12.

29. Lingenfelter and Gash, *Newspapers of Nevada,* 254.

30. *Gold Hill News,* October 23, 1873.

31. Drury, *Editor on the Comstock Lode,* 181.

32. Ronald James, "Territorial Enterprise," Online Nevada Encyclopedia, http://www.onlinenevada.org/territorial_enterprise.

33. Kemble, *History of California Newspapers,* 324; Lottie Roeder

Roth, ed., *History of Whatcom County*, 2 vols. (Chicago: Pioneer Historical Publishing, 1926), 1:573.

34. Quoted in Roth, *History of Whatcom County*, 1:94.

35. *Northern Light* (Whatcom, Washington), July 3, 1858.

36. Percival R. Jeffcott, *Nooksack Tales and Trails* (Ferndale, Wash.: Sedro-Woolley Courier-Times, 1949), 121, quoting from the *Puget Sound Herald* at Steilacoom, n.d.

37. Kemble, *History of California Newspapers*, 324.

38. David Fridtjof Halaas, *Boom Town Newspapers: Journalism on the Rocky Mountain Mining Frontier, 1859–1881* (Albuquerque: University of New Mexico Press, 1981), 3.

39. Ibid. See also Robert L. Perkin, *The First Hundred Years: An Informal History of Denver and the Rocky Mountain News* (Garden City, N.Y.: Doubleday, 1959), 32.

40. Halaas, *Boom Town Newspapers*, 3.

41. *Territorial Enterprise* (Virginia City, Nevada), March 19 and 26, 1859.

42. George S. Turnbull, *History of Oregon Newspapers* (Portland, Ore.: Binfords and Mort, 1939), 50.

43. See WPA Writers Program, "History of the Colorado Press Association and Early Newspapers in Colorado," *Colorado Editor* 17 (June 1942): 11; *Arizona Miner* (Prescott), January 10, 1866; and Kemble, *History of California Newspapers*, 138. One Seattle editor told of the time an Indian boy saw a freshly made ink roller left on the counter to dry. The lad nibbled at the roller, found the sweet taste to his liking, and proceeded to eat it. Clarence B. Bagley, *History of King County, Washington*, 3 vols. (Seattle: S. J. Clarke, 1929), 1:467.

44. Wendell J. Ashton, *Voice in the West: Biography of a Pioneer Newspaper* (New York: Duell, Sloan and Pearce, 1950), 63.

45. See Elmo Scott Watson, *History of Auxiliary Newspaper Service in the United States* (Champaign, Ill.: Illini, 1923); and Eugene C. Harter, *Boilerplating America: The Hidden Newspaper*, ed. Dorothy Harter (Lanham, Md.: University Press of America, 1991).

46. *Skagit News* (Mt. Vernon, Washington), quoted in Warren J. Brier, "A History of Newspapers in the Pacific Northwest, 1846–1896" (Ph.D. diss., State University of Iowa, 1957), 28.

47. These comments are quoted in Cloud, *Business of Newspapers,* 143.

48. For more on the economics of the preprints, see Cloud, *Business of Newspapers,* 140–44.

49. *Reese River Reveille* (Austin, Nevada), August 20, 1878.

50. Robin Troy, "When Speech Wasn't Free," *Vision,* 2004, http://www.umt.edu/urelations/vision/2004/24speech.htm. See also Dennis L. Swibold, *Copper Chorus: Mining, Politics, and the Montana Press, 1889–1959* (Helena, Mont.: Montana Historical Society, 2006).

51. Troy, "When Speech Wasn't Free."

52. Ibid.

53. Swibold, *Chopper Chorus,* 316.

54. Ibid., 328.

55. Ibid., 11.

56. Quoted ibid., 8.

57. Ibid., 16.

58. Ibid., 17.

CHAPTER FOUR

1. For more about the use of newspaper exchanges, see chapter 1.

2. Lyon, *Pioneer Editor,* 47.

3. John Cameron Sim, *The Grass Roots Press: America's Country Newspapers* (Ames: Iowa State University Press, 1969), 33.

4. Thomas H. Heuterman, *Movable Type: Biography of Legh R. Freeman* (Ames: Iowa State University Press, 1979), 47.

5. *Arizona Miner* (Prescott), January 10, 1866.

6. Robert G. Athearn, *Union Pacific Country* (Lincoln: University of Nebraska Press, 1971), 136.

7. *Oregonian* (Portland), March 8, 1873.

8. *Belmont Courier* (Belmont, Nevada), February 21, 1874.

9. Pomeroy, *Pacific Slope,* 39–40.

10. Louis J. Stellman, *Sam Brannan: Builder of San Francisco* (New York: Exposition, 1953), 95–96.

11. Actually, Brannan's competition, the *Californian,* had published short items about the discovery of gold, but Brannan's editor, Edward

Kemble, declared it to be "ALL SHAM!" (Stellman, *Sam Brannan*, 95–96).

12. Kemble says far more newspapers were started in the first decade of California journalism than show up on his list in 1858. He says his path in chronicling their history lay through a "literary grave-yard" (Kemble, *History of California Newspapers*, 98). See also S. N. D. North, "Catalogue of Periodical Publications," in *History and Present Condition of the Newspaper and Periodical Press of the United States*, Tenth U.S. Census, 1880 (Washington, D.C.: Government Printing Office, 1884), 8:207.

13. References to Brannan's life come from Stellman, *Sam Brannan*.

14. Ibid., 19.

15. Helen Harding Bretnor's foreword to the reprint of Kemble's *History of California Newspapers*, 20. Five pages earlier in her fore-word, Bretnor says an extra was issued on October 24, 1846, and that a number of historians, including Douglas C. McMurtrie, who cata-loged printing imprints throughout the West, had seen it.

16. Kemble, *History of California Newspapers*, 20.

17. Stellman, *Sam Brannan*, 114.

18. Kemble, *History of California Newspapers*, 28.

19. Ibid., 85–86.

20. Ibid., 15–16. The California Battalion was recruited by Frémont in fall 1846 to drive the Spanish-Mexican influence from California and establish the Bear Flag Republic.

21. Kemble, *History of California Newspapers*, 28.

22. Ibid., 30.

23. Ibid., 32.

24. Ibid., 33.

25. Ibid., 44.

26. *Alta California*, December 27, 1858, quoted in Kemble, *History of California Newspapers*, 33.

27. Kemble, *History of California Newspapers*, 34. Responding to a newspaper that underreported the length of Kemble's article as twenty-eight columns, Bretnor notes in her foreword that the work "told the story of more than three hundred newspapers throughout the State"

and "amounted to *thirty-five* columns of very small type which, in the present edition, occupy 200 very respectable pages."

28. Kemble, *History of California Newspapers,* 43.

29. See Barbara Cloud, "Oregon in the 1820s: The Congressional Perspective," *Western Historical Quarterly* 12 (April 1981): 145–64.

30. *National Intelligencer* (Washington, D.C.), January 10, 1829.

31. In 1845 journalist John L. O'Sullivan wrote in the *United States Magazine and Democratic Review* of "our manifest destiny to overspread the continent allotted by Providence for the free development of our yearly multiplying millions" (John L. O'Sullivan, "Annexation," *United States Magazine and Democratic Review* 17, no. 1 [July–August 1845]: 5).

32. M. L. Wardell, "Oregon Immigration Prior to 1846," *Oregon Historical Quarterly* 27 (1926): 42.

33. Robert Shortress, "First Emigrants to Oregon," *Oregon Pioneer Association Transactions, 1894–1903* (written c. 1840; published 1896), 93.

34. *National Intelligencer,* December 7, 1821.

35. Wardell, "Oregon Immigration," 57.

CHAPTER FIVE

1. Charles A. Beard and Mary Beard, *New Basic History of the United States* (Garden City, N.Y.: Doubleday, 1968), 270–71.

2. James B. Hedges, "Promotion of Immigration to the Pacific Northwest by the Railroads," *Mississippi Valley Historical Review* 15 (September 1925): 193.

3. Ibid., 185.

4. For descriptions of railroad immigration campaigns, see Richard C. Overton, *Burlington West: A Colonization History of the Burlington Railroad* (1941; reprint, New York: Russell and Russell, 1967), especially chapter 13; Paul Wallace Gates, *The Illinois Central Railroad and Its Colonization Work* (Cambridge, Mass.: Harvard University Press, 1934), chapter 9; Siegfried Mickelson, "Promotional Activities of the Northern Pacific Land Department," *Journalism Quarterly* 17, no. 4 (December 1940): 324–33; as well as Hedges, "Promotion of Immigration."

5. "Henry Villard," *Dictionary of American Biography Base Set* (American Council of Learned Societies, 1928–36), reproduced in Gale Group, "History Resource Center," http://galenet.galegroup.com/servlet/HistRC/. This brief biography of Villard is primarily from this source.

6. Ibid.

7. Henry Villard, *Memoirs,* 2 vols. (1904; reprint, New York: Da Capo, 1969), 1:277.

8. Stewart Holbrook, *The Story of American Railroads* (New York: Crown, 1947), 147, cited by Christopher Muller in "James J. Hill," at Railserv, http://www.railrserv.com/JJHill. html. Actually, there were numerous things labeled "Hill's Folly." When Hill built the Stone Arch Bridge across the Mississippi River in Minneapolis, Minnesota, his critics considered it "folly"; as of 2006, the bridge is the second oldest still spanning the Mississippi. When Hill's son-in-law Samuel built a castle overlooking the Columbia River, critics labeled it "Hill's Folly" as well. The castle, never occupied as a home, is thought to be the world's most isolated art museum.

9. Muller, "James J. Hill."

10. Martin's text adds "to an avail." It is unclear whether this is a typographic error or what Hill sought from this "provincial paper." Albro Martin, *James J. Hill and the Opening of the Northwest* (1976; reprint, St. Paul: Minnesota Historical Society, 1991), 428.

11. Ibid. Martin says Hill "growled ungraciously" when he told Nichols to dispose of his shares.

12. Ibid.

13. Edmund S. Meany, *Newspapers of Washington Territory* (1922–23; reprint, Seattle: University of Washington Press, 1923), 86n.

14. Quoted in the *Kalama Beacon* (Washington), May 19, 1871.

15. Ibid.

16. *Tacoma Herald* (Washington), January 21, 1879.

17. Meany, *Newspapers of Washington Territory,* 17; Charles Prosch, "The Press of Washington Territory," in *Annual Proceedings of the Washington Press Association, 1889* (Hoquiam, Wash.: Washington Steam Book, News and Job Print, 1891), 27.

18. Robert C. Notson, *Making the Day Begin: A Story of the Oregonian* (Portland, Ore.: Oregonian, 1976), 8.

19. Thomas Prosch, "The Early History of Tacoma," typed manu-

script no. 11, Northwest Collection, University of Washington Libraries.

20. *Bellingham Bay Mail,* July 5, 1873, cited in *An Illustrated History of Skagit and Snohomish Counties* (Chicago: Interstate, 1906), 426–27; and Roth, *History of Whatcom County,* 1:575.

21. James Power to Clarence Bagley, June 22, 1875, Clarence Bagley papers, box 2, Northwest Collection, University of Washington Libraries.

22. Charles Prosch, "Press of Washington Territory," 36.

23. *Northwest Enterprise* (Anacortes, Washington), March 25, 1882.

24. Frontier residents, including publishers, were not always consistent in spelling the names of their towns. Cook ignored the final *e* in Spokane, and actually called his newspaper the *Spokan Times.*

25. *Spokan Times,* April 24, 1879; Jonathan Edwards, A*n Illustrated History of Spokane County* (W. H. Lever, 1900), 202.

26. *Tacoma Herald,* January 21, 1879.

27. J. Orin Oliphant, introduction to "The Territory of Washington, 1879," by Francis H. Cook (1879; reprint, *Record* 32 [1971]: 108–9).

28. *Medical Lake Press* (Medical Lake, Washington), September 2, 1882.

29. Eugene P. Moehring, *Resort City in the Sunbelt: Las Vegas, 1930–1970* (Reno: University of Nevada Press, 1989), 3–4.

30. A. Underwood (secretary to Senator William Clark) to C. B. Irvine, *Salem Sentinel* (Salem, Oregon), February 9, 1903, University of Nevada, Las Vegas, Libraries Special Collections.

31. Lingenfelter and Gash, *Newspapers of Nevada,* 125–26.

32. Richard E. Lingenfelter, *Death Valley and the Amargosa: A Land of Illusion* (Berkeley: University of California Press, 1986), 317.

33. Ibid.

34. Ibid.

35. Sam Gilluly, *The Press Gang: A Century of Montana Newspapers, 1885–1985* (Helena, Mont.: Montana Press Association, 1985), 28. In *Burlington West* Overton discusses how the Burlington and Missouri line in Nebraska "diligently cultivated" editors for free publicity (371).

36. Athearn, *Union Pacific Country,* 261.

37. Ibid., 244.

38. Ibid., 317.

39. Howard Roberts Lamar, *The Far Southwest, 1846–1912: A Territorial History* (New Haven, Conn.: Yale University Press, 1966; New York: W. W. Norton, 1970), 373.

40. Athearn, *Union Pacific Country*, 91.

41. Ibid., 103.

42. Heuterman, *Movable Type*.

43. Ibid., 25.

44. Ibid., 29. George Francis Train, generally labeled "eccentric," is thought to have been the inspiration for Phineas Fogg in Jules Verne's novel *Around the World in Eighty Days*. Train actually made the trip in sixty-seven days in 1870; he made two more round-the-world trips by 1880. He wrote on many subjects, supported women's rights, and was jailed on obscenity charges while defending nineteenth-century reformer and feminist Victoria Woodhull.

45. Heuterman, *Movable Type*, 30.

46. Ibid., 31.

47. Quoted ibid. Heuterman says this came from a correspondent for the *Omaha Republican* who wanted an interview with "Vattel"; Heuterman cites the *Frontier Index*, August 24, 1868. The *Index* was then in Green River City, Wyoming Territory.

48. Heuterman, *Movable Type*, 35.

49. Quoted ibid., 38, from the *Frontier Index*, March 6, 1868, then located in Fort Sanders, Dakota Territory.

50. See, for example, Heuterman's discussion of their relationship with General John Gibbon at Fort Sanders, not far from Laramie, Wyoming (Heuterman, *Movable Type*, 45–46).

51. Quoted ibid., 47, from the *Frontier Index*, August 18, 1868, then in Green River City.

52. Heuterman, *Movable Type*, 49–52.

53. Ibid., 53.

54. See Stephen E. Ambrose, *Nothing Like It in the World: The Men Who Built the Transcontinental Railroad, 1863–1869* (New York: Simon

and Schuster, 2000), for a discussion of the challenges of constructing the western segment of the transcontinental line; and Oscar Lewis, *The Big Four* (New York: Alfred A. Knopf, 1966), about the newspapers' love-hate relationship with the Central Pacific, and the efforts by the line's owners to counteract their hostility.

55. Quoted in Lewis, *The Big Four,* 316.

56. Ibid.

57. Ibid., 349. Lewis is referring to the futility of bribing a millionaire.

58. Ibid., 252.

59. Ibid., 190–91. Actually, Hearst's father George had made a gubernatorial campaign speech opposing the railroad monopoly. After George lost the election, he continued his attacks in the *Examiner.* W. A. Swanberg, *Citizen Hearst: A Biography of William Randolph Hearst* (New York: Charles Scribner's Sons, 1961), 22–23. George died in 1891, just when his son's anti–Southern Pacific effort was picking up steam, and thereafter the young Hearst was dependent on his mother's good will and generosity, not his father's.

60. Swanberg, *Citizen Hearst.*

61. Ibid.

62. Ibid., 50.

63. Ibid., 92.

64. Ibid. Huntington made these attacks through California congressman Grove L. Johnson. Thanks at least in part to the *Examiner,* Johnson had lost his campaign for reelection, but he was happy to oblige his railroad friends during the remaining months of his term.

65. Ibid., 98.

66. Ibid.

67. Quoted ibid., 48–49. One of Hearst's writers who was present at the discussion said she didn't know whether Hearst meant it or not.

68. Swanberg describes him differently and would take issue with this characterization.

69. Ibid., 440.

70. Ibid., 469, quoting from *Social Frontier,* February 1935.

71. Swanberg, *Citizen Hearst,* 477.

72. Ibid., 483. Swanberg cites the *New York Times,* September 2, 1937.

73. Swanberg, *Citizen Hearst,* 486. They also put St. Donat's, his castle in Wales, on the auction block. Hearst had paid $120,000 for it and put $1.25 million into renovations. He had lived there four months (ibid., 487).

74. Ibid., 492.

75. Ibid., 494. Swanberg evidently writes from the perspective of a biographer who has come to know his subject well. His opinions here are not the usual view of the aging Hearst.

76. Ibid.

77. Ibid.

78. Ibid., 497.

79. Ibid., 498.

80. Ibid., 521.

CHAPTER SIX

1. Wiley and his friends first changed the newspaper's name to *Washington Pioneer,* but two months later they called it the *Pioneer and Democrat,* the name by which it was best known in Washington Territory. Thomas J. Dryer to Thornton F. McElroy, September 26, 1853, McElroy papers, University of Washington Libraries; *Washington Pioneer* (Olympia), December 3, 1853, quoted in Cloud, "A Party Press?" 54.

2. Ella Sterling Mighels, *The Story of the Files: A Review of California Writers and Literature* (San Francisco: Cooperative Printing, 1893), 80.

3. Ibid.

4. *Sacramento Union,* April 28, 1860. The plan was to pay reporters for the *Standard* and the *Union* three dollars a day.

5. Smith, *Mark Twain of the Enterprise,* 211–12.

6. Ibid.

7. Cloud, "Start the Presses," 47–49.

8. Jonas Winchester to Susan Winchester, May 13, 1850, Jonas

Winchester papers, Kemble Collection, California Historical Society, San Francisco.

9. Ibid., February 1, 28, and May 1, 1851.

10. W. A. Katz, "Public Printers of Washington Territory, 1863–1889," *Pacific Northwest Quarterly* 51 (October 1960): 175.

11. Doten, *Journals of Alfred Doten*, 2:1189.

12. Katz, "Public Printers," 172.

13. Ibid., 171.

14. Ibid., 173.

15. Ibid.

16. See Cloud, *Business of Newspapers*, 78–82; and Robert D. Armstrong, *Nevada Printing History* (Reno: University of Nevada Press, 1981).

17. William H. Lyon, *Those Old Yellow Dog Days: Frontier Journalism in Arizona, 1859–1912* (Tucson: Arizona Historical Society, 1994), 57.

18. Ibid., 52–63.

19. *Sacramento Union* quoting the *San Francisco Bulletin*, September 5, 1859.

20. *San Francisco Bulletin*, July 1, 1859.

21. Cloud, "A Party Press?" 72.

22. Legal documents, December 13, 1869, Clarence Bagley papers, University of Washington Libraries.

23. Quoted in Cloud, "A Party Press?" 72.

24. Selucius Garfielde to Clarence Bagley, January 10, 1870, Clarence Bagley papers, University of Washington Libraries.

25. Cloud, "A Party Press?" 73.

26. Lyon, *Yellow Dog Days*, 18. It worked for Washington. Washington Territory was formed in 1853, a year after its first newspaper, the *Columbian*, was established.

27. *Biographical Directory of the United States Congress*, Internet edition, http://bioguide.congress.gov/scripts/biodisplay.pl?index'M000371.

28. Lyon, *Yellow Dog Days*, 6.

29. Ibid., 22.

30. Ibid., 23.

31. *Biographical Directory of the United States Congress*.

32. Lyon, *Yellow Dog Days*, 20.

33. Ibid., 22.

34. Ibid., 21.

35. Ibid., 25.

36. Ibid., 69. In the meantime, the *Arizonian*'s name had been changed to *Democrat*. Marion attacked the new Republican owner so viciously that he went to San Francisco, where he hired a new editor who changed the paper's name again, this time to *Journal*. In 1885 the *Miner* and the *Journal* merged into the *Journal-Miner* (ibid., 70).

37. Ibid., 27.

38. Kenneth Leonard Robison, "Idaho Territorial Newspapers" (M.S. thesis, University of Oregon, 1966), 22.

39. Ibid.

40. Lyon, *Yellow Dog Days,* 32–33.

41. Porter A. Stratton, *The Territorial Press of New Mexico, 1834–1912* (Albuquerque: University of New Mexico Press, 1969), 199.

42. William H. Lyon, "Louis C. Hughes, Arizona's Editorial Gadfly," *Journal of Arizona History* 24 (Summer 1983): 171.

CHAPTER SEVEN

1. Ulf Jonas Bjork, "Ethnic Press," in *History of the Mass Media,* ed. Blanchard, 207.

2. William E. Huntzicker, "The Frontier Press, 1800–1900," in *The Media in America: A History,* ed. William David Sloan and James D. Startt, 3rd ed. (Northport, Ala.: Vision, 1996), 226.

3. North, "Catalog of Periodical Publications," Tenth U.S. Census, 1880, 8:206. This includes publications under the same ownership but issued on both a daily and a weekly basis, a common practice among city newspapers of the period.

4. Kemble, *History of California Newspapers,* 100.

5. North, "Catalog of Periodical Publications," Tenth U.S. Census, 1880, 8:206. By contrast, Boston, with which we have previously compared San Francisco as the heart of journalism for their respective areas, had only one foreign-language periodical among its 153 publications in 1880. New York State, the East Coast's second center of

journalism, had 131 foreign-language newspapers. It should be noted that 1880 census data was subject to whether publishers bothered to return the questionnaire, and may be incomplete.

6. Associated Press Analysis, "In New York and Elsewhere, Ethnic Press Blossoms as Diversity Grows," June 5, 2001, Freedom Forum, Newsroom Diversity, www.freedomforum.org/templates/document.asp?documentID=14070.

7. New America Media, http://news.newamericamedia.org/news/view_custom.html?custom_page_id=87.

8. Félix Gutiérrez, "Spanish-Language Media in America: Background, Resources, History," *Journalism History* 4, no. 2 (Summer 1977): 37. Gutiérrez notes there may have been an earlier publication because *El Misisipí* referenced *Diario de New York* in an item, but there is no other reference to a newspaper of that name in New York at that time. Even if there were, it may not have been a Spanish-language periodical, in spite of its name (*diario* is the Spanish word for *daily*).

9. Victoria Goff, "Spanish-Language Newspapers in California," in *Outsiders in 19th-Century Press History,* ed. Frankie Hutton and Barbara Straus Reed (Bowling Green, Ohio: Bowling Green State University Press, 1995), 59.

10. Ibid., 38.

11. Ibid., 41. Quotations are from *El Clamor Público,* August 28 and July 26, 1856, and April 26, 1857.

12. Goff, "Spanish-Language Newspapers," 61.

13. Ibid., 56.

14. *Tung-ngai san-luk* in Chinese, according to Wesley Norton, who says Chinese newspapers started even earlier—when Speer and his Old School Presbyterians issued the *Watchman* in 1850 for four issues. A fire of "suspicious origins" ended its run. The *Oriental* lasted two years. Wesley Norton, "'Like a Thousand Preachers Flying': Religious Newspapers on the Pacific Coast to 1865," *California Historical Quarterly* 56 (Fall 1977): 197.

15. William Huntzicker, "Chinese-American Newspapers," in *Outsiders in 19th-Century Press History,* ed. Hutton and Reed, 77. Kemble's *History of California Newspapers* has different dates for the *Golden Hill News,* which he says started in 1854 and "did not live long"

(117). Kemble dates the *Oriental* from January 1855; it was issued three times a week, and it survived two years (120). Kemble also says the only foreign-language newspaper in Sacramento prior to 1859 was the *Chinese News,* started in December 1856 and published for almost two years.

16. Quoted in Knight, "Frontier Newspaper," 78. "Tilting hoops" probably refers to the skirt style common in the nineteenth century, in which some of the skirts supported by metal or wooden hoops were wider to the side, rather than round; they were designed to be tilted when the wearer had to move in a narrow space. "Waterfalls" were the cascading lace jabots many women of the time wore, in contrast to the more austere dress of the Chinese women.

17. See also the discussion of utopian newspapers later in this chapter.

18. Clarence B. Bagley, *History of Seattle,* 3 vols. (Chicago: S. J. Clarke, 1916), 2:458.

19. See the next section of this chapter for the story of the *California Eagle*'s outstanding and controversial twentieth-century editor, Charlotta Spears Bass.

20. Kemble, *History of California Newspapers,* 284.

21. Alter, *Early Utah Journalism,* 274.

22. Ibid., 307–12.

23. See, for example, Kimberley Mangun, "The (Oregon) *Advocate:* Boosting the Race and Portland, Too," *American Journalism* 23 (Winter 2006): 7–34. The *Advocate* was started in 1903.

24. Kathleen A. Cairns, *Front-Page Women Journalists, 1920–1950* (Lincoln: University of Nebraska Press, 2003), 74.

25. Ibid., 80. According to Cairns, sources give Spears's birth date anywhere from 1874 to 1890, and her birthplace as South Carolina or Ohio, her siblings as three to ten in number, and her maiden name as Spear or Spears. She wrote an autobiography, but that, too, is apparently unreliable as to details of her life.

26. Ibid., 81.

27. Ibid., 83.

28. Ibid., 84.

29. Ibid., 85.

30. Quoted ibid. This was probably Bass's least successful boycott; usually she rallied the black community successfully.

31. Ibid., 36.

32. Ibid., 92–93.

33. Quoted in James Phillip Jeter, "Black Press Editorial Commentary on the Japanese Internment During World War II," paper delivered to the Association for Education in Journalism and Mass Communication, 1986, referencing the *California Eagle,* February 12, 1942.

34. Ibid., referencing the *California Eagle,* April 30, 1923.

35. Ibid., quoting from the *California Eagle,* January 1, 1942.

36. Southern California Library for Social Studies and Research, http://www.socallib.org/bass/story/candidate.html. This library in Los Angeles is the repository of Charlotta Bass's papers.

37. Rodger Streitmatter, *Raising Her Voice: African-American Women Journalists Who Changed History* (Lexington: University Press of Kentucky, 1994), 95.

38. Arlington Russell Mortenson, "The Deseret News and Utah, 1850–1867" (Ph.D. diss., University of California, Los Angeles, 1949), ii.

39. Alter, *Early Utah Journalism,* 90, 108.

40. Robert F. Karolevitz, *Newspapering in the Old West: A Pictorial History of Journalism and Printing on the Frontier* (New York: Bonanza Books, 1965), 60.

41. Quoted in Ashton, *Voice in the West,* 6.

42. Ibid., 42.

43. Ibid., 47.

44. Ibid., 62. Other western newspapers also took chickens and other food for payment on occasion. Cash generally was in short supply in the West during this period.

45. Ibid., 53–58.

46. Alter, *Early Utah Journalism,* 147.

47. Ibid., 146.

48. Ibid., 302–3.

49. Ibid., 304. Alter quotes the *Deseret News* of October 13, 1885: "By the time this reaches the eye of the Public the writer will be an inmate of the Utah Penitentiary. The power that put me there was

also instrumental in placing me during the present year in temporary charge of the editorial columns of this journal. It drove the chief of the staff into exile, and I, being his associate, have endeavored in my humble way with the help of God to fill his place during his enforced absence . . . John Nicholson."

50. Memoranda to various LDS leaders, "Charles W. Penrose Correspondence: 1887 Newspaper Campaign," http://jfs.saintswithouthalos.com/pri/cwp_1887media.htm.

51. Ibid.

52. Norton, " 'Like a Thousand Preachers Flying,' " 196.

53. Ibid., 198.

54. Ibid., 197.

55. *Daily Dramatic Chronicle,* February 15, 1865.

56. Kemble, *History of California Newspapers,* 112.

57. Bennion, *Equal to the Occasion,* 15.

58. Kemble, *History of California Newspapers,* 129.

59. Bennion, *Equal to the Occasion,* 19.

60. Kemble, *History of California Newspapers,* 128; Bennion, *Equal to the Occasion,* 131.

61. Bennion, *Equal to the Occasion,* 108–9.

62. Quoted ibid., 109.

63. Ibid., 113–14.

64. Ibid., 115.

65. Ibid., 116–17. Bennion relates more details of the lives of these remarkable women.

66. Barbara Cloud, "Cooperation and Printers Ink," *Rendezvous* 19, no. 1 (Fall 1983): 33–42. The account that follows is taken from this article.

67. This was done by taking the pieces of type usually used to print fine lines and turning them over so that the wider base was inked, resulting in a heavy border.

68. Charles Pierce LeWarne, *Utopias on Puget Sound, 1885–1915* (Seattle: University of Washington Press, 1975), 58. Equality Colony, formed in 1897, was named for utopian Edward Bellamy's book *Equality* (1897).

69. Quoted in LeWarne, *Utopias on Puget Sound,* 123.

70. Quoted ibid., 213. The story of the Home Colony is related in chapter 6 of LeWarne's study.

71. Sherilyn Cox Bennion, "The Woman Suffrage Press of the West," in *Outsiders in 19th-Century Press History,* ed. Hutton and Reed, 169.

72. Ibid., 170. These are periodicals of which copies survive. Others are mentioned in directories and by other newspapers.

73. Ibid., 171.

74. Ibid.

75. Ibid.

76. Ibid., 173.

77. Bennion, *Equal to the Occasion,* 74.

78. Ibid., 75.

79. Ibid.

80. Quoted ibid.

81. Ibid., 77.

82. North, "Catalog of Periodical Publications," Tenth U.S. Census, 1880, 8:285.

CHAPTER EIGHT

1. *World Almanac and Book of Facts, 2006* (New York: World Almanac Education Group, 2006), 475.

2. Charles C. Mann, *1491: New Revelations of the Americas Before Columbus* (New York: Alfred A. Knopf, 2005). Mann's discussion of native cultures extends into the post-Columbus era and thus is relevant to the history of the frontier, as well as to the Atlantic seaboard.

3. See chapter 1.

4. Robert E. Huffman, "Newspaper Art in Stockton, 1850–1892," *California Historical Society Quarterly* 34 (December 1955): 345–46.

5. *Oregonian* (Portland), January 7, 1873.

6. Ibid.

7. Ashton, *Voice in the West,* 74.

8. George N. Belknap, "*Oregon Sentinel* Extras—1858–1864," *Pacific Northwest Quarterly* 70 (October 1979): 180.

9. *Arizona Miner* (Prescott), January 24, 1867.

10. *Reese River Reveille* (Austin, Nevada), September 7, 1878.

11. *Oakland Tribune,* May 17, 1874.

12. Quoted in Turnbull, *History of Oregon Newspapers,* 73.

13. Ibid., 150.

14. See chapter 6, in particular the example of Arizona.

15. Quoted in Turnbull, *History of Oregon Newspapers,* 74.

16. *Idaho Avalanche,* September 28, 1878.

17. Knight, "Frontier Newspaper," 77.

18. *Seattle Daily Call,* September 1885–February 1886.

19. *Sonora Union Democrat,* June 26, 1875, quoted in Helen Rocca Goss, "The Fourth Estate in Old Tuolumne," *Historical Society of Southern California Quarterly* 40 (June 1958): 128.

20. *Mariposa Gazette,* January 1, 1869, also quoted by Goss, "Fourth Estate," 129.

21. *White Pine News* (Hamilton, Nevada), February 27, 1875.

22. Jack A. Nelson, "The Missing Social Conscience of the Frontier Press," paper presented at the West Coast Journalism Historians conference, January 20, 1982.

23. Ibid., 1.

24. Ibid., 6.

25. Ibid., 9. Nelson seems to share Mrs. Leslie's lack of enthusiasm for Nevada.

26. Ibid., citing Lucius Beebe, *Comstock Commotion* (Stanford, Calif.: Stanford University Press, 1954), 49.

27. Nelson, "Missing Social Conscience," 10.

28. Ibid., 10–11.

29. The *San Francisco Bulletin* printed the doctor's letter on February 11, 1859, essentially ending the ruckus.

30. Jack A. Nelson, "Tall Tales, Wild Lies and Hoaxes: Those Comical Frontier Editors," paper presented at the American Journalism Historians Association conference, October 1985, 2, quoting the *Nye County News* in Ione, Nevada, June 15, 1866.

31. Nelson, "Tall Tales," 2, quoting from *Bill Nye: His Own Life Story,* ed. Frank Wilson Nye (New York: Century, 1926), 82.

32. Nelson, "Tall Tales," 3.

33. Ibid.

CHAPTER NINE

1. "O young Lochinvar is come out of the West / Through all the wide Border his steed was the best"—a reference to a section in Sir Walter Scott's long narrative poem *Marmion*. The young Highlander arrives too late to prevent the wedding of his love to another man but rides off with her anyway, an example of the boldness and creativity of westerners in getting what they want. The poem can be found in many collections of Scott's works or at http://homepages.wmich .edu/~cooney/poems/Scott.Lochinvar.html.

2. *Associated Press et al. v. United States,* 326 U.S. 1; 65 S.Ct. 1416; 89 L.ED. 2013 (1945).

3. *United States v. Citizen Publishing Co.,* 280 F. Supp. 978 (D. Ariz. 1968).

4. *Citizen Publishing v. U.S.,* 394 U.S. 131 (1969).

5. *U.S. Code* 15 § 1801.

6. Data about current JOAs are taken from the Detroit *Free Press's* Web site freep.com, "Jobs Page," http://www.freep.com/legacy/ jobspage/links/joa.htm. The list of terminated JOAs, as of November 2006, contains an error. The two Las Vegas newspapers continue their agreement, although it is correct that the *Sun* is published as an insert in the *Review-Journal,* not as a separate newspaper.

7. *Las Vegas Review-Journal,* June 15, 2005, 1.

8. Congress passed the Clayton Act in 1914 to strengthen the nineteenth-century Sherman Antitrust Act. Section 7 of the Act (*U.S. Code* 15 § 18) has to do with lessening competition.

9. See chapter 10 for the role of the *Los Angeles Times* in western history.

10. Michael S. Green, "Valley Times," Online Nevada Encyclo- pedia, www.onlinenevada.org/valley-times.

11. Michael Green, "The *Valley Times:* A Personal History," in *Change in the American West: Exploring the Human Dimension,* ed. Stephen Tchudi (Reno: University of Nevada Press, 1996), 214. Green worked at the *Valley Times* in the 1980s. The account of the newspaper is taken from this book chapter unless otherwise cited.

12. Ibid.

13. Greenspun bought the *News* in 1955; in 1959 the paper was combined with Yacenda's *North Las Vegas and Moapa Valley Times* (Lingenfelter and Gash, *Newspapers of Nevada,* 158–59).

14. Moapa is an agricultural community about sixty miles east of the Las Vegas Valley.

15. Green, "A Personal History," 217.

16. See the next section of this chapter for the history of the *Las Vegas Sun.*

17. Gibbons, who was elected on the heels of accusations of sexual improprieties—no charges were ever brought—has also been accused of using his former position of U.S. representative to help a longtime friend get secret government defense contracts in exchange for campaign contributions. Again, no charges had been filed as of spring 2008.

18. Hank Greenspun with Alex Pelle, *Where I Stand: The Record of a Reckless Man* (New York: David McKay, 1966), 2. Full disclosure: the author, though retired, is still associated with the Hank Greenspun School of Journalism and Media Studies at the University of Nevada, Las Vegas, for which the family is a major benefactor.

19. Ibid., 4–5. Unless otherwise cited, Greenspun's biographical information comes from his autobiography, *Where I Stand.*

20. Ibid., 5.

21. Ibid.

22. Ibid., 68.

23. Ibid. By this time, the Greenspuns had a daughter, Susan, and another child on the way.

24. Ibid., 181.

25. Ibid., 184–85. See also Jennifer Robison, "Sun's History Dates to 1950," *Las Vegas Review-Journal,* June 15, 2005, 5A.

26. Greenspun, *Where I Stand,* 187. Greenspun ultimately paid $104,000 for the newspaper and its equipment (Moehring, *Resort City,* 90).

27. Greenspun, *Where I Stand,* 200.

28. Ibid., 203. See also Moehring, *Resort City,* 91.

29. Greenspun, *Where I Stand,* 217.

30. Moehring, *Resort City,* 91.

31. Robison, "Sun's History."

32. Moehring, *Resort City,* 91. Contrary to popular opinion, prostitution is not legal in Las Vegas or Clark County.

33. Circulation growth of the *Review-Journal* has not kept pace with the population growth of the Las Vegas Valley. The *Review-Journal*'s circulation is about 220,000 in the valley, which has a population of 1.8 million. However, a high rate of transience is often blamed for the disproportionately small number of subscribers.

34. J. M. Kalil, "Agreement Keeps LV Two-Newspaper Town," *Las Vegas Review-Journal,* June 15, 2005, 5A.

35. Brian Greenspun, "Where I Stand," *Las Vegas Sun,* June 15, 2005.

36. With a population of more than two hundred thousand, the "bedroom" suburb of Henderson has become Nevada's second-largest city, surpassing Reno. When a population of 1.8 million is cited for Las Vegas, as it often is, the number is for the metropolitan area, which includes Henderson and North Las Vegas.

37. Jake Highton, *Nevada Newspaper Days: A History of Journalism in the Silver State* (Stockton, Calif.: Heritage West Books, 1990), 254.

38. Ibid., 255.

39. Ibid.

40. Ibid.

41. Quoted ibid.

42. Quoted ibid.

43. Quoted ibid., 257.

44. In addition, the journalism school at the University of Nevada, Reno, bears Reynolds's name, while its counterpart at the University of Nevada, Las Vegas, is named for Greenspun. A gift from the Reynolds Foundation helped fund the University of Nevada, Las Vegas, Student Services Center, while a Greenspun Family Foundation gift helped fund the Greenspun College of Urban Affairs and the new ninety-four-million-dollar Greenspun Hall, expected to open in 2008.

CHAPTER TEN

1. Kemble, *History of California Newspapers*, 232.

2. Ibid., 233.

3. Ibid., 328, 357.

4. Ibid., 92–93.

5. Ibid., 359. I have not been able to establish whether this McElroy is related to the McElroy who started the *Columbian*, the first newspaper in Washington Territory.

6. *Los Angeles Star*, May 24, 1851.

7. Kemble, *History of California Newspapers*, 347. Since Kemble wrote his history in 1858, it's hard to see how he would have had enough information to know whether Hamilton's career was either long or successful.

8. Ibid., 234–35.

9. Ibid., 254.

10. McDougal, *Privileged Son*, 8. Most of the Chandler story is drawn from McDougal's book. Full-page views of the first issue of the *Times* can be found on ProQuest, a full-text library service.

11. Ketupa.net, http://www.ketupa.net/latimes.htm.

12. David Halberstam, *The Powers That Be* (New York: Alfred A. Knopf, 1979), 104.

13. McDougal, *Privileged Son*, 10–11.

14. Ibid.

15. California State Military Museum, http://www.militarymuseum .org/Otis.html.

16. California State Military Museum; McDougal, *Privileged Son*, 12.

17. McDougal, *Privileged Son*, 13.

18. Ibid.

19. Ibid., 14.

20. Ibid., 15.

21. Ibid.

22. Halberstam, *Powers That Be*, 110. According to McDougal's account, the Bridge and Structural Iron Workers union even had a supervisor of dynamite operations (McDougal, *Privileged Son*, 52).

23. McDougal, *Privileged Son*, 21.

24. Ibid., 24.

25. Ibid., 29.

26. Ibid., 37.

27. Ibid., 40.

28. Ibid., 65.

29. Ibid., 72–73.

30. Ibid., 90.

31. Ibid., 89.

32. Ibid.

33. Ibid., 219.

34. The *Los Angeles Times* has won some thirty Pulitzers, the most recent in 2007 for explanatory reporting. Seven were awarded during Otis Chandler's years.

35. McDougal, *Privileged Son,* 221.

36. Ibid., 222.

37. Ibid., 260.

38. Ibid., 344.

39. *New York Times,* September 21, 2006, http://www.nytimes .com/2006/9/21/business/media/21tribune.html?ex'1316491200&en.

40. Ibid.

41. Drake Bennett, "Return of the Press Barons: As a New Breed of Aspiring Press Moguls Talk About Buying Big City Dailies, There's More Than Just an Industry at Stake," *Boston Globe,* November 19, 2006, E1, available through ProQuest.

42. *New York Times,* November 29, 2006, online edition, available through ProQuest.

43. Katharine Q. Seelye and Terry Pristin, "Sam Zell, the 'Grave Dancer,' Sees Profit in Newspapers," *International Herald Tribune,* March 25, 2007, http://www.iht.com/articles/2007/03/25/business/ zell.php.

44. Richard Pérez-Peña, "Los Angeles Times Editor Forced Out," *New York Times,* January 21, 2008, http://www.nytimers/2008/01/ 021/business/media/21latimes-web.html?ex=1358571600&en= 0ff3a4690fb5e51c&ei=5088&partner=rssnyt&emc=rss.

45. Ibid.

46. Seelye and Pristin, "Sam Zell."

47. Kemble, *History of California Newspapers*, 133–37.

48. Ibid., 138–39.

49. Ibid., 143.

50. Ibid., 144.

51. Ibid., 145–46.

52. Ibid., 146–47.

53. Ibid., 162.

54. Ibid., 359.

55. The post–gold rush era McClatchy history is taken from the McClatchy Company's Web site at http://www.mcclatchy.com/100/story/179.html.

56. Ibid. Of the thirty-two dailies, McClatchy "announced its intentions to sell twelve that didn't fit its longstanding acquisition philosophy of buying newspapers in fast-growing markets," according to the company Web site.

57. The numbers are from MediaNews Group's Web site, at http://www.medianewsgroup.com/home.

58. Scott Sherman, "The Evolution of Dean Singleton," *Columbia Journalism Review* 41, no. 6 (March/April 2003), http://www.cjr.org/issues/2003/dean-sherman.asp?printerfriendly=yes.

59. Ibid.

60. Ibid.

61. Carolyn Said, "2 Bay Area Papers to Join Growing Media Group," *San Francisco Chronicle*, April 27, 2006, http://www.sfgate.com/cgi-bin/article.cgi?f=/c/a/2006/04/47/MNG52IG4I.T1.DTL.

62. Ibid.

63. Ibid.

CHAPTER ELEVEN

1. John L. O'Sullivan, "The Great Nation of Futurity," *United States Magazine and Democratic Review* 6, no. 23 (November 1839): 427.

2. *Silver State* (Unionville, Nevada), March 22, 1870.

3. O'Sullivan, "Annexation," 5.

4. Interestingly, linking the attribution of "Go West, young man"

to Greeley can be as confusing as trying to track "manifest destiny" to O'Sullivan. In spring 2007, an Internet search on O'Sullivan's phrase takes the researcher primarily to the 1839 article in which, as noted, he wrote around it but did not actually use the phrase "manifest destiny." Greeley gets credit, most sources agree, for an editorial "To Aspiring Young Men" in which he advises those struggling with the hardships of the 1830s that "if you have no family or friends to aid you, and no prospect opened to you there, turn your face to the Great West, and there build up a home and fortune" (quoted by his primary biographer, James Parton, *Life of Horace Greeley* [New York: Mason Brothers, 1855], 414). The real originator of the phrase, according to most sources other than Parton, was John B. L. Soule, editor of the *Terre Haute* (Indiana) *Express,* who, in 1851, wrote an editorial titled "Go West, young man, and grow up with the country." In either case, the phrase as generally cited has been simplified. Thomas Fuller has probably done the most exhaustive research on the source of the phrase. See his article "Go West, Young Man—An Elusive Slogan" in the *Indiana Magazine of History* 100, no. 3 (September 2004): 231–42.

5. See the 1630 sermon by Congregationalist John Winthrop, "A Model of Christian Charity," in which he tells the Puritans that "we shall be as a City upon a Hill, the eyes of all people are upon us." This sermon has been reprinted in many sources, including Perry Miller, ed., *The American Puritans: Their Prose and Poetry* (Garden City, N.Y.: Doubleday Anchor Books, 1956), 83.

6. William H. Lyon, "The Significance of Newspapers on the American Frontier," in *Journalism in the West,* ed. William H. Lyon (Manhattan, Kans.: Sunflower University, 1980), 9.

7. The professor shall be anonymous to protect him from western publishers who are not so cynical about their motives.

8. Edgar Eugene Eaton, "A History of Olympia Newspapers" (M.A. thesis, University of Washington, 1963), 130.

9. While Thornton McElroy was publisher of the *Columbian* in Olympia, Washington, he attended at least one printers' convention in Portland.

10. "Ratting" was a form of blacklisting.

11. *Journalist,* March 16, 1889.

12. Meany, *Newspapers of Washington Territory,* 48.

13. See, for example, *Seattle Times,* http://archives.seattletimes
.nwsource.com/cgi_bin/texis.cgi/web/vortex/display?slug=joa211&
date=20070221&query=pryne.

14. For example, a reporter from the *Los Angeles Times* is often
part of the panel on programs like *Washington Week in Review,* on PBS
television.

15. Larry McMurtry, *Sacagawea's Nickname: Essays on the American
West* (New York: New York Review of Books, 2001), 21.

SELECTED BIBLIOGRAPHY

BOOKS AND ARTICLES

Alter, J. Cecil. *Early Utah Journalism: A Half Century of Forensic Warfare, Waged by the West's Most Militant Press.* 1938; reprint, Westport, Conn.: Greenwood, 1970.

Ambrose, Stephen E. *Nothing Like It in the World: The Men Who Built the Transcontinental Railroad, 1863–1869.* New York: Simon and Schuster, 2000.

American National Biography, s.v. "Joseph Thompson Goodman," 9:244. New York: Oxford University Press, 1999.

Armstrong, Robert D. *Nevada Printing History.* Reno: University of Nevada Press, 1981.

Ashton, Wendell J. *Voice in the West: Biography of a Pioneer Newspaper.* New York: Duell, Sloan and Pearce, 1950.

Associated Press Analysis. "In New York and Elsewhere, Ethnic Press Blossoms as Diversity Grows." June 5, 2001. Freedom Forum, Newsroom Diversity. www.freedomforum.org/ templates/document.asp?documentID=14070.

Athearn, Robert G. *Union Pacific Country.* Lincoln: University of Nebraska Press, 1971.

Atwood, Roy Alden. "Handwritten Newspapers on the Iowa Frontier, 1844–1854." *Journalism History* 7, no. 2 (Summer 1980): 56–59.

Bagley, Clarence B. Personal papers. Northwest Collection, University of Washington Libraries.

———. *History of King County, Washington.* 3 vols. Seattle: S. J. Clarke, 1929.

———. *History of Seattle.* 3 vols. Chicago: S. J. Clarke, 1916.

Baldasty, Gerald J. *The Commercialization of News in the Nineteenth Century.* Madison: University of Wisconsin Press, 1992.

————. *E. W. Scripps and the Business of Newspapers.* Urbana: University of Illinois Press, 1999.

————. "The Press and Politics in the Gilded Age." Paper presented at the West Coast Journalism Historians conference, February 1987.

Beard, Charles A., and Mary Beard. *New Basic History of the United States.* New York: Doubleday, 1968.

Beebe, Lucius. *Comstock Commotion: The Story of the Territorial Enterprise.* Stanford, Calif.: Stanford University Press, 1954.

Belknap, George N. "*Oregon Sentinel* Extras—1858–1864." *Pacific Northwest Quarterly* 70 (October 1979): 180.

Bennett, Drake. "Return of the Press Barons: As a New Breed of Aspiring Press Moguls Talk About Buying Big City Dailies, There's More Than Just an Industry at Stake." *Boston Globe,* November 19, 2006, E1. Available through ProQuest.

Bennion, Sherilyn Cox. *Equal to the Occasion: Women Editors of the Nineteenth-Century West.* Reno: University of Nevada Press, 1990.

Billington, Ray Allen. *America's Frontier Heritage.* 1963; reprint, Albuquerque: University of New Mexico Press, 1974.

————. *The Far Western Frontier: 1830–1860.* New York: Harper, 1956.

Biographical Directory of the United States Congress. Internet edition. http://bioguide.congress.gov/scripts/biodisplay.pl?index=M000371.

Blainey, Geoffrey. *The Tyranny of Distance.* Melbourne, Australia: Sun Books, 1966.

Blair, Walter, ed. *Mark Twain's West: The Author's Memoirs About His Boyhood, Riverboats and Western Adventures.* Chicago: Lakeside, 1983.

Blanchard, Margaret A., ed. *History of the Mass Media in the United States: An Encyclopedia.* Chicago: Fitzroy Dearborn, 1998.

Blankenship, Mrs. George E., comp. and ed. *Early History of Thurston County, Washington.* Olympia, 1914.

Boorstin, Daniel J. *The Americans: The National Experience.* New York: Vintage Books, 1965.

Boswell, Sharon A., and Lorraine McConaghy. *Raise Hell and Sell Newspapers: Alden J. Blethen and the Seattle Times.* Pullman: Washington State University Press, 1996.

Brier, Warren, J. "A History of Newspapers in the Pacific Northwest, 1846–1896." Ph.D. dissertation, State University of Iowa, 1957.

Brier, Warren J., and Nathan B. Blumberg, eds. *A Century of Montana Journalism.* Missoula, Mont.: Mountain Press, 1971.

Bruce, John. *Gaudy Century: The Story of San Francisco's Hundred Years of Robust Journalism.* New York: Random House, 1948.

Cairns, Kathleen A. *Front-Page Women Journalists, 1920–1950.* Lincoln: University of Nebraska Press, 2003.

Chandler, Robert J. "The California News-Telegraph Monopoly, 1860–1870." *Southern California Quarterly* 58 (Winter 1976): 459–84.

Cloud, Barbara. *The Business of Newspapers on the Western Frontier.* Reno: University of Nevada Press, 1992.

————. "Cooperation and Printer's Ink." *Rendezvous* 19, no. 1 (Fall 1983): 33–42.

————. "News: Public Service or Profitable Property?" *American Journalism* 13 (Spring 1996): 141–56.

————. "Oregon in the 1820s: The Congressional Perspective." *Western Historical Quarterly* 12 (April 1981): 145–64.

————. "A Party Press? You Bet, but Not Just Yet! Political Publishing on the Frontier." *Journalism History* 7, no. 2 (Summer 1980): 54–55, 72–73.

————. "Photographic Technology." In *History of the Mass Media in the United States: An Encyclopedia,* edited by Margaret A. Blanchard. Chicago: Fitzroy, Dearborn, 1998.

————. "Start the Presses: The Birth of Journalism in Washington Territory." Ph.D. diss., University of Washington, 1979.

Connelly, Dolly. "Gold Rush Produced Northwest Washington's First Newspaper." *Seattle Times Magazine,* February 22, 1959, 4.

Copeland, David A. *The Idea of a Free Press: The Enlightenment and Its Unruly Legacy.* Evanston, Ill.: Northwestern University Press, 2006.

Dary, David. *Red Blood and Black Ink: Journalism in the Old West.* New York: Alfred A. Knopf, 1998.

Dicken-Garcia, Hazel. "News Manufacturing in Late Nineteenth-Century America." Paper presented at the American Journalism Historians Association conference, Wichita, Kans., October 2006.

Dictionary of American Biography Base Set, s.v. "Henry Villard." American Council of Learned Societies, 1928–36. Reproduced in Gale Group, "History Resource Center," http://galenet.galegroup.com/servlet/HistRC/.

Doten, Alfred. *The Journals of Alfred Doten, 1849–1903.* Edited by Walter Van Tilburg Clark. Reno: University of Nevada Press, 1973.

Drury, Wells. *An Editor on the Comstock Lode.* New York: Farrar and Rinehart, 1936.

Eaton, Edgar Eugene. "A History of Olympia Newspapers." M.A. thesis, University of Washington, 1963.

Edwards, Jonathan. *An Illustrated History of Spokane County.* W. H. Lever, 1900.

Elliott, Russell R. *History of Nevada.* Lincoln: University of Nebraska Press, 1973.

Evensen, Bruce. "Yellow Gold for a Yellow Press." Research in progress paper presented at the American Journalism Historians Association conference, October 2004.

Fatout, Paul. *Mark Twain in Virginia City.* Bloomington: Indiana University Press, 1964.

Gates, Paul Wallace. *The Illinois Central Railroad and Its Colonization Work.* Cambridge, Mass.: Harvard University Press, 1934.

Gilbert, Frank T. *Historic Sketches of Walla Walla, Whitman, Columbia and Garfield Counties, Washington Territory.* Portland, Ore.: A. G. Walling, 1882.

Gilluly, Sam. *The Press Gang: A Century of Montana Newspapers, 1885–1985.* Helena, Mont.: Montana Press Association, 1985.

Goff, Victoria. "Spanish-Language Newspapers in California." In *Outsiders in 19th-Century Press History,* edited by Frankie Hutton and Barbara Straus Reed. Bowling Green, Ohio: Bowling Green State University Press, 1995.

Goss, Helen Rocca. "The Fourth Estate in Old Tuolumne." *Historical Society of Southern California Quarterly* 40 (June 1958): 128.

Green, Michael S. "Valley Times." Online Nevada Encyclopedia. www.onlinenevada.org/valley-times.

————. "The *Valley Times*: A Personal History." In *Change in the American West: Exploring the Human Dimension,* edited by Stephen Tchudi. Reno: University of Nevada Press, 1996.

Greenspun, Brian. "Where I Stand." *Las Vegas Sun,* June 15, 2005.

Greenspun, Hank, with Alex Pelle. *Where I Stand: The Record of a Reckless Man.* New York: David McKay, 1966.

Gutiérrez, Félix. "Spanish-Language Media in America: Background, Resources, History." *Journalism History* 4, no. 2 (Summer 1977): 34–47.

Gutiérrez, Félix, and Ernesto Ballesteros. "The 1541 Earthquake: Dawn of Latin American Journalism." *Journalism History* 6, no. 3 (Autumn 1979): 78–83.

Halaas, David Fridtjof. *Boom Town Newspapers: Journalism on the Rocky Mountain Mining Frontier, 1859–1881.* Albuquerque: University of New Mexico Press, 1981.

Halberstam, David. *The Powers That Be.* New York: Alfred A. Knopf, 1979.

Harter, Eugene C. *Boilerplating America: The Hidden Newspaper.* Edited by Dorothy Harter. Lanham, Md.: University Press of America, 1991.

Hedges, James B. "Promotion of Immigration to the Pacific Northwest by the Railroads." *Mississippi Valley Historical Review* 15 (September 1925): 183–203.

Hester, Al. "Newspapers and Newspaper Prototypes in Spanish America, 1541–1750." *Journalism History* 6, no. 3 (Autumn 1979): 73–77, 88.

Heuterman, Thomas H. *Movable Type: Biography of Legh R. Freeman.* Ames: Iowa State University Press, 1979.

Highton, Jake. *Nevada Newspaper Days: A History of Journalism in the Silver State.* Stockton, Calif.: Heritage West Books, 1990.

Holbrook, Stewart. *The Story of American Railroads.* New York: Crown, 1947.

Hudson, Frederic. *Journalism in the United States*. 1873; reprint, Grosse Pointe, Mich.: Scholarly Press, 1968.

Huffman, Robert E. "Newspaper Art in Stockton, 1850–1892." *California Historical Society Quarterly* 34 (December 1955): 345–46.

Huntzicker, William. "Chinese-American Newspapers." In *Outsiders in 19th-Century Press History,* edited by Frankie Hutton and Barbara Straus Reed. Bowling Green, Ohio: Bowling Green State University Press, 1995.

Hutton, Frankie, and Barbara Straus Reed, eds. *Outsiders in 19th-Century Press History*. Bowling Green, Ohio: Bowling Green State University Press, 1995.

Illustrated History of Skagit and Snohomish Counties. Chicago: Interstate, 1906.

James, Ronald. "Territorial Enterprise." Online Nevada Encyclopedia. http://www.onlinenevada.org/territorial_enterprise.

James, Ronald M., and Elizabeth Raymond. *Comstock Women: The Making of a Mining Community*. Reno: University of Nevada Press, 1998.

Jeffcott, Percival R. *Nooksack Tales and Trails*. Ferndale, Wash.: Sedro-Woolley Courier-Times, 1949.

Johansen, Dorothy O. *Empire of the Columbia: A History of the Pacific Northwest*. 2nd ed. New York: Harper and Row, 1967.

Kalil, J. M. "Agreement Keeps LV Two-Newspaper Town." *Las Vegas Review-Journal,* June 15, 2005.

Karolevitz, Robert F. *Newspapering in the Old West: A Pictorial History of Journalism and Printing on the Frontier*. New York: Bonanza Books, 1965.

Katz, W. A. "Public Printers of Washington Territory, 1863–1889." *Pacific Northwest Quarterly* 51 (October 1960): 171–81.

Kemble, Edward C. *A History of California Newspapers*. 1858. Edited with a foreword by Helen Harding Bretnor. Los Gatos, Calif.: Talisman, 1962.

Knight, Oliver. "The Frontier Newspaper as a Catalyst in Social Change." *Pacific Northwest Quarterly* 58, no. 2 (April 1967): 74–81.

————. Review of *The Pioneer Editor in Missouri, 1808–1860,* by William H. Lyon. *Journalism Quarterly* 42, no. 3 (Summer 1965): 478–79.

Kuykendall, Ralph S. "History of Early California Journalism." M.A. thesis, University of California, Berkeley, 1918.

Lamar, Howard Roberts. *The Far Southwest, 1846–1912: A Territorial History.* New Haven, Conn.: Yale University Press, 1966; New York: W. W. Norton, 1970.

Lee, Alfred McClung. *The Daily Newspaper in America.* New York: Macmillan, 1937.

Leubke, Frederick C. "Regionalism and the Great Plains: Problems of Concept and Method." *Western Historical Quarterly* 15 (1984): 19–38.

Levy, JoAnn. *They Saw the Elephant: Women in the California Gold Rush.* Norman: University of Oklahoma Press, 1992.

LeWarne, Charles Pierce. *Utopias on Puget Sound, 1885–1915.* Seattle: University of Washington Press, 1975.

Lewis, Oscar. *The Big Four.* New York: Alfred A. Knopf, 1966.

Limerick, Patricia Nelson. *The Legacy of Conquest: The Unbroken Past of the American West.* New York: W. W. Norton, 1987.

Lingenfelter, Richard E. *Death Valley and the Amargosa: A Land of Illusion.* Berkeley: University of California Press, 1986.

Lingenfelter, Richard E., and Karen Rix Gash. *The Newspapers of Nevada: A History and Bibliography, 1854–1979.* Reno: University of Nevada Press, 1984.

Lotchin, Roger W. *San Francisco, 1846–1856: From Hamlet to City.* New York: Oxford University Press, 1974.

Lyon, William H. "Louis C. Hughes, Arizona's Editorial Gadfly." *Journal of Arizona History* 24 (Summer 1983): 171–200.

———. *Those Old Yellow Dog Days: Frontier Journalism in Arizona, 1859–1912.* Tucson: Arizona Historical Society, 1994.

———. *The Pioneer Editor in Missouri, 1808–1860.* Columbia: University of Missouri Press, 1965.

———. "The Significance of Newspapers on the American Frontier." In *Journalism in the West,* edited by William H. Lyon. Manhattan, Kans.: Sunflower University, 1980.

Mangun, Kimberley. "The (Oregon) *Advocate:* Boosting the Race and Portland, Too." *American Journalism* 23 (Winter 2006): 7–34.

Mann, Charles C. *1491: New Revelations of the Americas Before Columbus.* New York: Alfred A. Knopf, 2005.

Martin, Albro. *James J. Hill and the Opening of the Northwest.* 1976; reprint, St. Paul: Minnesota Historical Society, 1991.

Martin, Douglas D. *Tombstone's Epitaph.* Albuquerque: University of New Mexico Press, 1951.

McDougal, Dennis. *Privileged Son: Otis Chandler and the Rise and Fall of the L.A. Times Dynasty.* Cambridge, Mass.: Perseus, 2001.

McElroy, Thornton F. Family papers, University of Washington Libraries.

McIntyre, Jerilyn. "Communication on a Western Frontier—Some Questions About Context." *Journalism History* 3, no. 2 (Summer 1976): 53–55.

McMurtry, Larry. *Sacagawea's Nickname: Essays on the American West.* New York: New York Review of Books, 2001.

Meany, Edmund S. *Newspapers of Washington Territory.* 1922–23; reprint, Seattle: University of Washington Press, 1923.

Mickelson, Siegfried. "Promotional Activities of the Northern Pacific Land Department." *Journalism Quarterly* 17, no. 4 (December 1940): 324–33.

Mighels, Ella Sterling. *The Story of the Files: A Review of California Writers and Literature.* San Francisco: Cooperative Printing, 1893.

Milner, Clyde A., II, Patricia Nelson Limerick, and Charles E. Rankin, eds. *Trails: Toward a New Western History.* Lawrence: University of Kansas Press, 1991.

Moehring, Eugene P. *Resort City in the Sunbelt: Las Vegas, 1930–1970.* Reno: University of Nevada Press, 1989.

Moehring, Eugene P., and Michael S. Green. *Las Vegas: A Centennial History.* Reno: University of Nevada Press, 2005.

———. *Urbanism and Empire in the Far West, 1840–1890.* Reno: University of Nevada Press, 2004.

Mortenson, Arlington Russell. "The Deseret News and Utah, 1850–1867." Ph.D. diss., University of California, Los Angeles, 1949.

Nelson, Jack A. "The Missing Social Conscience of the Frontier Press." Paper presented at the West Coast Journalism Historians conference, January 20, 1982.

———. "Tall Tales, Wild Lies and Hoaxes: Those Comical Frontier Editors." Paper presented at the American Journalism Historians Association conference, October 1985.

Nevins, Allan. Review of *Gold Rush: The Journals, Drawings and Other Papers of J. Goldsborough Bruff 1849–1851*, edited by Georgia Willis Reed and Ruth Gaines. *Saturday Review of Literature* 32 (May 14, 1949): 52–53.

Newell, Gordon. *Rogues, Buffoons and Statesmen: The Inside Story of Washington's Capital City and the Hilarious History of 120 Years of State Politics*. Seattle: Hangman, 1975.

Norton, Wesley. " 'Like a Thousand Preachers Flying': Religious Newspapers on the Pacific Coast to 1865." *California Historical Quarterly* 56 (Fall 1977): 194–209.

Notson, Robert C. *Making the Day Begin: A Story of the Oregonian*. Portland, Ore.: Oregonian, 1976.

Oliphant, J. Orin. Introduction to "The Territory of Washington, 1879," by Francis H. Cook. 1879; reprint, *Record* 32 (1971): 107–47.

O'Sullivan, John L. "Annexation." *United States Magazine and Democratic Review* 17, no. 1 (July–August 1845): 5–10.

———. "The Great Nation of Futurity." *United States Magazine and Democratic Review* 6, no. 23 (November 1839): 426–30.

Overton, Richard C. *Burlington West: A Colonization History of the Burlington Railroad*. 1941; reprint, New York: Russell and Russell, 1967.

Pérez-Peña, Richard. "Los Angeles Times Editor Forced Out." *New York Times,* January 21, 2008. http://www.nytimers/2008/01/021/business/media/21latimes-web.html?ex=1358571600&en=off3a4690fb5e51c&ei=5088&partner=rssnyt&emc=rss.

Perkin, Robert L. *The First Hundred Years: An Informal History of Denver and the Rocky Mountain News*. Garden City, N.Y.: Doubleday, 1959.

Pomeroy, Earl. *The Pacific Slope: A History of California, Oregon, Washington, Idaho, Utah and Nevada*. 1965; reprint, Seattle: University of Washington Press, 1973.

Powell, Lawrence Clark. *Philosopher Pickett: The Life and Writings of Charles Edward Pickett Esq. of Virginia, Who Came Overland to the Pacific Coast in 1842–43, and for Fifty Years Waged War with Pen and Pamphlet.* Berkeley: University of California Press, 1942.

Prosch, Charles. "The Press of Washington Territory." In *Annual Proceedings of the Washington Press Association, 1889.* Hoquiam, Wash.: Washington Steam Book, News and Job Print, 1891.

Prosch, Thomas. "The Early History of Tacoma." Typed manuscript no. 11, Northwest Collection, University of Washington Libraries.

Robison, Jennifer. "Sun's History Dates to 1950." *Las Vegas Review-Journal,* June 15, 2005.

Robison, Kenneth Leonard. "Idaho Territorial Newspapers." M.S. thesis, University of Oregon, 1966.

Roth, Lottie Roeder, ed. *History of Whatcom County.* 2 vols. Chicago: Pioneer Historical Publishing, 1926.

Said, Carolyn. "2 Bay Area Papers to Join Growing Media Group." *San Francisco Chronicle,* April 27, 2006. http://www.sfgate.com/cgi-bin/article.cgi?f=/c/a/2006/04/47/MNG52IG4I.T1.DTL.

Seelye, Katharine Q., and Terry Pristin. "Sam Zell, the 'Grave Dancer,' Sees Profit in Newspapers." *International Herald Tribune,* March 25, 2007. http://www.iht.com/articles/2007/03/25/business/zell.php.

Sherman, Scott. "The Evolution of Dean Singleton." *Columbia Journalism Review* 41, no. 6 (March/April 2003): 32–41. http://www.cjr.org/issues/2003/dean-sherman.asp?printerfriendly=yes.

Shortress, Robert. "First Emigrants to Oregon." *Oregon Pioneer Association Transactions, 1894–1903.* Written c. 1840, published 1896.

Sim, John Cameron. *The Grass Roots Press: America's Country Newspapers.* Ames: Iowa State University Press, 1969.

Sloan, William David, and James D. Startt, eds. *The Media in America: A History.* 3rd ed. Northport, Ala.: Vision, 1996.

Smith, Henry Nash, ed. *Mark Twain of the Enterprise.* Berkeley: University of California Press, 1957.

Stellman, Louis J. *Sam Brannan: Builder of San Francisco.* New York: Exposition, 1953.

Stratton, Porter A. *The Territorial Press of New Mexico, 1834–1912.* Albuquerque: University of New Mexico Press, 1969.

Streitmatter, Rodger. *Raising Her Voice: African-American Women Journalists Who Changed History*. Lexington: University Press of Kentucky, 1994.

Sugar, Max. *Regional Identity and Behavior*. New York: Kluwer Academic, Plenum, 2002.

Swanberg, W. A. *Citizen Hearst: A Biography of William Randolph Hearst*. New York: Charles Scribner's Sons, 1961.

Swibold, Dennis L. *Copper Chorus: Mining, Politics, and the Montana Press, 1889–1959*. Helena, Mont.: Montana Historical Society, 2006.

Troy, Robin. "When Speech Wasn't Free: Professors Delve into Montana's Troubled Past." *Vision*, 2004. http://www.umt.edu/urelations/vision/2004/24speech.htm.

Turnbull, George S. *History of Oregon Newspapers*. Portland, Ore.: Binfords and Mort, 1939.

Twain, Mark. *Roughing It*. 2 vols. 1871; reprint, New York: Books, Inc., 1913.

U.S. Bureau of the Census. *History and Present Condition of the Newspaper and Periodical Press of the United States*, vol. 8, Tenth U.S. Census, 1880. Prepared by S. N. D. North, special agent for the Bureau of the Census. Washington, D.C., 1884.

———. *Manufacturing Industries, Newspapers and Periodicals*, vol. 6, pt. 3, Eleventh U.S. Census, 1890. Washington, D.C., 1895.

Villard, Henry. *Memoirs*. 2 vols. 1904; reprint: New York: Da Capo, 1969.

Wardell, M. L. "Oregon Immigration Prior to 1846." *Oregon Historical Quarterly* 27 (1926): 41–64.

Watson, Elmo Scott. *History of Auxiliary Newspaper Service in the United States*. Champaign, Ill.: Illini, 1923.

Winchester, Jonas. Papers, Kemble Collection, California Historical Society, San Francisco.

Winthrop, John. "A Model of Christian Charity." In *The American Puritans: Their Prose and Poetry*, edited by Perry Miller. Garden City, N.Y.: Doubleday Anchor Books, 1956.

World Almanac and Book of Facts, 2005. New York: World Almanac Books, 2005.

WPA Writers Program. "History of the Colorado Press Association and Early Newspapers in Colorado." *Colorado Editor* 17 (June 1942): 11.

LEGAL CASES

Associated Press et al. v. United States. 326 U.S. 1; 65 S.Ct. 1416; 89 L.ED. 2013 (1945).
Citizen Publishing v. U.S. 394 U.S. 131 (1969).
United States v. Citizen Publishing Co. 280 F. Supp. 978 (D. Ariz. 1968).

WEB SITES

California State Military Museum. http://www.militarymuseum.org/ Otis.html.
Detroit Free Press, freep.com. "Jobs Page." http://www.freep.com/legacy/ jobspage/links/joa.htm.
Ketupa.net. http://www.ketupa.net/latimes.htm.
McClatchy Company. http://www.mcclatchy.com/100/story/179.html.
MediaNews Group. http://www.medianewsgroup.com/home.
New America Media. http://news.newamericamedia.org/news/view _custom.html?custom_page_id=87.
New York Times, September 21, 2006. http://www.nytimes.com/2006/ 9/21/business/media/21tribune.html?ex'1316491200&en.
Palace of the Governors. "The Palace Print Shop and Bindery." http:// palaceofthegovernors.org/PrintShop/coll.html.
Southern California Library for Social Studies and Research. http:// www.socallib.org/bass/story/candidate.html.

INDEX

Barbara Cloud is a professor emeritus of journalism at the Hank Greenspun School of Journalism and Media Studies and the former associate provost for academic affairs at the University of Nevada, Las Vegas. She is also the author of *The Business of Newspapers on the Western Frontier.*

Alan K. Simpson is a former U.S. senator and former director of the Institute of Politics at Harvard University's John F. Kennedy School of Government. He is also the author of *Right in the Old Gazoo: A Lifetime of Scrapping with the Press.*